Welsh Sea Kayaking

FIFTY-ONE GREAT SEA KAYAK VOYAGES

2nd Edition

Jim Krawiecki & Andy Biggs

PESDA PRESS
WWW.PESDAPRESS.COM

2nd Edition 2022

First published in Great Britain 2006 by Pesda Press
Reprinted with minor updates 2009
Reprinted 2013

Tan y Coed Canol
Ceunant
Caernarfon
Gwynedd
LL55 4RN
Wales

Copyright © 2005 and 2022 Jim Krawiecki and Andy Biggs
ISBN: 9781906095826

The authors assert the moral right to be identified as the authors of this work.

All rights reserved. No part of this publication may be reproduced or transmitted, in any form or by any means, electronic or mechanical, including photocopying, recording or otherwise, without the prior written permission of the publisher.

Printed in Poland. www.lfbookservices.co.uk

Foreword

When this book was first published it had been a long time coming! Wales has a spectacular coastline with the added complication of strong tides. Rugged coastlines often make access difficult and expeditions exposed to the elements. This guide certainly goes a long way in providing essential information, making the planning of trips less stressful, and is within the reach of all.

The severity of the trips often depends on wind strength and direction. Being on neap or spring tides may turn a benign expedition into a mini-epic, so local knowledge of the kind that helped compile this book can be essential. The book will provide you with a lot of valuable information so if you plan to paddle our coastline it is an essential read. I only wish I'd had the benefit of this guide in my early days as it would have certainly made life easier and probably safer.

Jim and Andy have added stories and tales intertwined with historic facts. This makes the book more than just a guide; it is an interesting and motivational read as well. The photographs are of high quality and the book has been designed for ease of reading and referencing, to include essential information on tidal streams, launch and landing spots, places of interest, campsites and friendly hostelries.

I would like to take this opportunity of congratulating the authors for all their hard work. I can think of no better way to spend hours of research time. 'Welsh Sea Kayaking' will be of great benefit to sea kayakers. It is wonderful to have such enthusiastic people who are prepared to impart valuable information and experiences to fellow paddlers. With updated information, new photographs and an inspiring additional route, this guide is more essential than ever. Fantastic!

Nigel Dennis

Dedication

This book is dedicated to the memory of Peter Hatt – initiator, and motivator of North West Sea Kayakers ... 'Hattie' enjoyed paddling with others to discover the sounds, views and moods of the sea. I hope that this guide will encourage all its readers to share and develop those ideals and in doing so be a fitting tribute to a memorable character.

Peter Roscoe

Contents

Foreword and Dedication 3
Coastal Access in Wales 6
Important Notice 7
Acknowledgements 7
How to Use the Guide 8
About the Authors 10

The North Coast 11

  1   Dee Estuary 13
  2   The Ormes 19
  3   Conwy Estuary 25

Anglesey / Ynys Môn 29

  4   Puffin Island 31
  5   Menai Strait 35
  6   South-west Anglesey 41
  7   Cymyran Strait and Rhoscolyn 45
  8   The Stacks 51
  9   Irish Sea Crossing 57
  10 Holy Island Circumnavigation 61
  11 Carmel Head 67
  12 The Skerries 71
  13 Porth Wen 75
  14 Point Lynas 81
  15 Bull Bay to Isle of Man 87

The Lleyn Peninsula 91

  16 Trefor to Porth Dinllaen 93
  17 Porth Dinllaen to Porth Oer 97
  18 Bardsey Sound 101
  19 Bardsey Island 107
  20 South-west Lleyn 113
  21 St Tudwal's Islands 119
  22 Pwllheli to Criccieth 123

Cardigan Bay 129

  23 Dwyryd Estuary 131
  24 Mawddach Estuary 135
  25 Aberdovey to Aberystwyth 139
  26 Ynys-Lochtyn 145
  27 Mwnt 151

Pembrokeshire ... 155

28 Cemaes Head ... 157
29 Dinas Head ... 161
30 Strumble Head ... 165
31 Penclegyr ... 169
32 St David's Head ... 173
33 Ramsey Island ... 177
34 Bishops and Clerks ... 183
35 Grassholm ... 187
36 Green Scar ... 191
37 St Brides Bay ... 195
38 Stack Rocks ... 199
39 Skomer and Skokholm ... 203
40 St Ann's Head ... 209
41 Milford Haven ... 213
42 St Govan's Head ... 217
43 Caldey Island ... 221
44 Carmarthen Bay ... 225

Gower & Bristol Channel ... 229

45 Burry Holms ... 231
46 Worms Head ... 235
47 Mumbles Head ... 239
48 Tusker Rock ... 243
49 The Most Southerly Point ... 247
50 Flat Holm and Steep Holm ... 251
51 Bristol Channel ... 257

Appendices ... 263

A Coastguard & Emergency Services ... 263
B Weather ... 263
C Pilots ... 264
D Mean Tidal Ranges ... 264
E Glossary of Welsh Language Place Names ... 265
F Recommended Reading ... 266
G Trip Planning Route Card - User's Guide ... 266
H Trip Planning Route Card ... 269
I Index ... 270

Coastal Access in Wales

Access to the outdoors in Wales is becoming increasingly encouraged and the Countryside and Rights of Way Act of 2000 brought access to many additional areas of coastal land. While engaged in sea kayaking it is rare to encounter access problems. Most of the routes described in this book start and finish at beaches or small harbours where public access to the foreshore is already established. Areas of the coast between the high and low water mark are often described as 'foreshore', and most of this is owned by the Crown Estate. Neither the Crown Estate nor any other owners normally restrict access to the foreshore.

Access on the sea is restricted only in rare and extreme cases and information is given by the coastguard during regular maritime safety information broadcasts. Access is frequently restricted in the vicinity of artillery firing ranges. These areas are often patrolled by staff from the Ministry of Defence. Further information and firing times can always be obtained from the coastguard.

At the busy ports of Holyhead and Milford Haven permission should be sought from the relevant authority, either by VHF or mobile phone, before entering or crossing harbour entrances.

The coasts of Anglesey, the Lleyn Peninsula and Pembrokeshire have greatly improved public access due to the development of coastal footpaths. Following on from the success of these paths, the Wales Coast Path was developed. It was officially launched in 2012 and runs the entire length of the Welsh coast from Chester to Chepstow.

Respect the Interests of Other People

Acting with courtesy, consideration and awareness is very important. If you are exercising access rights make sure you respect the privacy, safety and livelihoods of those living and working in the outdoors, and the needs of people enjoying the outdoors.

Care for the Environment

Sea kayakers are able to access remote places others cannot. Many of these places have sensitive plant, animal and bird life. Be aware of, and respect, landing restrictions around nature reserves. Look after the places you visit and enjoy and leave the land as you find it.

Take responsibility for your own actions.

Remember that the outdoors cannot be made risk free and that you should act with care at all times for your own safety and that of others.

Wild Camping

This guide provides information on many 'paddler friendly' commercial campsites. However, wild camping provides a special experience and forms an integral part of sea touring. There is no right to camp on the Welsh coast, and areas that lend themselves to wild camping for sea kayakers in Wales are few and far between. If you do decide to add a wild camp to your journey plan, be sure to choose a remote location away from dwellings, roads and paths. Always arrive late in the day and do not pitch your tent until dusk. You should take your tent down early the following morning. "Leave nothing but footprints and take nothing but photographs".

Further information on access to coastal areas can be had from Natural Resources Wales at www.naturalresources.wales

Important Notice

As with many outdoor activities that take place in remote and potentially hostile environments, technical ability, understanding of the environment and good planning are essential. The sea is one of the most committing environments of all, and with this considered it should be treated with the constant respect that it deserves. This guide is designed to provide information that will inspire the sea kayaker to venture into this amazing environment, however it cannot provide the essential ingredients of ability, environmental awareness and good planning. Before venturing out on any of the trips described in this book ensure that your knowledge and ability are appropriate to the seriousness of the trip. If you are unsure, then look for appropriate advice before embarking on the trips described. The book is purely a guide to provide information about the sea kayaking trips. For the additional essential knowledge of safety at sea, personal paddling, environmental considerations and tidal planning the authors recommend gaining the appropriate training from experienced and qualified individuals.

Warning

Sea kayaking is inherently a potentially dangerous sport, and with this considered, users of this guide should take the appropriate precautions before undertaking any of the trips. The information supplied in this book has been well researched, however the authors can take no responsibility if tidal times differ or information supplied is not sufficient. Conditions can change quickly and dramatically on the sea and there is no substitute for personal experience and judgment when kayaking or during the planning stages of a sea trip.

The guide is no substitute for personal ability, personal risk assessment and good judgement. The decision on whether to go out sea kayaking or not, and any consequences arising from that decision, remain yours and yours alone.

Acknowledgements

The authors would like to express their thanks to those who have contributed anecdotes and photographs which are credited throughout the book. Two people who are not mentioned by name are David Roberts and John Rowlands from pixaerial.com. Their spectacular aerial photography provides a unique perspective and we wish them all the best in their projects.

Throughout the time it took to compile information, take and source photographs, and write text for this guide the authors have had the benefit of help and support from others without whom this book would not have been possible. The authors would like to acknowledge the efforts of, and extend special thanks to: Penny Excell, Chris Krawiecki, Simon Fenton, Kirstine Pearson, Peter Roscoe and Trevor Shepherd. Their continued practical support and encouragement throughout the project has been invaluable.

Finally, thanks are due to Franco Ferrero and his team at Pesda Press. Franco's patience, and dedication to this project has been immeasurable and the team at Pesda Press have worked together to produce a publication of the highest quality that meets the aspirations of the authors.

For the 2nd edition a special thanks to Mark Rainsley for the Grassholm chapter and numerous photographs, Eurion Brown for his photographs, and to Mike Mayberry for his piece about The Smalls.

Photographs

All photos by Jim Krawiecki and Andy Biggs except where acknowledged in the captions.

How to Use the Guide

To use the guide all that you will need are up-to-date tide timetables of the relevant area, the appropriate Ordnance Survey map and the knowledge to use these. There is also a Trip Planning Route Card at the end of the book that can be used to help plan your chosen trip. There is a full explanation of how to use this alongside the route card. Each of the fifty trip chapters is set out into six sections:

Tidal & Route Information - This is designed as a quick reference for all the 'must know' information on which to plan the trip yourself.

Introduction - This is designed to give the reader a brief overview of what to expect from the trip and to whet the appetite.

Description - This provides further detail on the trip including coastline information, launching / landing information, about the wildlife and environment, historical information and the views to expect.

Tide & Weather - Giving further tidal information and how best to plan the trip, taking the tides, weather and local knowledge into consideration.

Map of Route - An outline of the route's start / finish points, landing places, points of interest and tidal information.

Additional Information - Further information that will help complete the trip, or is of interest if in the area.

Using the Tidal & Route Information

Each route begins with an overview of pertinent details beginning with the following information;
Trip name; Trip number; Grade of difficulty - (Colour scheme indicated)

Grade A - Trips from 6 – 20 kilometres in distance. Relatively easy landings with escape routes available. Offering relative shelter from extreme conditions and little affected by ocean swell. Some tidal movement may be found, but easy to predict with no tidal races or overfalls.

Grade B - Trips from 10 – 30 kilometres in distance. Some awkward landings and sections of coastline with no escape routes should be expected. Tidal movement, tidal races, overfalls, crossings, ocean swell and surf may be found on these trips. They will also be exposed to the weather and associated conditions.

Grade C - These trips will have difficult landings and will have no escape routes for the majority of the trip. Fast tidal movement, tidal races, overfalls, extended crossings, ocean swell and surf will be found on all these trips. They will be very exposed to the weather and conditions, therefore requiring detailed planning. With this considered they will all require good conditions for the trip to be viable.

Distance - Total distance for the trip.

OS Sheet - Number of Ordnance Survey 1:50,000 Landranger map required.

Tidal Port - The port for which tide timetables will be required to work out the tidal streams.

Start - Map symbol, name, six-figure grid reference and postcode of starting point.

Finish - Map symbol, name, six-figure grid reference and postcode of finishing point.

HW/LW - The tidal time difference from the tidal port of high water and low water for the local port nearest to the trip.

Tidal times - Position of tidal stream movement; followed by the direction to which the tidal stream flows and the time it starts flowing in relation to the tidal port high water.

Tidal rates - The areas in which the tidal streams are fastest and the speed in knots of the average spring rate.

Coastguard - Name of relevant Coastguard Station. Telephone number and the time the three-hourly weather forecast starts being announced on the VHF radio on Channel 16.

Below is an example:

St Tudwal's Islands

No. 21 | **Grade A** | **10km** | **OS Sheet 123** | **Tidal Port Liverpool**

Start	 Abersoch Beach SH314277 – LL53 7EF
Finish	Abersoch Beach SH314277 – LL53 7EF
HW/LW	are around 3 hours 20 minutes before Liverpool.
Tidal times	The south-going stream starts around 3 hours before HW Liverpool.
	The north-going stream starts around 3 hours after HW Liverpool.
Tidal rates	Tidal streams are generally weak, less than 2 knots maximum at springs.
Coastguard	Holyhead, Tel. 01407-762-051, VHF weather 0150 UT repeated every 3 hours

Map Symbols Used

- △ - Start
- ◎ - Finish
- →- - Described Route
- ○ - Landing Place
- ⋀ - Campsite
- 🮲 - Lighthouse
- ⩓ - Beacon

- ♜ - Castle
- ■ - Building or Built-up Area
- ⌒ - Possible Rough Water
- → - Tidal Stream Direction
- +0550 HW Liv - Time in relation to High Water of Tidal Port
- 2.5kn Sp - Average Spring Rate

About the Authors

Jim Krawiecki

Jim's involvement in the outdoors and in particular the Welsh coastline started on family holidays spent at the unique Polish ex-servicemen's home near Pwllheli. Beachcombing, investigating the sea life in rock pools and walks along the dramatic headlands of the Lleyn developed an interest in the outdoors. An introduction to canoes and kayaks at school led Jim to join a local canoe club in the mid 1990s, predominately a white-water club, as members suggested that sea kayaking was both dangerous and boring! Undeterred, and finding better-informed company through North West Sea Kayakers, a passion for the sea was rekindled and encouraged. In return Jim is now a prominent member of that group and regularly organizes meets and sea trips.

Sea kayaking in Scotland, Brittany, the Greek Isles, Norway, Iceland and Greenland as well as numerous excursions to Wales have prompted him to share his enthusiasm for sea touring by putting pen to paper and hopefully opening up opportunities for others to enjoy the delights of North Wales.

Jim is also a passionate mountaineer, which in turn led to his current employment at the offices of the British Mountaineering Council.

Andy Biggs

Andy has always had a strong affinity with the sea. Those who have paddled with him comment on, and benefit from, his understanding and analysis of tidal movements and anomalies, often ensuring the most efficient and enjoyable trips with the tide and wind being allies rather than obstacles.

Fascinated by the journeying nature of sea kayaking, Andy has completed many memorable trips around the UK, including trips in Ireland, Scotland and extensively in Wales. He has circumnavigated the islands of Skye and Mull and recently paddled multi-day trips in Alaska and New Zealand.

Andy loves remote places and has completed many challenging trips, either as a solo traveller or with his long-suffering college friend, Simon. These adventures have included trekking in the Himalayas, alpine climbing, cycling across Iceland and also crossing Eastern Europe soon after the collapse of the Eastern Bloc.

Andy has been a free-lance photographer and has in the past enjoyed teaching students. Recently he has returned to his previous passion of sailing.

The North Coast

An Introduction

This section holds some of Wales's forgotten backwaters and a stunning classic that many drive past on their way to Anglesey and the Lleyn Peninsula. There is a total distance of 48km of coastal paddling from West Kirby, on the Wirral in England, across the Dee Estuary and along the Welsh north coast to Conwy. Although this section does not readily lend itself to a journey along its entire length, there are areas of great natural and historical importance, and interest to sea kayaking.

Paddling on the Dee Estuary offers the chance to visit the nature reserves at Hilbre Island, Talacre and Point of Ayr. Most of the coastline to the west of Point of Ayr is best known for the beach holiday resorts of Prestatyn, Rhyl, Abergele and Colwyn Bay. Broad beaches of sand and shingle backed by amusement arcades and fairground rides offer little to the adventurous paddler seeking wilderness. These beaches stretch nearly 28km from Point of Ayr to Rhos-on-Sea where the coastline begins to show far more promise. A short hop across Penrhyn Bay, to the west of Rhos will introduce you to an often forgotten classic paddle around the towering limestone cliffs of Little Orme, along the elegant Victorian sea front at Llandudno and round the Great Orme. South of the Great Orme are the friendly waters of Conwy. The estuary offers sheltered paddling in bad weather and plays host to an annual canoe and kayak race held each spring.

Tide & Weather

Tides for this section are generally weak with the exception of Point of Ayr, the waters around the Great Orme and the lower reaches of the Conwy Estuary. In the Conwy and Dee estuaries the flood stream runs generally south (upriver). For the rest of this section the flood stream runs east, parallel to the coast between Llandudno and Point of Ayr. The ebb stream runs north out of the Dee and Conwy to join the main west-going stream, which runs parallel to the coast.

Background Reading

Coast - A Celebration of Britain's Coastal Heritage, Christopher Somerville, BBC Books, 2005, ISBN 9780563522799

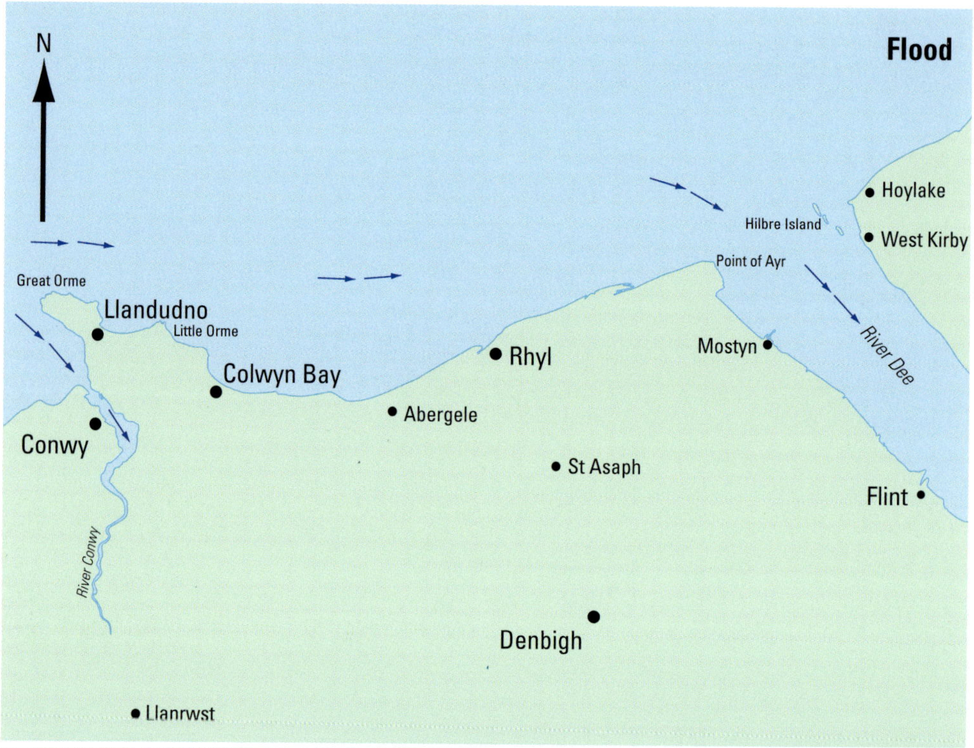

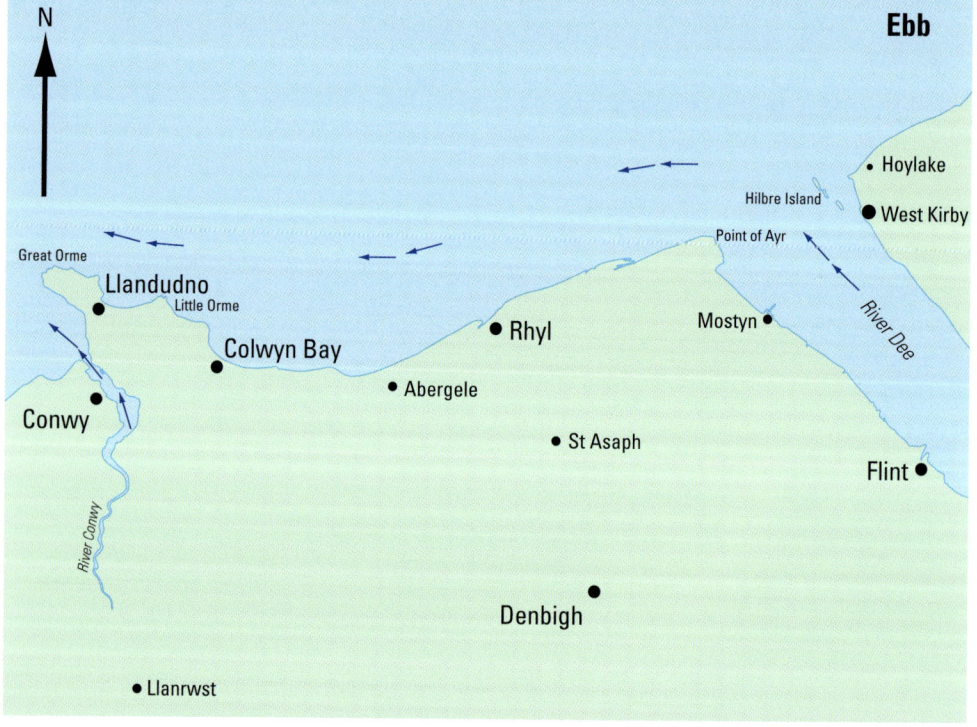

The above charts are intended to give a general overview. Consult the relevant chapters and other sources for more precise information.

Sunset on the Dee Estuary

Dee Estuary

| No. 1 | Grade B | 10 or 20km | OS Sheets 108 &116 | Tidal Port Liverpool |

Start	△ West Kirby Sailing Club slipway SJ 215 859 / CH48 0RR
Finish	○ West Kirby Sailing Club slipway SJ 215 859 / CH48 0RR
HW / LW	are 12 minutes before Liverpool.
Tidal times	The NW going stream (ebb) runs out of the estuary and starts at around HW Liverpool. The SE going stream (flood) runs up the estuary and starts around 6 hours before HW Liverpool.
Tidal rates	The average spring rate for this area is 1.5 knots but can reach 3 knots in the vicinity of Hilbre Island and Point of Ayr.
Coastguard	Holyhead, Tel. 01407-762-051, VHF weather 0150 UT repeated every 3 hours

Introduction

A journey from England to Wales!

At low water you can stand on the promenade at West Kirby and gaze across the expanse of sand towards Hilbre Island and find it difficult to imagine that the tide will ever come in. During

13

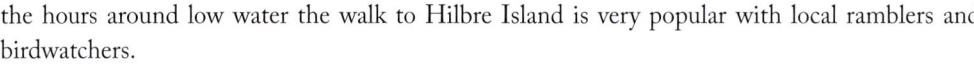
The slipway at West Kirby

Dee Estuary

the hours around low water the walk to Hilbre Island is very popular with local ramblers and birdwatchers.

There is a strong community of local paddlers that frequent the Dee Estuary and on weekends, when high water occurs in the middle of the day, small groups often paddle to Hilbre Island. Having done this, the next obvious step is to paddle the 9km to the lighthouse at Point of Ayr, across the sea to Wales. The return trip can be done on one tide, but requires some fast paddling, as there will only be sufficient water in the estuary for less than 4 hours. Timing is crucial with this trip, the main hazard is becoming grounded on a drying sandbank or stuck in mud. Local Dee Estuary paddlers have gained a reputation for speed due to the nature of the waters of their backyard.

Description (West Kirby)

Access to the water is by means of a slipway, beside the West Kirby Sailing Club, at the southern end of West Kirby promenade. There is plenty of parking along the promenade but this is quickly taken up at weekends. If spaces are hard to come by on the promenade you can unload your boat by the slipway and find parking in the nearby streets.

Ideally there should be a tide reaching 9m or more at Liverpool. You should launch at the slipway as soon as there is enough water to float, usually about 2 hours 20 minutes before high water at Liverpool. Tanskey Rocks lie 1km west of the slipway and will be just becoming covered as you leave. Whether you are going to Point of Ayr or Hilbre Island you should pass to the south of the rocks in order to find deeper water.

Description (Hilbre Island and back, 10km)

Hilbre Island marks the north-west end of an outcrop of red Bunter sandstone, which is very much in evidence as rocky outcrops, but also in many grand buildings along the Wirral west coast. Hilbre itself is no more than 1km long, and little more than 200m at its widest and forms the end of a chain of smaller islets: Little Hilbre, Little Eye and Tanskey Rocks. The distance from the slipway at West Kirby to its southern end is no more than 4km. Having passed to the south of Tanskey Rocks, getting to Hilbre is a simple matter of paddling north-west, keeping well to the west of Little Eye and Little Hilbre Island, and landing on the shingle beach on the southern end. The southern beach on Hilbre is the only practical landing at high water, and can be completely covered by the height of a tide exceeding 10m at Liverpool. In very calm conditions it is possible to land on a slipway 30m to the west of the beach. Paddling round to the north end of Hilbre provides better views of the red sandstone cliffs but sea conditions can get quite choppy due to groundswell and clapotis. When wind opposes tide, overfalls can develop to the north of the island, particularly beside the old lifeboat slipway. This can be a challenging playground for the adventurous.

Leave plenty of time for the return, you could be paddling against up to 1 knot of tide at times and the approach to the slipway at West Kirby dries quickly 2 hours after local high water.

Description (Point of Ayr and back, 18km)

The lighthouse at Point of Ayr is just over 9km due west of the slipway at West Kirby. As you approach the deeper water beyond Tanskey Rocks, check your transit, as the flood stream will tend to push you south. Salisbury Bank lies in the middle of the estuary; if this is visible, pass it to the north and take note of your route for the return journey.

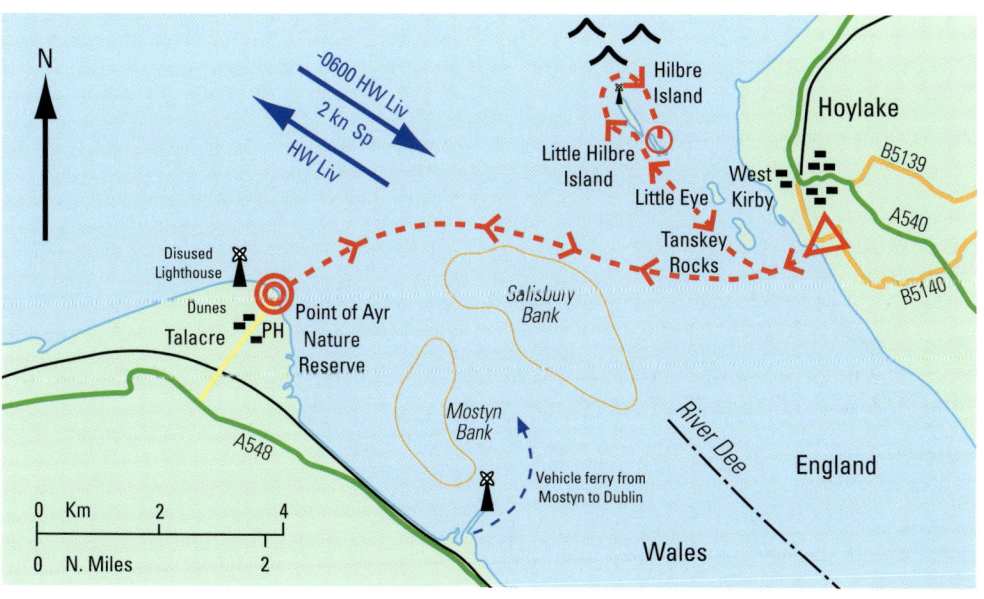

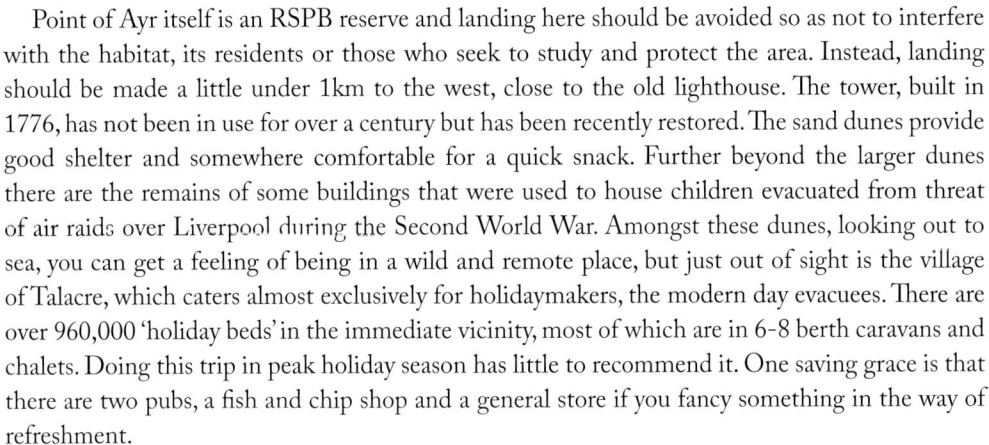

Disused lighthouse, Point of Ayr

Point of Ayr itself is an RSPB reserve and landing here should be avoided so as not to interfere with the habitat, its residents or those who seek to study and protect the area. Instead, landing should be made a little under 1km to the west, close to the old lighthouse. The tower, built in 1776, has not been in use for over a century but has been recently restored. The sand dunes provide good shelter and somewhere comfortable for a quick snack. Further beyond the larger dunes there are the remains of some buildings that were used to house children evacuated from threat of air raids over Liverpool during the Second World War. Amongst these dunes, looking out to sea, you can get a feeling of being in a wild and remote place, but just out of sight is the village of Talacre, which caters almost exclusively for holidaymakers, the modern day evacuees. There are over 960,000 'holiday beds' in the immediate vicinity, most of which are in 6-8 berth caravans and chalets. Doing this trip in peak holiday season has little to recommend it. One saving grace is that there are two pubs, a fish and chip shop and a general store if you fancy something in the way of refreshment.

Leave plenty of time for the return and be mindful of your previous route across Salisbury Bank. As you approach the slipway at West Kirby remember to pass to the south of Tanskey Rocks.

Tide and weather

Make a note of precisely when water reaches the slipway at West Kirby. Using the interval of this time added to the time of local high water will give a good indication of the time by which you should return. The punishment for a late return is a slippery, smelly boat drag through Dee Estuary mud. Your performance will almost certainly provide amusement to an audience of locals, who will have seen it all before.

Turnstones

A matter of survival

In the spring or autumn, this area provides the potential to witness bird migration in huge numbers at close quarters. The Hilbre group of islands, Point of Ayr and Talacre Marsh are Sites of Special Scientific Interest. The Dee Estuary is one of the ten most important estuaries in Europe for the over-wintering of wildfowl and waders. The islands are used as roost sites when the tide covers the thousands of acres of flats upon which the birds feed at low water. If birds are disturbed from the islands during the winter months it causes them to use up valuable energy reserves; the resulting fatigue can prove fatal to them. It is for this reason that local sea kayakers have voluntarily agreed not to paddle close to the Hilbre Islands during the winter months without first contacting the island ranger.

email: westkirbyhoylakemeolsparks@wirral.gov.uk

There should be no problem, nor need to contact the Hilbre Island Ranger with regard to bird disturbance in the spring and summer months (April to September).

The land surrounding the Dee Estuary is mostly low-lying, leaving the waters exposed to winds from any direction. The crossings from West Kirby to Point of Ayr and to Hilbre Island are especially exposed to winds from the north and west. The waters in the estuary are shallow, making wind against tide conditions particularly choppy, especially at the north end of Hilbre and close to Point of Ayr.

The southern beach on Hilbre Island

Additional information

West Kirby can be a bleak place to return to, as there is little in the way of natural shelter from any sort of inclement weather. Rather than hide in your car with the heating fan on full, have a look along the promenade for Tanskey's for a hot drink and a snack. At the north end of the promenade there is a supermarket and large car park. If you feel the need for something stronger, there is the Ring O' Bells pub, which serves fine ales and excellent meals and is less than 500m from the slipway. Head east along Sandy Lane, then turn left onto Village Road. The pub is on the left and has a large car park.

Great Orme's Head and old lighthouse

The Ormes

No. 2	**Grade B**	**16km**	**OS Sheet 115 &116**	**Tidal Port Liverpool**
Start	△ Rhos on Sea / Llandrillo yn Rhos SH 843 807 / LL28 4NH
Finish	○ Llandudno West Shore SH 769 821 / LL30 2AG
HW / LW	are around 30 minutes before Liverpool.
Tidal times	The west-going stream starts 30 minutes before HW Liverpool. The east-going stream starts 6 hours before HW Liverpool.
Tidal rates	The spring rate for this area is no more than 2 knots.
Coastguard	Holyhead, Tel. 01407 762051, VHF Weather 0150 UT repeated every 3 hours

Introduction

The A55 North Wales coast expressway is for many the road to the seaside. As the road descends Rhuallt Hill you will have your first view of Colwyn Bay. In the distance, the Little Orme stands proud from the otherwise flat coastline, and forms the eastern end of Llandudno Bay. The Great Orme towers over Llandudno, and guards the bay and its 3km of Victorian promenade from the west. These magnificent headlands are part of the Clwyd Limestone band that runs from the east coast of Anglesey to Llangollen. The limestone forms towering cliffs teeming with life.

19

The harbour and beach at Rhos-on-Sea

In the springtime swarms of seabirds compete with seals and fishermen for the catch of the day. This route will take you round the wildest scenery on the Welsh north coast but with Deganwy, Llandudno and Rhos-on-Sea so close by, the opportunity for tea and cakes is never too far away.

Description

Rhos-on-Sea is signposted from the A55 North Wales expressway and is just to the west of Colwyn Bay. The promenade leads to a beach and shallow harbour, which is protected from the east by a breakwater. If you arrive a little early it is worth paying a visit to the tiny Chapel of St Trillo. The Welsh name for this town, Llandrillo yn Rhos, is derived from St Trillo's name and describes this as his holy land. The chapel is just a short walk along the promenade from Rhos Point and, with room for a congregation of only 6, is thought to be the smallest church in the British Isles.

Access to the harbour beach is via a small set of steps. There is limited roadside parking by Rhos Point but there is also a public car park close by, along Abbey Road. It is possible to paddle north from the harbour but only close to high water; at other times you will have to use the main harbour entrance to the south. The best time to start this trip is about one hour before HW Liverpool. By the time you reach Little Orme the east-flowing stream will be dying away and the west-flowing stream will provide assistance for the remainder of the trip. As you pass Rhos Point and St Trillo's Chapel, the Little Orme will come into view some 3km across the shallow waters of Penrhyn Bay.

Upon closer inspection the Little Orme is actually rather more impressive than the name suggests. After passing the first headland there is Porth Dyniewaid, a small, steep-sided bay with a pebbly beach. Beyond the next headland is a sight that often brings a gasp to any first timer here. The limestone cliffs rise vertically from the sea, reaching a height of 141m, and during the early summer months the noise and stench from the seabird colonies can be quite overpowering. Kittiwakes and guillemots capitalise on any small ledges for nesting, row upon row of terraced housing for seabirds. At other times of the year this limestone metropolis can be strangely quiet, only the cormorants standing on the lower rocks to offer a sign that bird life on these cliffs continues all year round.

There are some rockhopping opportunities here at high water, but closer to low water can be even better when some caves become exposed. The cliffs give way abruptly to the steep shingles of Llandudno Beach and about halfway along the beach from here there is a café and toilets beside a children's paddling pool and play area (SH 769 821 / LL30 2AG). This is an ideal spot for a break, and also an alternative start / finish for shorter trips.

Looking to the west from the café gives the classic view of the Great Orme, Pen-trwyn and Llandudno Pier. The pier was built in 1878 and is still in use today. Beware of sea anglers' lines when passing beneath or around the end.

The distance by water from Llandudno promenade to the west shore is 10km. The cliffs and rugged steep ground of the Great Orme are continuous for all but the last 3km. Having described the Little Orme as a limestone metropolis, the Great Orme must be equivalent to an entire county! It has its coast road, cable car and tramway, parish church and ski slope! More significantly the Great Orme boasts unique sub-species of butterflies and plants. If you look up every now and then you may be able to catch a glimpse of a few of the unique Great Orme Kashmir goats. This herd is descended from animals given to King George IV at a time when their wool was much in demand for cashmere shawls. This herd of feral goats has roamed freely amongst crags without much human intervention for well over 100 years. Down at sea level, we are better equipped to enjoy more of the delights of sea-weathered limestone. The cliffs are blocky and narrow cracks run deep

Llandudno Pier and the Great Orme at dawn

into the rock. Sea water gurgles and surges its way through small gaps, channels, and sea caves. It is easy to imagine that sea serpents or some such mad creatures of children's nightmares dwell here.

The Great Orme lighthouse was constructed in 1862 by the Mersey Docks and Harbour Company and marks the northern extremity. The lighthouse was decommissioned in 1985 and now serves as a small, spectacularly located bed and breakfast hotel. The cliffs beneath are sheer and jagged, ideal for the thousands of seabirds that nest here every spring. You can be assured a superb aerial display beneath these cliffs during the breeding season.

As you approach the western side the cliffs become less imposing but there are still caves to explore and channels for rockhopping. The cliffs soon give way to a boulder-strewn beach, which leads the way to the sands of Llandudno's west shore. Shortly before you arrive at your destination you may find two rocky pinnacles; these are left high and dry at low water and are covered by high spring tides. If you can paddle between these pinnacles, your walk up the nearby beach will be tolerable. If the gap between them is too small, you may have to carry your boat some considerable distance.

Tide and weather

The tidal streams tend not to exceed 2 knots in this area and can be paddled against, even in the strength of the tide. Progress against the direction of the tidal stream is easier if you take advantage of the many eddies that exist close to the cliffs. The beaches at Rhos-on-Sea and the west shore of Llandudno have large expanses of sand, shingle and rocks exposed at low water. You should plan trips round the Ormes so that you launch and land above half tide.

Llandudno West Shore

This section includes some fairly committing paddling, which is exposed to all but southerly winds. Wind and swell from the north will produce clapotis around the cliffs and dumping surf on any of the north-facing beaches. Strong southerly winds can produce awkward downdraughts beneath the cliffs.

Additional information

The VHF aerial that Holyhead Coastguard uses is located on the summit of the Great Orme. You may have difficulty communicating with the coastguard if you are immediately beneath the cliffs of the Great Orme or to the east of Little Orme.

Variations

If this trip is to be done in the opposite direction the best time to leave Llandudno West Shore is around 2–3 hours before HW Liverpool.

A trip round the Great Orme starting from, and finishing at the west shore of Llandudno is a less committing alternative and ideal if you are using just one car. If by the time you reach Llandudno Pier you have had enough, a car parked at west shore will be a little over a kilometre walk away along Gloddaeth Avenue (A546).

Paddling to either the Great Orme or Little Orme from the café (SH 800 821 / LL30 3AA) on the Llandudno promenade beach is less committing still. The cliffs of the Little Orme are a mere 1km away and when explored close to low water there are some interesting caves to explore and plenty of rockhopping possibilities.

St Trillo

The mouth of the Conwy Estuary by Deganwy

Conwy Estuary

No. 3　Grade A　28km　OS Sheet 115　Tidal Port Liverpool	
Start	△ Beacons Car Park, Conwy　SH 774 789 / LL32 8GJ
Finish	○ Beacons Car Park, Conwy　SH 774 789 / LL32 8GJ
HW / LW	at Conwy are around 30 minutes before Liverpool, at Dolgarrog Bridge 30 minutes after Liverpool.
Tidal times	The south-going stream (flood) runs up the estuary and begins 5 hours before HW Liverpool. The north-going stream (ebb) runs north out of the estuary and begins around HW Liverpool.
Tidal rates	In Conwy Harbour and beneath the Conwy bridges the average spring rate can exceed 6 knots. The rest of the estuary tidal rates tend to be 3-4 knots.
Coastguard	Holyhead, Tel. 01407 762051, VHF Weather 0150 UT repeated every 3 hours

Introduction

One Saturday each spring, a hundred or more paddlers hurriedly launch various boats at 'The Beacons' by Conwy, in the quest to be the first to reach Dolgarrog Bridge, 14km upstream. The

The start of the Conwy Ascent Race

Conwy Ascent Race and Tour is an annual event organised by local enthusiasts from Dyffryn Conwy Paddlers. The race and touring event begins at the beach and car park known as 'The Beacons' at the western shores of the entrance to the Conwy Estuary. Paddlers use the strong tidal streams generated as the rising waters flood in from the Irish Sea. The scenery is varied and beautiful, taking in historic monuments, river banks designated as Sites of Special Scientific Interest and spectacular views of the Carneddau, the majestic mountains of northern Snowdonia.

Description

The Beacons car park is quite easily reached from the A55 by following signs for Conwy Marina then taking a left at the mini-roundabout, signposted 'Car Park'. Launching here during the middle hours of the flood will give a swift ride past the marinas of Conwy and Deganwy. When picking your way through Conwy Harbour, dodging the many moorings in midstream will become an art learnt with great haste. A passage close to the west shore will be easier going and will provide more opportunity to enjoy the views of the walled town of Conwy and its historic castle. Conwy Castle is one of several that were built by Edward I during the late 1200's to play a key role in his struggles with the Welsh. Once under the bridges and past the castle the strong currents ease as the estuary becomes wider. The east shore is a nature reserve managed by the RSPB and is an important site for wading birds and ducks. The estuary is at its widest as you pass the town of Llansanffraid Glan Conwy. From here the estuary becomes much narrower and the rolling countryside closes in all around you, invoking a strange feeling of travelling on a river gently flowing the wrong way!

After 8km you will pass beneath the bridge that connects Tal y Cafn on the east bank with Ty'n-y-groes to the west. It is possible to egress from here but parking along the road beside the bridge is minimal. Less than 1km after the bridge the river becomes even narrower, bound into a shallow rocky gorge, known as the Tal y Cafn rapids. In deep water there is nothing here but a few gentle boils but at lower levels rougher water may be encountered and some rocks may have to be avoided.

In the last 4km to Dolgarrog the river winds its way through low-lying farmland and the banks become hidden from view by tall, dense reed-beds. A couple of reed-infested islands make route finding a little more interesting but the bridge at Dolgarrog is not far away.

Dolgarrog Bridge is the official finish for the Conwy Ascent Race and Tour event. There are public rights of way from Dolgarrog, 1km to the west and from the A470, via Dolgarrog Station 300m to the east. Dyffryn Conwy Paddlers hold the award presentations for the Conwy Ascent Race in the grounds of the aluminium works. Vehicular access can be gained via the aluminium works to Dolgarrog Bridge on race day but at other times this must be specially arranged in advance with the landowner, as the gates are often locked.

Upstream has less to recommend it; if you have got this far you will have seen the best of the tidal stretch of the Conwy. The normal tidal limit is another 4km upstream, close to Trefriw. Exceptional spring tides can reach the historic town of Llanrwst.

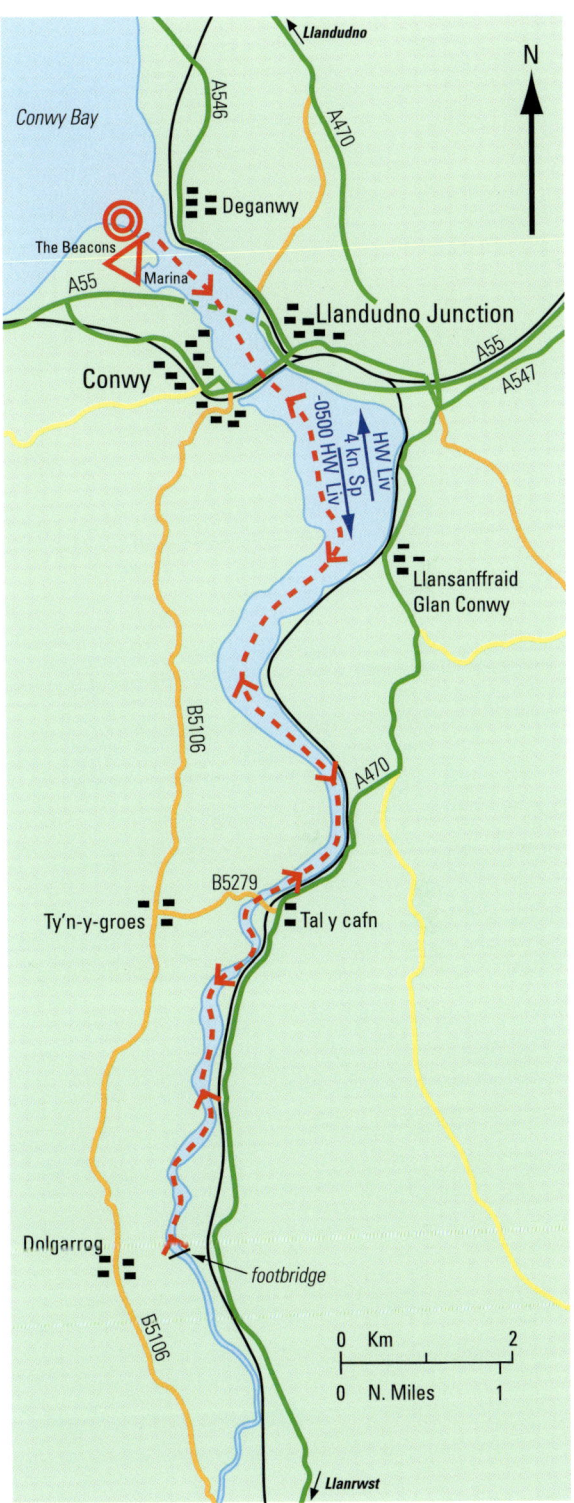

The Conwy by Tal y Cafn and Ty'n-y-groes

However far you choose to paddle up the estuary, you should begin your return as the water begins to flow downstream. An early return will reduce the risk of becoming grounded on sand or mud banks in the lower reaches of the estuary.

Tide and weather

The Conwy Estuary is generally well sheltered and can make a bad weather alternative to paddling around the Ormes. Strong winds from the north-west can produce gusty conditions around the Conwy bridges. When coupled with an ebbing spring tide, large standing waves or confused water conditions may be encountered in the harbour area. The tidal stream running through Conwy Harbour runs up to 6 knots. Swift action is needed to avoid mooring buoys and moored craft.

In recent years harbour traffic has increased dramatically. Both new marinas have tidal gates and there is often congestion around half tide when these gates open and close. The Conwy Estuary is becoming increasingly popular with pleasure craft, jet skis and powerboats.

Additional information

There are all the amenities a paddler could want in this area. Beside the marina there is a large pub and restaurant called Mulberrys. The name refers to the floating harbours used as part of the D-Day landings operation at the end of the Second World War. The Mulberry harbours were designed and tested in Conwy by local engineer, Hugh Ioris Hughes. The Sunday carvery is wonderful value and makes the perfect end to a day out on the water. The old town of Conwy boasts an abundance of shops, pubs and cafés. There is a youth hostel and plenty of camping nearby.

Anglesey/Ynys Môn

An Introduction

Anglesey / Ynys Môn is the largest of the Welsh islands and was all but isolated from the Welsh mainland by the turbulent waters of the Menai Strait. The isolation came to an end when the engineer Thomas Telford built what was the largest suspension bridge of its time in 1826. Robert Stephenson's Britannia railway bridge followed and in more recent times was adapted to carry the island's main A55 road and rail link.

Evidence of human habitation on Anglesey has been found dating as far back as the Stone Age. Standing stones and hut circles such as those at Porth Dafarch date back to the Bronze Age. During the Roman occupation of Wales, Anglesey remained a stronghold for the Celts and Druids. Following a prolonged and bloody battle along the shores of the northern Menai Strait, the Celts were defeated and Druids' sacred groves destroyed as the Romans marched on to occupy Anglesey. In medieval times the Celtic Christian Church flourished; this is when the monasteries of St Gybi at Holyhead/Caergybi and St Seiriol at Puffin Island/Ynys Seiriol were established. Many other churches were built during this era such as the Church of St Dwynwen on Llanddwyn Island and the Church of St Eilian at Llaneilian, close to Point Lynas.

The 200km of coastline is immensely varied, most of which can be accessed on foot by means of the Anglesey Coast Path. The tidal races and towering cliffs of Holy Island provide committing paddling of an extreme nature. The north coast of Anglesey has a challenging combination of steep cliffs, strong tidal streams, offshore islands and intriguing bays. Tidal streams on the east and south-west coasts are weaker, making the paddling there much more suited to short easy day trips and introductory sessions. Trips to Puffin Island and Ynys Dulas are popular for wildlife enthusiasts, whereas Llanddwyn Island and Porth Cyfan provide trips that offer more in the way of historical interest. Anglesey's island status means that during periods of inclement weather there is usually enough sheltered coastline for a day's paddling in the lee of the land. These attributes have led to Anglesey becoming extremely popular for sea kayakers the world over. There are a number of excellent guiding outfits offering instruction and courses. There is also a well-stocked paddling shop called Summit to Sea in Holyhead.

The following chapters describe the paddling around the Anglesey coastline and include information on the major crossings to Ireland and the Isle of Man. Another major undertaking is the circumnavigation of Anglesey. Guided trips are often completed in 3-5 days but circumnavigations have been completed in less than 24 hours. When this book was first published, the record (what then seemed an amazing time of 11 hours 30 minutes and 15 seconds) was held by local paddler John Willacy. The current time is well under 10 hours! Clockwise is generally the direction of choice. This is because the south-west going ebb stream in the Menai Strait is more powerful than the north-east flood. On the north and west coasts the north-east going flood is stronger than the ebb.

Background Reading

Cruising Anglesey and Adjoining Waters, Ralph Morris, Imray, 2021, ISBN 9781786791825

The above charts are intended to give a general overview. Consult the relevant chapters and other sources for more precise information.

Trwyn Du and Puffin Island

Puffin Island

No. 4	**Grade B**	**22km**	**OS Sheet 114 & 115**	**Tidal Port Liverpool**
Start	Moelfre Beach SH 512 863 / LL72 8HP
Finish	Trwyn y Penrhyn SH 627 795 / LL58 8RW
HW / LW	are around 30 minutes before Liverpool.
Tidal times	The SE going stream turns S through Puffin Sound, and starts around 5 hours 30 minutes after HW Liverpool. The north-going stream runs through Puffin Sound then runs NW, and starts around 30 minutes before HW Liverpool.
Tidal rates	Tide streams are strongest in Puffin Sound and reach 4 knots during spring tides.
Coastguard	Holyhead, Tel 01407 762051, VHF Weather 0150 UT repeated every 3 hours

Introduction

Most of this trip can be seen from the beach at Moelfre. Blocky limestone cliffs dominate the scenery along the east coast of Anglesey and provide both shelter and good potential for exploring. The main focus for this section is Puffin Island / Ynys Seiriol. Its ease of access and plentiful wildlife has made this island a popular destination for kayaking trips for many years.

31

Curious grey seal | Mark Rainsley

Description

Moelfre is a charming, sleepy town on the east coast of Anglesey, just off the A5025, 4km north of Benllech. There is a car park by the beach for which there is a charge during the summer months. The sea front is overlooked by the Kinmel Arms and there is also a kiosk which sells hot drinks and snacks. The car park by the sea front is small and quickly fills up. It is easy enough to unload kayaks and kit beside the beach and park in a larger (free) car park, clearly signposted and less than a 5 minute walk up the hill. Paddling south from the beach is mostly beneath limestone cliffs amongst which small rock ledges are exposed at low water. Just over a kilometre south of Moelfre is a small sheltered beach called Traeth Bychan. There is a car park with public toilets, and a campsite nearby with direct access to the sea. Either Traeth Bychan or the Nant Bychan Farm campsite can be used as an alternative start or finish.

As you continue along the coast, the limestone cliffs become more dominant, rising to almost 30m, but any illusions of wilderness are short-lived along this coast. Before long the popular holiday resort of Benllech will be within reach and during the school holidays Benllech fizzes to the relentless sound of motorboats and jet skis. The cafés beside the beach can provide a short, sheltered break on a cold day and there are also local shops in case you are in need of supplies. Trwyn Dwlban is little more than 1km along the coast and divides Benllech Sand from the huge expanse of Red Wharf Bay. Before crossing the 4km of the bay you may wish to stop for replenishment at the Ship Inn beside the moorings at the village of Red Wharf Bay. The pub grub and hot chocolate here are excellent. The wooded slopes of Mynydd Llwydiarth dominate the east side of the bay. The slopes break to limestone cliffs with small coves and secluded pebbly beaches. The coastline continues like this for another 7km until Trwyn Dinmor is passed and the beach at Penmon can be seen.

The Trwyn Du Lighthouse was completed in 1838 and marks the narrow channel between Trwyn Du and Puffin Island. The clang of the fog signal bell along with the boldly written words, "No Passage Landward", on the side of the tower will send a shiver through anyone approaching the Puffin Straits for the first time. Paddling here in the gloom of a misty morning can be a most haunting experience.

The steep shingle beach to the west of the lighthouse is a convenient place to land but can be tricky close to high water or in rough conditions. If you paddle round to the eastern side of Trwyn Du there is a more sheltered landing close to the old lifeboat station. A path, intially hidden amongst wild rose bushes, leads from the beach past some cottages to a small café with a sheltered garden on the headland.

Puffin Island has steep rocky shores and rugged slopes with coarse vegetation and, when viewed from the north-western side, has a distinctive whale-back shape. The Vikings called the island Priestholm. The Welsh name, 'Ynys Seiriol', refers to St Seiriol who established a monastery here during the 6th Century. There are many and varied stories about Seiriol walking to meet his good friend St Gybi who lived at Caergybi / Holyhead. The two friends often used to meet in the middle of Anglesey. Seiriol would walk west in the morning, and then return home walking east in the afternoon. With the sun on his back for most of his travels his face never tanned and he became known as the pale saint. St Gybi walked east in the mornings and west in the afternoons and always had the sun in his face and became known as the dark saint.

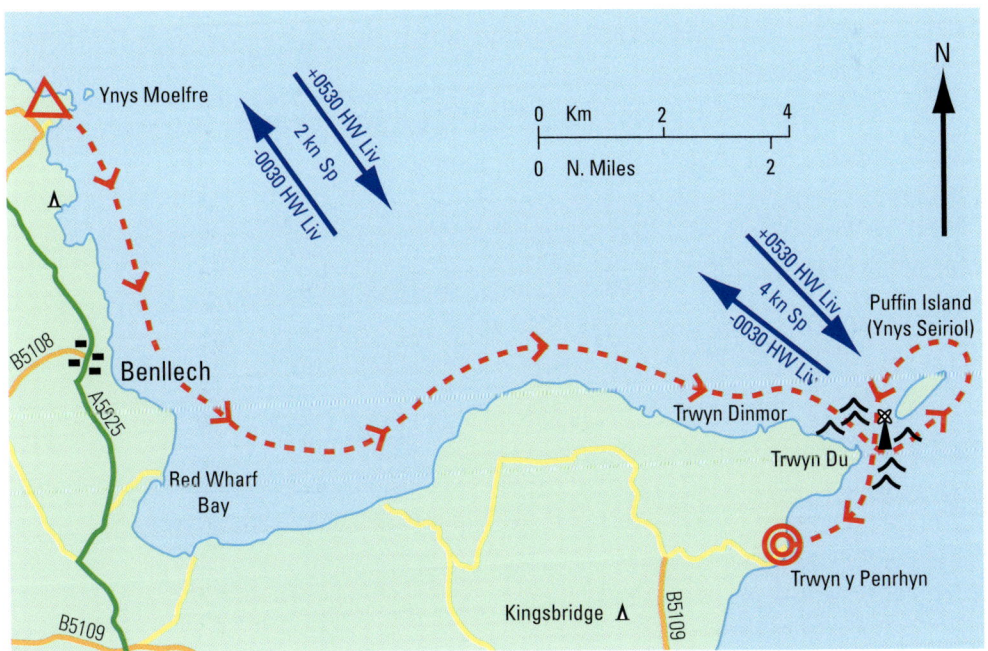

The only buildings visible from the sea are the remains of an old telegraphy station at the north-east end of the island. With little disturbance from man, life on the island was perfect for seabirds, especially puffins. However, in the late 1800's a plague of rats decimated the population of breeding birds and puffins were no longer to be seen in the area. This remained the case for nearly two centuries until the late 1990's when the Countryside Council for Wales (now Natural Resources Wales) undertook a programme to rid the island of rats. Puffins are now beginning to make a return and can be seen in small numbers around the island once more. The seal colony on the north end of the island provides by far the most special reason to come here. Over years of close contact with man, possibly through the local boat trips from Beaumaris, the seals have become less timid than in other places. If you have the patience to sit still in your boat for a while you may be surprised how close these curious creatures will come.

To the south of Puffin Island is the entrance to the Menai Strait. The nearest convenient landing with public road access is along the Anglesey shore, where there is a substantial lay-by on the road to Penmon Priory. The lay-by is at Trwyn y Penrhyn, which is a low headland with boulders on the beach and can be seen across the bay beyond the last of the quarried limestone cliffs.

Tide & Weather

The cliffs along the east coast give good shelter from the prevailing south-westerlies but in these conditions Red Wharf Bay creates a wind tunnel effect. You may be lulled into a false sense of security in sheltered conditions beneath the cliffs and paddlers have been caught out by unexpected offshore winds whilst crossing the bay.

The tidal streams between Moelfre and Red Wharf Bay are weak and insignificant. The effect of tidal streams is felt most strongly in the vicinity of Puffin Sound where there can be overfalls and confused seas when wind opposes tide. The north-western side of Puffin Island is exposed to more wind and swell than any other part of this section and can be rougher than you might expect.

Additional Information

There is camping at Nant Bychan Farm with direct access to the sea 1km south of Moelfre, Tel. 01248 410269. There is the added advantage of a fish and chip shop, bakery and the Kinmel Arms close by in the town. There is an extensive but charming campsite called Kingsbridge Caravan and Camping Park, Tel. 01248 490636, just off the B5109, north from Beaumaris. In good weather the Ship Inn at Red Wharf Bay is a pleasant place to stop for a refreshing beer. In bad weather the hot chocolate and warming fire are hard to resist. The beach beside the lighthouse at Trwyn Penmon can be used for access to the water; the charge for using the toll road to the headland and car park is not extravagant but paddlers might also be asked for launching fees here.

Variations

A trip round Puffin Island that starts and finishes at Trwyn y Penrhyn is a popular choice because, at around 9km, it is relatively short and affords some shelter from westerly winds.

Menai Strait

No. 5 | Grade B | 24km | OS Sheet 115 | Tidal Port Liverpool

Start	△ Trwyn y Penrhyn SH 629 796 / LL58 8RW
Finish	◎ Lay-by close to the Anglesey Sea Zoo, Brynsiencyn SH 478 651/ LL61 6TQ
HW / LW	HW and LW at Beaumaris are around 30 minutes before Liverpool. HW and LW at Caernarfon are around 1 hour 20 minutes before Liverpool.
Tidal times	For description of tidal times see diagram.
Tidal rates	In the vicinity of 'The Swellies' the spring rate can exceed 8 knots. For the rest of this section 2-4 knots is more typical.
Coastguard	Holyhead, Tel. 01407 762051, VHF Weather 0150 UT repeated every 3 hours

Introduction

Standing on the shores of the Menai Strait / Afon Menai, beneath Thomas Telford's famous suspension bridge, it becomes obvious why the Welsh name for this stretch of water describes it as a river. These treacherous waters all but isolated Anglesey from the Welsh mainland until the completion of the Menai Suspension Bridge in 1826. Paddling the length of 'The Strait' offers

Grey heron with Bangor Pier in the background

Menai Strait

wonderful variety in one day. The open estuarine feel and gentle flows of the Beaumaris area could not be in more contrast with the steep-sided narrows and tide races of 'The Swellies'. Much of this section is well sheltered and can be paddled in relative safety when bad weather prevents paddling elsewhere. The complex nature of the tidal streams that run through the Menai Strait makes trip planning challenging, especially when paddling this section as part of a longer trip. Getting it right here is essential when planning a circumnavigation of Anglesey.

Description

Trwyn y Penrhyn is reached by driving north from Beaumaris along the B5109 for 3km, then turning right onto a narrow lane which eventually leads to Penmon Priory. Before reaching the priory there is access to a pebbly shore via two lay-bys where cars can be parked. The sturdy sea wall separates the road from the shore for most of the year. Occasionally the combination of a strong easterly wind and a high spring tide can bring seaweed and debris onto the road.

The northern part of 'The Straits' is broad and exposed. There is over 7km of shallow water and sandbanks between this launching site and Llanfairfechan on the North Wales mainland coast. As the water recedes over these gently shelving shores, mud flats and sandbanks become exposed which make rich feeding grounds for wading birds such as turnstone and oystercatcher.

If you launch around 2 hours before HW Liverpool, Beaumaris will be reached quickly after paddling 4km on the rising waters. The summer months bring Arctic terns to the shallows of Lavan Sands. The terns hover, dance and dive the waters in search of their staple food, sand eels.

Beaumaris is a busy seaside town popular with tourists, especially in summer. There is plenty of parking close to the shore, and the shingle beach beside the lifeboat station provides one of many alternative access points for this trip. There is a quieter landing at Gallows Point where there is a boat yard, chandler and petrol station that sells basic groceries. If the inner self requires something a little stronger, the Gazelle Hotel stands directly opposite Bangor Pier. Aside from the expected alcoholic medley, hot drinks and pub grub can be well appreciated on a cold day.

Between Beaumaris and the town of Menai Bridge, the straits become narrower and the Anglesey shore is adorned by some spectacular real estate clinging precariously to the steep slopes. Two small, inhabited islands herald the northern edge of Menai Bridge and one could be forgiven for wondering who lives here. You would be unlikely to make friends by landing here to explore but the waters between these islands offer a welcome diversion and shelter from the strengthening tidal stream in the main channel. A good spot for landing for a break is a slipway and small beach known locally as Porth Wrach (SH 558 718 / LL59 5DE). This is also a good start / finish for a shorter trip. Parking in the narrow streets can be tricky, especially in the summer months. A short walk up Water Street will bring you to the High Street and all you could wish for in the way of pubs, shops and cafés plus a car park with public toilets.

The narrowest point in 'The Straits' was capitalised by Thomas Telford when he completed his revolutionary suspension bridge in 1826. Between this and Robert Stephenson's Britannia Bridge lies a stretch of water famously known as 'The Swellies'. Passage through this section by kayak is often exciting as the water surges and boils its way towards Caernarfon. The tidal race in 'The Swellies' is one of the fastest in Wales but the shelter provided by the steep shores and close proximity to easy landings makes trips to this area less serious. Swellies Rock is marked by a cardinal mark because it is a hazard to shipping, but good sport can be had on the standing waves here by fun-seeking paddlers. The waters around the nearby, inhabited island of Gored Goch can also be good sport and are often used for coaching by local outdoor centres. Special care should be taken here, as the water can be deceptively shallow and fast moving. There are also submerged remains of broken concrete fish traps and moorings. All of this excitement can happily be exchanged for a more gentle passage close to the Anglesey shore. Weaving your way between Church Island and Ynys Benlas will keep you away from most of the turbulent waters and bring you to a pleasant picnic spot in the woods to the north of Britannia Bridge.

Once through 'The Swellies' and under Britannia Bridge, the Menai Strait takes on a more open, rural feel. For the first time since passing Beaumaris, green fields and mountain views can be seen. The Anglesey shore is adorned with a statue of the Admiral Lord Nelson, close to an old jetty. Public access to the jetty can be gained via a rough track to the main A4080. As you draw level with the impressive house at Plas Newydd, the marina and town of Y Felinheli will come into view on the mainland shore. If you need to stop for a rest, there are public toilets, a pub and a café. Y Felinheli can also be used as an alternative start/finish. If you are aiming to pass by quickly, be aware that this part of the Menai Strait can be busy with pleasure craft. Once you pass the national watersports centre at Plas Menai, you should begin to make your way towards the Anglesey shore. Take care not to get stuck on the wrong side of a drying sandbank. The flags flying at the entrance to the Anglesey Sea Zoo make a good target to aim for. The Lay-by is less than 200 metres further on as you head south along the shore.

High Water Liverpool -6

High Water Liverpool -5

High Water Liverpool -4

High Water Liverpool -3

High Water Liverpool -

High Water Liverpool -

High Water Liverpool

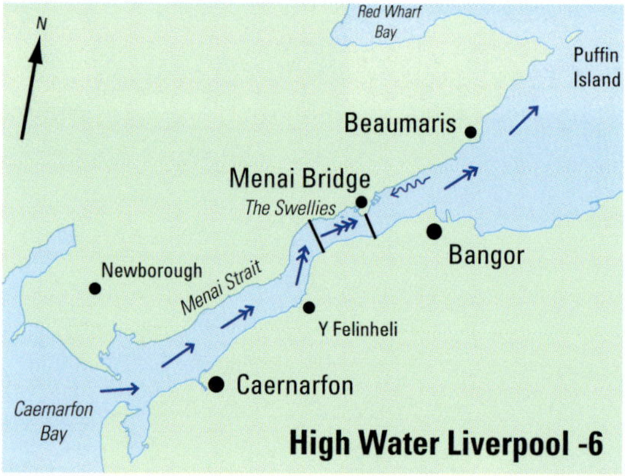

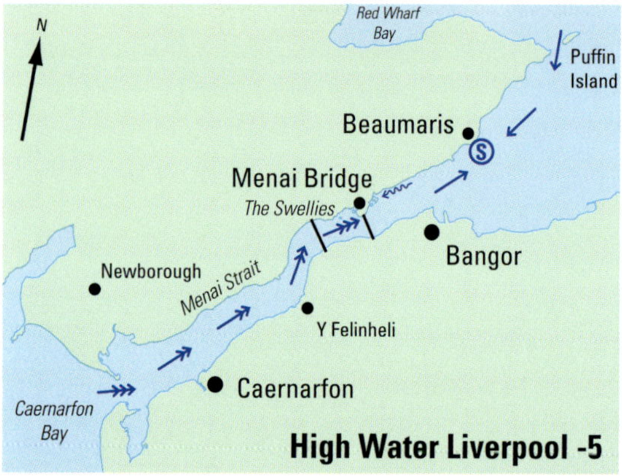

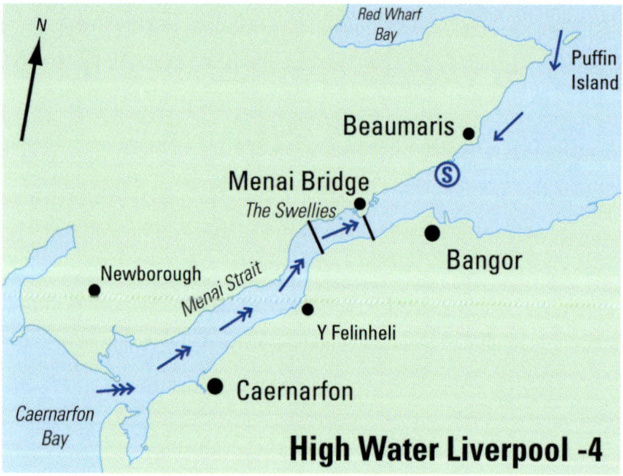

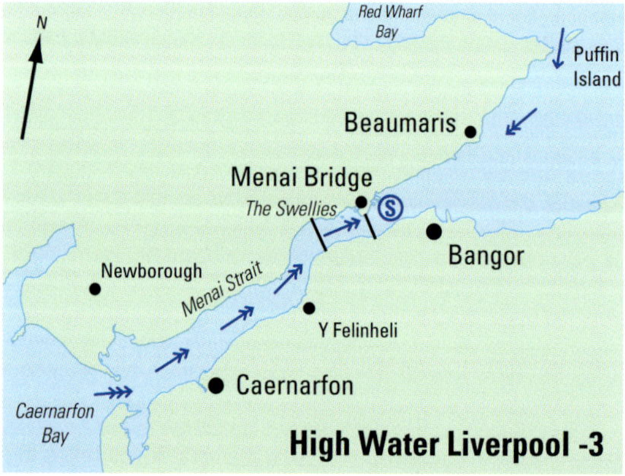

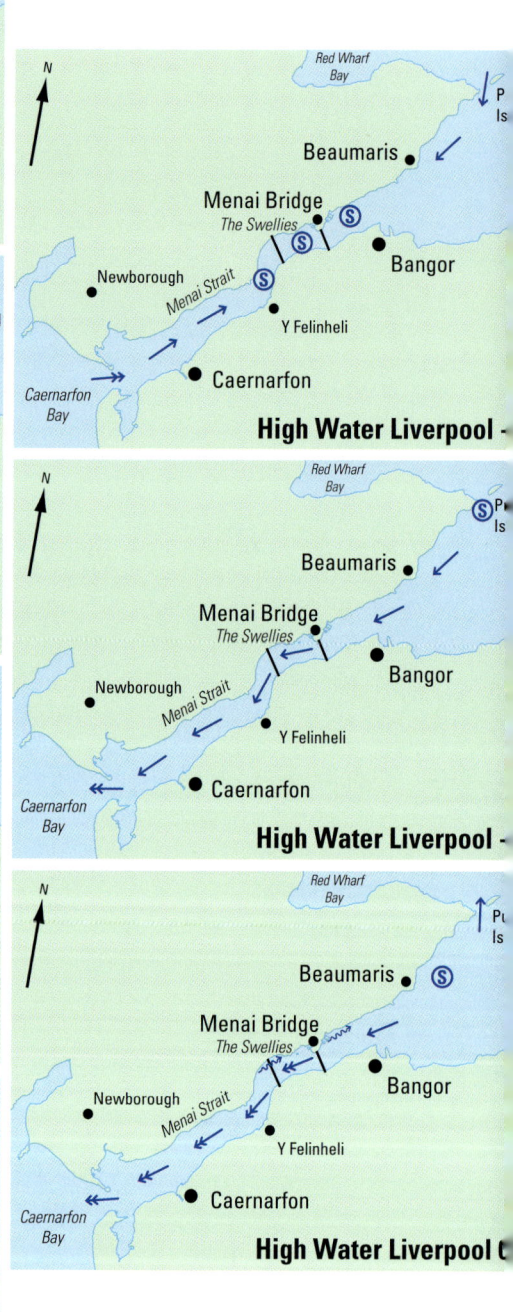

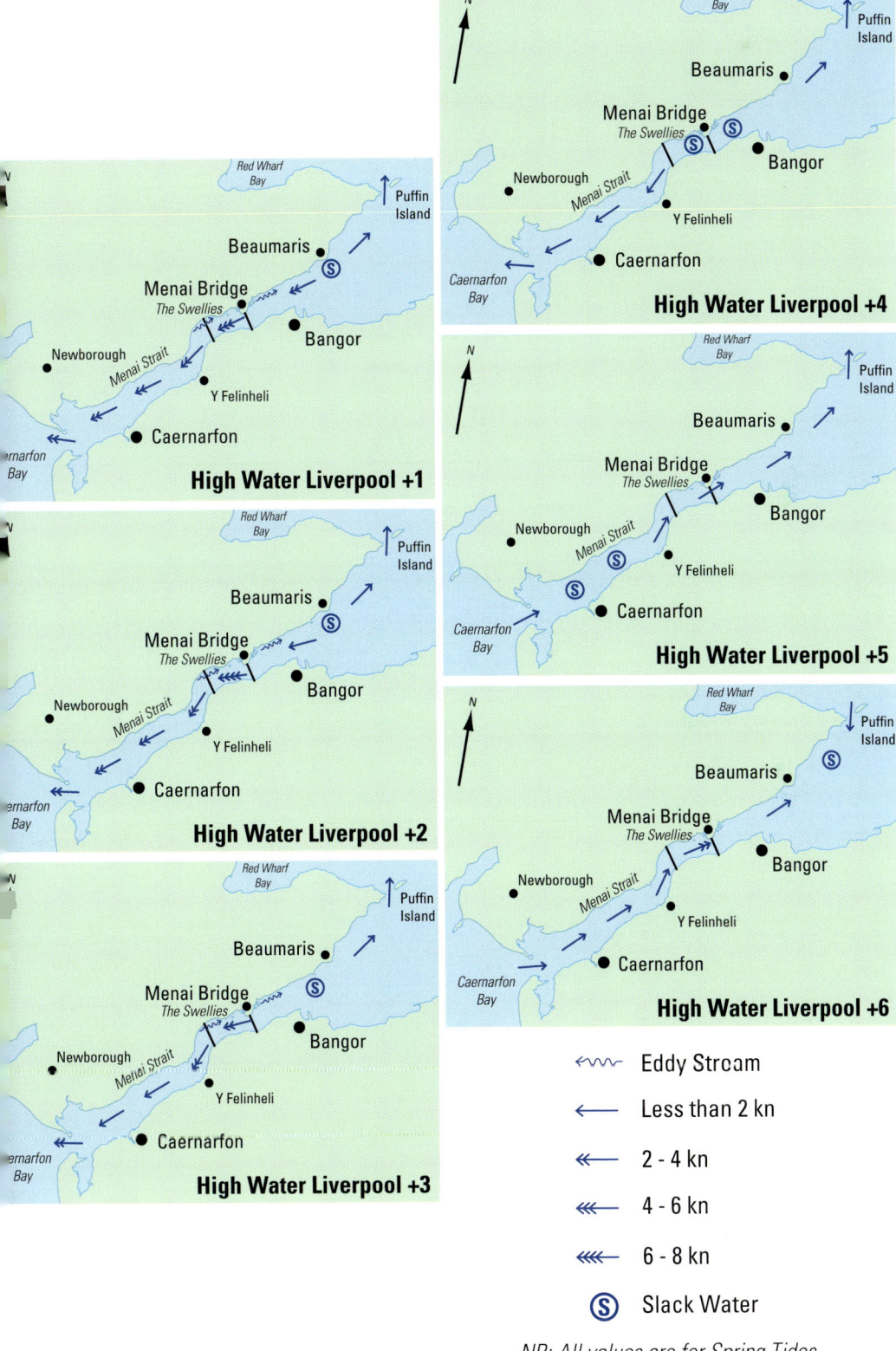

© Playing in The Swellies

Menai Strait

Tide & Weather

The tidal streams are strong for most of the length of the Menai Strait. Wind against tide conditions can create choppy conditions almost anywhere but 'The Straits' are well sheltered in winds from most directions. Special care should be taken with novices around 'The Swellies' and the two bridges. Tides can run up to 8 knots and there can be surprisingly gusty conditions beneath Britannia Bridge on a windy day.

Additional Information

There is camping at the Kingsbridge Caravan and Camping Park, Tel. 01248 490636, just off the B5109, north from Beaumaris. There is also a well sheltered site with good facilities at Treborth Hall Farm just off the A487 to the west of Bangor, Tel. 01248 364399.

Plas Menai is the Welsh National Watersports Centre and provides courses in sea kayaking for beginners and experienced paddlers alike.

© Llanddwyn Island | www.pixaerial.com

South-west Anglesey

No. 6 | Grade B | 26km | OS Sheet 114 | Tidal Port Liverpool

Start	△ Lay-by close to the Anglesey Sea Zoo, Brynsiencyn SH 478 651 / LL61 6TQ
Finish	◎ Rhosneigr Beach SH 316 732 / LL64 5QB
HW / LW	are around 1 hour 25 minutes before Liverpool.
Tidal times	In the Menai Strait and at Abermenai Point the SW going stream starts around 1hour 15 minutes before HW Liverpool, the NE going stream starts 4 hours 45 minutes after HW Liverpool.
	Between Llanddwyn and Rhosneigr the NW going stream starts around 4 hours 10 minutes after HW Liverpool, the SE going stream starts around 1 hour 15 minutes before HW Liverpool.
Tidal rates	The average spring rate for the southern end of the Menai Strait is 2-4 knots and is strongest in the vicinity of Abermenai Point. The tides between Llanddwyn and Rhosneigr are less significant, normally not exceeding 1.5 knots.
Coastguard	Holyhead, Tel. 01407 762051, VHF Weather 0150 UT repeated every 3 hours

Introduction

This low-lying corner of Anglesey is frequently ravaged and therefore shaped by Atlantic winter storms. There are few roads to the south-west coast which adds to the remote feel of the area. These

Looking across to the Lleyn from Twr Mawr (disused) lighthouse | Mark Rainsley

shores have broad sandy beaches, backed with towering dunes, slung between low rocky headlands and islets from Snowdonia's violent, volcanic prehistory. Celtic crosses and ancient churches stand as monuments to religion and legend. All of this creates a magical atmosphere for those of us who wish for the simplicity of a peaceful day away from our modern-day battles.

Description

The Anglesey Sea Zoo can be found by following the narrow road that leads south, south-west. There is a sharp right turn as the road meets the shore of the Menai Strait and the entrance to the Anglesey Sea Zoo is 200 metres on the right. The lay-by is less than 200 metres further on the left. To reach Rhosneigr by kayak from here you first must pass Abermenai Point, at the southern end of the Menai Strait. This is best done early in the ebb so you should leave shortly after local high water. This will enable you to easily avoid any sandbanks and find deeper, fast-running water. Caernarfon lies across 'The Straits' and is well worth the added distance for a humbling trawl beneath the looming ramparts of its famous castle.

Abermenai Point is a spit of land made up from sand and pebbles and forms the southernmost tip of Anglesey. Just across 'The Straits' from here lies Fort Belan. Thomas Wynn, later to become the first Lord Newborough, built the fort in the late 18th Century in response to the threat of invasion by the French. The fort has been recently restored, parts of which are available as self-catering accommodation.

Heading north-west, sand dunes and eventually the Newborough Forest are reached, heralding the ancient home and ruined chapel of Saint Dwynwen, the patron saint of Welsh lovers.

Llanddwyn Island lies 6km to the west of Abermenai Point and is part of a low ridge that was formed as a result of a submarine volcanic eruption. Llanddwyn is not strictly an island as you can walk there at most states of the tide. This mini-peninsula and its associated rocky islets extend nearly 2km south-west from Newborough Forest into Caernarfon Bay. It is easy to spend an hour or more wandering around and exploring. More information can be found on notice boards by the narrow sand spit that joins Llanddwyn to Newborough Forest. To the north of Llanddwyn is Malltraeth Bay and, when ocean swell runs in from the south-west, there is excellent surf here. The lack of road access here means that you may well have this beach to yourself.

Between the bay at Malltraeth and Aberffraw is a series of narrow coves with sandy beaches divided by low rocky headlands. To the west of Aberffraw the theme of churches by the sea continues at Porth Cwyfan. There has been a church on this site since the 7th Century. The present building and the sea wall which protects the site were more recently built in the 19th Century. St Cwyfan's Church in the Sea is cut off from the mainland at high tide but a causeway gives access at mid to low tide. Services are still held here at Easter and Christmas.

After Porth Cwyfan the coastline turns to the north and, with Rhosneigr in sight, has a less remote, sportier feel. Porth Trecastell and the nearby Porth Nobla are popular beaches for surfing. These small bays do well to pick out the best of any residual swell from the south-west approaches. Porth Trecastell, sometimes known as Cable Bay, has a narrowing entrance which helps to steepen the waves. The waters around Rhosneigr are popular with just about anybody who owns something that floats. On a calm summer's day the sea will be infested with sailing dinghies, motorboats, jet skis and fishing boats. On windier days kite and wind surfing are the sport of choice. Whatever the weather, take care and keep a sharp look out.

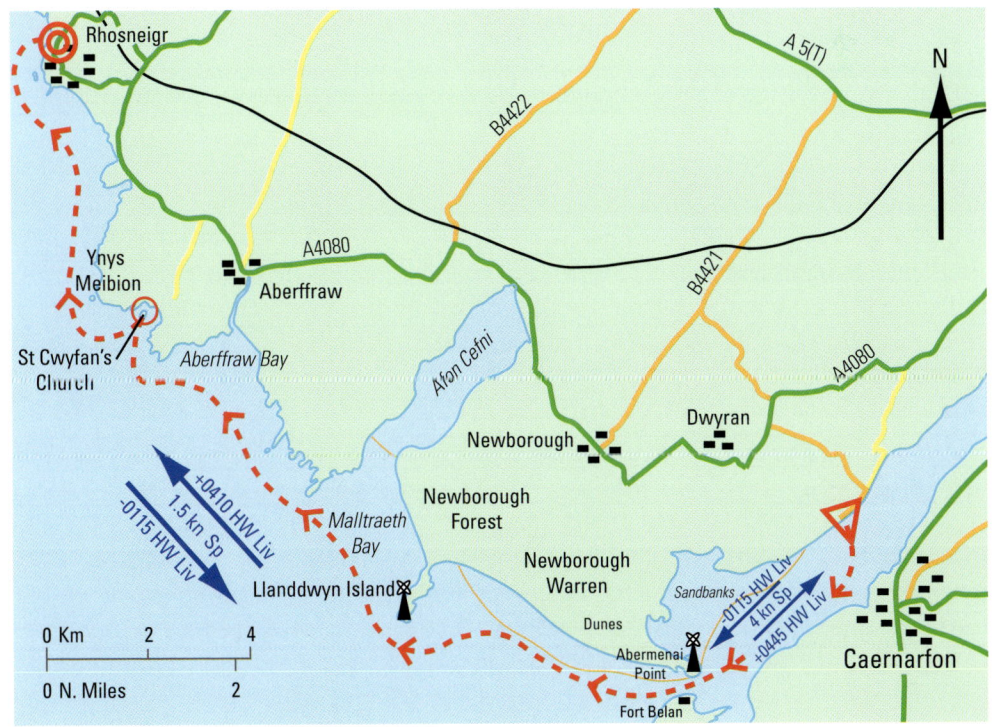

The Church of St Cwyfan | Trevor Shepherd

Access to the beach at Rhosneigr is via Beach Road which is narrow and has little or no space for parking but enough room for kayaks to be loaded onto cars. There is a car park which is a 5 minute walk into the town just off the High Street.

Tide & Weather

Although the Menai Strait is a narrow stretch of water, the surrounding land is low-lying, leaving this southernmost section exposed to winds from any direction. Wind against tide conditions can create awkward, choppy conditions close to Abermenai Point.

Additional Information

There is camping at Awelfryn Caravan Park close to Newborough, Tel 01248 440230, and Fron Caravan and Camping Site near Dwyran, Tel. 01248 430310. Rhosneigr has a watersports shop which could be useful should you need to make any emergency repairs. There is also a café, fish and chip shop and a post office. The visitor centre and café at Halen Môn – Anglesey Sea Salt Company is well worth a visit. Coffee, cake and flapjacks are very popular here.

Variations

This trip can easily be reversed as long as you arrive at Abermenai Point when the tide is flooding north-east into the Menai Strait. A return trip to St Cwyfan's Church in the Sea from Rhosneigr or Porth Trecastell can be a pleasant way to spend a couple of hours in the afternoon. There are little or no tidal streams to deal with but there will be less boat carrying if you plan your trips around high water.

Cymyran Strait and Rhoscolyn

No. 7 | Grade B | 18km | OS Sheet 114 | Tidal Port Liverpool

Start	△ Four Mile Bridge SH 280 783) / LL65 3HB
Finish	◎ Porth Dafarch SH 234 800 / LL65 2LS
HW / LW	are around 1 hour 30 minutes before Liverpool .
Tidal times	At Four Mile Bridge the south-going stream begins around 1 hour after HW Liverpool, the north-going stream begins around 3 hours 30 minutes before HW Liverpool.
	In the southern entrance to the Cymyran Strait the south-going stream begins 1 hour 30 minutes before HW Liverpool, the north-going stream begins around 4 hours 30 minutes after HW Liverpool.
	Offshore from Rhoscolyn the SE going stream begins around 1 hour 30 minutes before HW Liverpool, the NW going stream begins around 4 hour 30 minutes after HW Liverpool.
	In Rhoscolyn Sound the SE going stream begins around 1 hour 30 minutes before HW Liverpool, the NW going stream starts around 3 hours after HW Liverpool.
Tidal rates	The strongest tidal streams in the Cymyran Strait are in the narrows, close to where it opens out into Cymyran Bay and can reach 5 knots. In the vicinity of Rhoscolyn Beacon and Rhoscolyn Head tidal streams are around 3-4 knots.
Coastguard	Holyhead, Tel. 01407 762051, VHF Weather 0150 UT repeated every 3 hours

Four Mile Bridge

Introduction

This is a trip with tremendous variety and repeated visits to this area always turn up something new. The start at Four Mile Bridge has an estuary feel with salt marshes patrolled by terns, curlews and oystercatchers. Once out of the Cymyran Strait into deeper water the cormorant is king and you can embark upon a festival of rockhopping in one of the most popular sea kayaking destinations of the United Kingdom. Borthwen is a sheltered bay at Rhoscolyn and makes an ideal spot for a lunch stop before exploring more offshore islands, caves and gullies. Trearddur Bay is all too often plagued by jet skis and powerboats but has shops and cafes, so provides a useful opportunity to stock up on essential goodies. The finish at Porth Dafarch often has surf, especially following a few days of strong south-westerlies. Upon arrival you may be able to reward yourself with a steaming mug of tea from the food wagon that is often in attendance.

Description

Four Mile Bridge is on the B4545 between Valley and Trearddur Bay. To the north lies the Inland Sea; to the south is the Cymyran Strait. There are no car parks at Four Mile Bridge but parking is possible on the roadside; remember to be considerate to other road users and people who live and work locally. Access can be gained to the water at either end of the bridge. The chute of water that develops as water levels change on either side of the bridge is sometimes used for fishing, but is also a popular spot for paddlers to practise moving-water skills.

If you leave Four Mile Bridge as water begins to flow south through the arch you should have reasonable tidal assistance along the Cymyran Strait to the open sea.

The shores of the Cymyran Strait are low-lying and marshy, making this an ideal setting for a lazy warm-up to an exciting day's paddling. The estuarine environment is home to wading birds such as oystercatcher, curlew and redshank. Herons can often be seen standing over drying pools, waiting for the next easy meal of freshly stranded fish. We might be relatively oblivious to the life under the water but during the summer months terns enjoy many a day fishing for sand eels here. The southern end of the Strait leads through some small overfalls and on to the open waters of Cymyran Bay. There is often surf here too, all of which combines well for a place to stop and play for a while. Just to the west is Silver Bay, a beautiful little beach with a slipway at its western end. From here to the next bay is some of the finest rockhopping in North Wales. The Precambrian rock that makes up this coastline has been eroded by the action of the sea, exposing any weaknesses and widening cracks to reveal a myriad of gullies and channels. Hours can be spent rock dodging your way along the coastline towards Borthwen.

Borthwen is a charming little bay with sandy beaches and a narrow rocky entrance to its south. The whitewashed cottages and the old lifeboat station help to give this place an old-fashioned and remote feel, reminiscent of small fishing villages on the west coast of Scotland. The bay is well sheltered and has a car park with public toilets. The road to the beach is narrow and winding with few passing places. At busy times you may need to dig deep into your driving skills and patience in order to reach Borthwen by road. The combination of sheltered water and the abundance of interesting rocky gullies and islets close by makes this a popular venue for introducing novices to kayaking. The coast of Rhoscolyn is dominated by the presence of Rhoscolyn Beacon which stands upon a set of rocky islets called Ynysoedd Gwylanod. The beacon is a useful landmark and can be seen from as far away as Penrhyn Mawr and Llanddwyn Island. The overfalls and tidal races around the rocks can provide good sport in the middle hours of the north-west flowing flood.

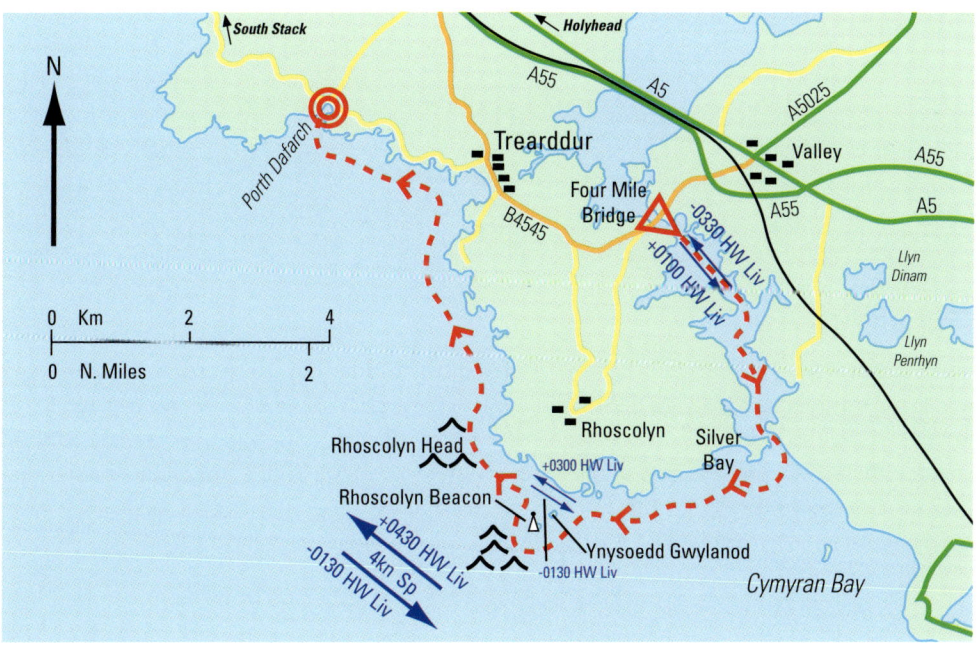

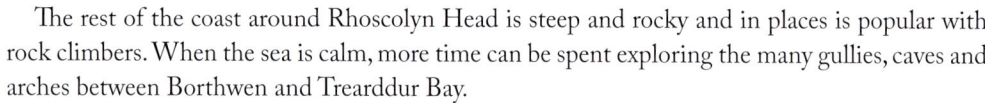
The Cymyran Strait

The rest of the coast around Rhoscolyn Head is steep and rocky and in places is popular with rock climbers. When the sea is calm, more time can be spent exploring the many gullies, caves and arches between Borthwen and Trearddur Bay.

Trearddur Bay lies beyond the caravan sites at Porth Y Garan and Ravens Point. The bay is popular with holidaymakers because of its broad sandy beach and good car parking facilities. The main street has a post office and a well-stocked general store with an integral bakery. During the summer months Trearddur can get rather busy with jet skis and dive boat traffic. At the southern entrance of Trearddur Bay there is a quieter, sheltered beach at Porth Diana where there is a useful watersports shop and chandlers.

Porth Dafarch lies about 2km to the west of Trearddur along a section of yet more intriguing coastline with rocky coves and small beaches. Take care when landing at Porth Dafarch; there is often surf in this narrow rocky bay.

Tide & Weather

You will need to make use of two tidal phases to complete the trip from Four Mile Bridge to Porth Dafarch. The ebb from the Inland Sea and the Cymyran Strait will help you on your way towards the open sea at Cymyran Bay. Between Cymyran Bay and Borthwen tidal movement is of little

◎ *Rhoscolyn Beacon*

◎ *The 'haunted house' Treardˆur Bay*

"Surf's up!" Silver Bay

importance, especially if you stay close to shore. Borthwen is an ideal spot for a lunch stop and a place to wait for the flood stream to begin running north-west to assist your passage to Trearddur and Porth Dafarch.

Additional Information

There is a campsite by the Inland Sea close to Four Mile Bridge at Pen y Bont Farm, Tel. 01407 740481. Outdoor Alternative is a centre used by schools, university groups and outdoor pursuits clubs. They do not generally advertise their camping facilities but sea kayakers are usually made very welcome, Tel. 01407 860469, www.outdooralternative.co.uk.

Variations

Borthwen is a good place to start and finish short rockhopping trips, or excursions to the tidal races at Rhoscolyn Beacon. The sheltered bay here is an excellent spot for warming up and for skills practice.

South Stack and Gogarth Bay, North Stack in the distance

The Stacks

No. 8 | Grade C | 12km | OS Sheet 114 | Tidal Port Liverpool

Start	△ Porth Dafarch SH 234 800 / LL65 2LS
Finish	◎ Soldiers' Point, Holyhead SH 236 837 / LL65 1YG
HW / LW	High and low water at Porth Dafarch occur around 1 hour 20 minutes before Liverpool. High and low water at Holyhead are around 48 minutes before Liverpool.
Tidal times	At Penrhyn Mawr the NW going stream (flood) starts around 3 hours 30 minutes after HW Liverpool, the SE going stream (ebb) starts around 1 hour 15 minutes before HW Liverpool.
	At South Stack the NNE going stream (flood) starts around 4 hours 50 minutes after HW Liverpool, the SSW going stream (ebb) starts around 1 hour 10 minutes before HW Liverpool.
	At North Stack the NE going stream (flood) starts around 5 hours after HW Liverpool, the SW going stream (ebb) starts 2 hours before HW Liverpool.
Tidal rates	This area has a reputation for fast tidal streams, which can exceed 6 knots on spring tides.
Coastguard	Holyhead, Tel. 01407 762051, VHF Weather 0150 UT repeated every 3 hours

Jagged reefs near Trearddur Bay, Snowdon in the background

Introduction

On the Friday before the May bank holiday sea kayaking enthusiasts from around the world are congregating at 'The Paddlers Return' bar, in readiness for the immensely popular Anglesey Sea Symposium. The event attracts over 200 paddlers of varying ability and experience each year. Workshops, seminars, slide shows and guided trips will keep everyone entertained for over a week. Back in the bar, you are bound to hear the words, "Have you ever been round 'The Stacks' before?" The trip from Porth Dafarch to Soldiers' Point is a conversation piece for good reason. Feelings of anticipation and excitement mixed with a little fear give rise to butterflies in the stomach for many, as a group of first timers assemble upon the sheltered sandy beach at Porth Dafarch. Having negotiated the jagged headland and associated overfalls of Penrhyn Mawr you will be committed for the rest of this awe-inspiring journey around South and North Stack, and beneath the famous cliffs of Gogarth Bay.

Description

The winding road from Trearddur Bay to South Stack passes Porth Dafarch. The narrow rocky bay with its gently shelving sandy beach makes this an ideal place to launch. There is a good deal of parking but this beach is popular and is often busy on summer weekends. Launch at Porth Dafarch soon after the flood stream begins and you will arrive at Penrhyn Mawr in plenty of time to watch the overfalls build.

The coastline between Porth Dafarch and Penrhyn Mawr is jagged and riddled with gullies and caves waiting to be explored. Porth Ruffydd, once home to a lifeboat station, has a small pebbly beach. It is possible to land here and walk the short distance to the headland, if you feel the need to check the mood of the sea before fully committing yourself to the tide race. The overfalls at Penrhyn Mawr are the 'gate to the stacks', an exciting roller-coaster ride and a lively welcome to Anglesey's wild west coast. There are plenty of eddies amongst the rocks, this is an exhilarating playground for confident paddlers with a good roll.

As you emerge from the overfalls into smoother water, South Stack and the lighthouse appear reassuringly bold but still over 2km away. The route to South Stack from here becomes a matter of choice. The quick way is to stay offshore. Follow the tidal stream flowing north-west, then north, giving swift passage through more overfalls at South Stack. The slower, more interesting route is to stay close to the shore. Abraham's Bosom is the rocky bay to the north of Penrhyn Mawr.

Kayakers are known to use this as an escape route, or temporary resting place, having suffered the chaotic waters of South Stack or Penrhyn Mawr. It is possible to land on a pebbly beach here and, if necessary, escape to the coast road above the cliffs. This is the only possible escape route on this trip and is via a set of steep steps up the cliff. It is possible to carry a kayak up these steps, but not without considerable difficulty. Paddling north from Abraham's Bosom the scenery becomes more dramatic with vertical cliffs rising 80m from the sea. Beneath the cliffs there are lagoons shielded from the open sea by huge blocky reefs and towering sea stacks.

South Stack / Ynys Lawd is a small island separated from the mainland by a narrow gully, less than 3m wide. This is the most westerly point of Holy Island. The lighthouse was built in 1809 by

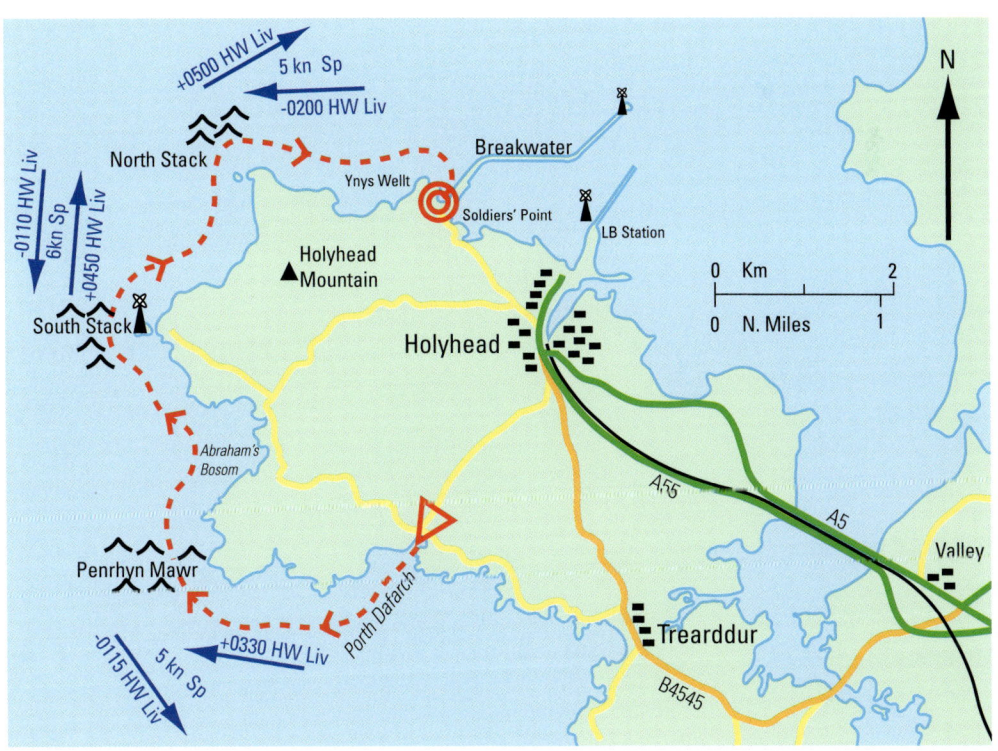

© Gogarth Bay, approaching North Stack | Mark Rainsley

Trinity House, is nearly 28m high and open to the public during the summer months. Access is via a bridge that spans South Stack Gully.

South Stack and the cliffs beneath Ellin's Tower are important seabird colonies and the Royal Society for the Protection of Birds have asked that kayakers help the breeding seabirds by keeping well back from the cliffs during the breeding season between May and August.

With South Stack behind you Gogarth Bay opens up ahead like a huge amphitheatre. The southern half has steep slopes where heather and tough grass cling desperately. The north part has vertical cliffs that rise over 100m straight from the water. The Gogarth cliffs are popular with climbers. One of the most famous climbs on these cliffs is called 'A Dream of White Horses' beneath which is a cave known as 'Annie's Arch' that can be paddled in one entrance and out of another. The largest and most impressive cave is Parliament House Cave and on a calm day it is possible to land on the steep pebbly beach within. At the top of the beach within Parliament House Cave there is a dark passage which runs right through to the north side of North Stack. There are further caves and gullies around North Stack that are perfect for the inquisitive paddler but it is important to be aware of dangerous waves created by car ferries approaching or leaving Holyhead Harbour.

The overfalls that develop at North Stack during the middle hours of the SW going ebb are just as spectacular as those that form at Penrhyn Mawr on the flood. The crux of this trip is to arrive at North Stack before the tide turns here.

Porth Namarch is the closest beach to North Stack but offers little more than a temporary landing to someone in desperate need to stretch their legs. The final landing is little more than 1km

Overfalls at Penrhyn Mawr | Mike Webb – www.rockpoolkayaks.com

The Power of the Sea

I always watch my back at Penrhyn Mawr. It's not the fear of someone surfing into me, nor the local amorous seal who likes to whack passing hulls. It's a place where I'm often reminded that the sea is much more powerful than me.

Aled Williams - www.tideraceseakayaks.com

beyond Ynys Wellt. Waves breaking on the reef here often catch out paddlers who have become weary or even complacent towards the end of their journey. The beach at Soldiers' Point is steep and pebbly and landing can be a little awkward. The land beside Soldiers' Point is privately owned. The track leading to the breakwater is frequently used by kayakers and divers without objection, however if in doubt there is a public car park a short walk away at the Holyhead Breakwater Country Park.

Tide & Weather

As with any stretch of coastline with strong tidal streams, numerous back eddies form within sheltered bays and coves. A significant back eddy forms during both flood and ebb within Abraham's Bosom.

Playing in the rough stuff, Porth Ruffydd

Although the races at North and South Stack are not far away the strength of the tide is not felt in the depth of Gogarth Bay.

Anything more than a gentle breeze with a southerly, westerly or northerly component can have a significant effect on the tidal races. Wind against tide conditions around these headlands can produce huge breaking seas that are, for most mortals, better observed from land.

Additional Information

There is camping and bunkhouse accommodation available at Anglesey Outdoors, Tel. 01407 769351, www.angleseyoutdoors.com. There is also a bar with a kayaking theme on site called 'The Paddlers Return' where you can get a refreshing drink and a hearty meal.

Variations

The trip round 'The Stacks' can be and often is done from Soldiers' Point to Porth Dafarch using the south-going ebb stream.

Paddling into the sunset, shortly after launching | Jonny Eldridge

Irish Sea Crossing

No. 9 | Grade C | 104km | Admiralty Chart SC 1411 | Tidal Port Liverpool

Start	△ Porth Dafarch SH 234 800 / LL65 2LS (53° 17' N, 04° 39' W)
Finish	◎ Bullock Harbour (53° 17' N, 06° 06' W)
HW / LW	HW and LW at Porth Dafarch are 1 hour 20 minutes before Liverpool. HW and LW at Bullock Harbour are 30 minutes after Liverpool.
Tidal times	For Penrhyn Mawr and South Stack see No. 8. The offshore ebb stream runs south and begins soon after HW Liverpool. The offshore flood stream runs north and begins 6 hours before HW Liverpool.
Tidal rates	For Penrhyn Mawr and South Stack see No. 8. The offshore tidal streams only exceed 3 knots close to Penrhyn Mawr, 'The Stacks' and Dalkey Island, which lies 2.5 kilometres south-east of Bullock Harbour.
Coastguard	Holyhead, Tel. 01407 762051, VHF 0150 UT repeated every 3 hours; Dublin, Tel. 00353-1-662-0922/3

Introduction

This is an immense open crossing that has been completed several times by very experienced paddlers. The crossing has been done in as little as 11 hours but can take over 20 hours depending

Kish Bank Lighthouse, on the approach to Dublin Bay | Jonny Eldridge

upon conditions and fitness. The sense of achievement gained from completing such a trip will fill you with pride for many years to come, but paddling a kayak for this length of time without landing is an endurance challenge of a very serious nature. Prior to 2015, it was possible to paddle into Dun Laoghaire Harbour and make use of the slipway and marina facilities at the East Pier.

Commitment

Out in the middle of a big open crossing with no sign of land in any direction you really understand the true meaning of commitment.

Crossing the Irish Sea from Holyhead to Dun Laoghaire is one of those trips that I think is regularly planned over a few pints and then put on the back burner until next time. For me things were a little bit different; when I first met my good friend Harry we discussed the crossing and I soon realised it wasn't going to go away until we'd done it.

Five months later I was leaning over Harry's rear deck in a big following sea getting my first taste of being sick out of a kayak. Another few hours later and we were paddling like mad in the dark trying to get out the way of the 'Sea Cat'.

The Irish Sea crossing certainly isn't a trip for the faint-hearted but I hope that anyone who attempts it will be left with memories as good as the ones I have.

Speak to anybody who has done this crossing and they'll all have a story or two to tell.

Barry Shaw

The advantage of landing here was the proximity of the ferry terminal. It was quite straightforward to trolley your kayak from the slipway to the ferry terminal and onto a boat to Holyhead. Sadly, this service has now ended making logistics more complex.

Description

This trip is normally done from Anglesey to Ireland because the strong tides around Penrhyn Mawr and South Stack can be dealt with early in the voyage. Dublin Bay, with the Wicklow Mountains beyond is a big target to aim for and there are plenty of lights, both on land and on the sea, to guide you in case you approach the Irish coast after dark. June and July are the best months for this trip, not only because of the good weather associated with these months, but just as importantly there can be daylight for more than 18 hours.

Apart from the natural hazards that an open crossing can provide possibly the greatest immediate hazard is from high-speed ferries, but this is greatly reduced if you use VHF to keep in touch with the coastguard, are paddling in daylight and there is good visibility. Information on the arrival and departure times of ferries can be obtained from the coastguard and port authorities.

The narrow entrance to Bullock Harbour is at the southern end of Dublin Bay, 2 kilometres south-east of Dun Laoghaire. This is a quiet place with a small number of moorings and little in the way of facilities. The gently sloping slipway will make for an easy landing at high water, but at low water the harbour dries out all the way to the entrance.

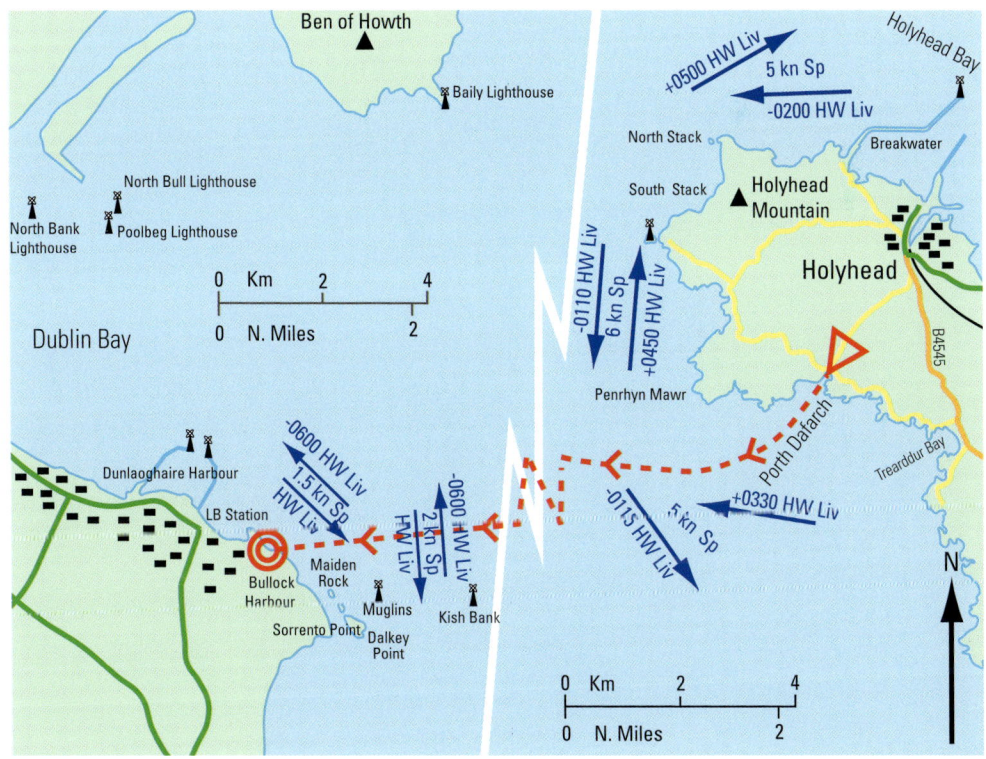

It is possible to paddle to the Dublin Port View Point but landing on this steep man-made shore of broken concrete, rocks and boulders is tricky, and would still leave you more than 500 metres from the ferry terminal. If you plan to land here you should contact the Dublin Port VTS beforehand.

Tide & Weather

An accurate weather forecast is more important on an extended sea crossing than for any other kind of sea kayaking trip.

Doing this voyage on a neap tide will reduce the amount you will drift north and south during the crossing. If you leave Porth Dafarch to catch the last 2 hours of the flood, then the ebb will carry you initially south, away from major ferry routes.

Additional Information

There is a company called Kayaking.ie that provides kayaking and canoeing trips and courses. They have a base at Bullock Harbour and can be approached for help with your arrival, and transport to the ferry terminal at Dublin Port.

It is not necessary to show your passport to enter Ireland from the UK, but Irish immigration officials may ask you to confirm your identity. It is therefore important to take your passport or similar proof of identity with you. Further details and updates on entry requirements can be found on the website of the British Foreign, Commonwealth and Development Office (FCDO).

Holyhead Mountain and Abraham's Bosom

Holy Island Circumnavigation

No. 10 | Grade C | 32km | OS Sheet 114 | Tidal Port Liverpool

Start	△ Porth Dafarch SH 234 800 / LL65 2LS – Borthwen SH 272 751 / LL65 2NJ
Finish	◎ Porth Dafarch SH 234 800 / LL65 2LS – Borthwen SH 272 751 / LL65 2NJ
HW / LW	HW in the Inland Sea is 1 hour after HW Liverpool. Low water is 2 hours after LW Liverpool. High and low water at Holyhead occur 48 minutes before Liverpool. At Porth Dafarch they occur 1 hour 20 minutes before Liverpool. At Rhoscolyn they are 1 hour 30 minutes before Liverpool.
Tidal times	For Rhoscolyn, southern Cymyran Strait and Four Mile Bridge see No. 7. At Stanley Embankment the flood stream flows south through the tunnel and begins 4 hours before HW Liverpool. The ebb stream flows north through the tunnel and begins 1 hour after HW Liverpool. For North Stack, South Stack and Penrhyn Mawr see No.8.
Tidal rates	The strongest tidal streams in the Cymyran Strait are in the narrows, close to the entrance at Cymyran Bay and can reach 5 knots. In the vicinity of Rhoscolyn Beacon and Rhoscolyn Head tidal streams are around 3–4 knots. Around the major headlands at Penrhyn Mawr, South Stack and North Stack tidal streams are strongest and reach 6 knots.
Coastguard	Holyhead, Tel. 01407 762051, VHF 0150 UT repeated every 3 hours. Holyhead Port Control, Tel. 01407 606700, VHF 14

© Four Mile Bridge

Introduction

Holy Island / Ynys Gybi is barely separated from the western shores of Anglesey by the shallow waters of the Cymyran Strait and the Inland Sea. The north-west part of the island ends dramatically as the slopes of Holyhead Mountain crash abruptly into the Irish Sea at North Stack, Gogarth Bay and South Stack. In contrast, the southern half of the island has small cliffs riddled with gullies and caves, and sheltered bays with sandy beaches.

The circumnavigation of Holy Island presents a challenge of stamina for the distance but accurate tidal planning and navigation will also be required. A safe circumnavigation should also include liaison with the coastguard and Port Control at Holyhead so as to avoid becoming tangled with busy harbour traffic.

The key to a successful circumnavigation is crossing the Inland Sea and passing beneath Stanley Embankment at the time of slack water at high tide.

Description (anticlockwise) from Porth Dafarch

As soon as you leave the shelter of Porth Dafarch you will be able to see Rhoscolyn Head, and the Beacon Rocks just over 6km to the south-east. Leaving 2 ½ hours before HW Liverpool you will be paddling in the opposite direction to the dying NW going flood stream. Paddling close in to the shore will keep you away from the effects of the tide and may bring some benefits from gentle back eddies as you approach Rhoscolyn Head.

By the time you reach the Rhoscolyn area tidal streams will be dying away and you will be able to enter the Cymyran Strait shortly after local high water. If you arrive a little late it is possible to use some of the many eddies and hop your way between them to make your way upstream. Any tidal flow is strongest in the lower reaches close to Plas Cymyran and the closer you get to Four Mile Bridge the weaker the flow will become.

Four Mile Bridge carries the B4545 road between Trearddur Bay and Valley / Dyffryn over the southern entrance to the Inland Sea. The bridge has one small arch, just under 3m wide. Water flows through the arch, creating a shoot popular for practising basic white-water skills. This is another popular place to start a circumnavigation of Holy Island. Access to the water is easy at either end of the bridge, and on either side via small gravely beaches. The pleasant paddle across the shallow waters of the Inland Sea brings you to the new A55 road bridge and Stanley Embankment, after just over 2km.

Stanley Embankment was built in 1823 and carries the A5 road and the Holyhead to London railway. The embankment is far longer than Four Mile Bridge but also has only one arch. The newer A55 dual carriageway embankment runs parallel and was completed in March 2001. The rising waters from Holyhead Bay flow through the tunnel into the Inland Sea and within the

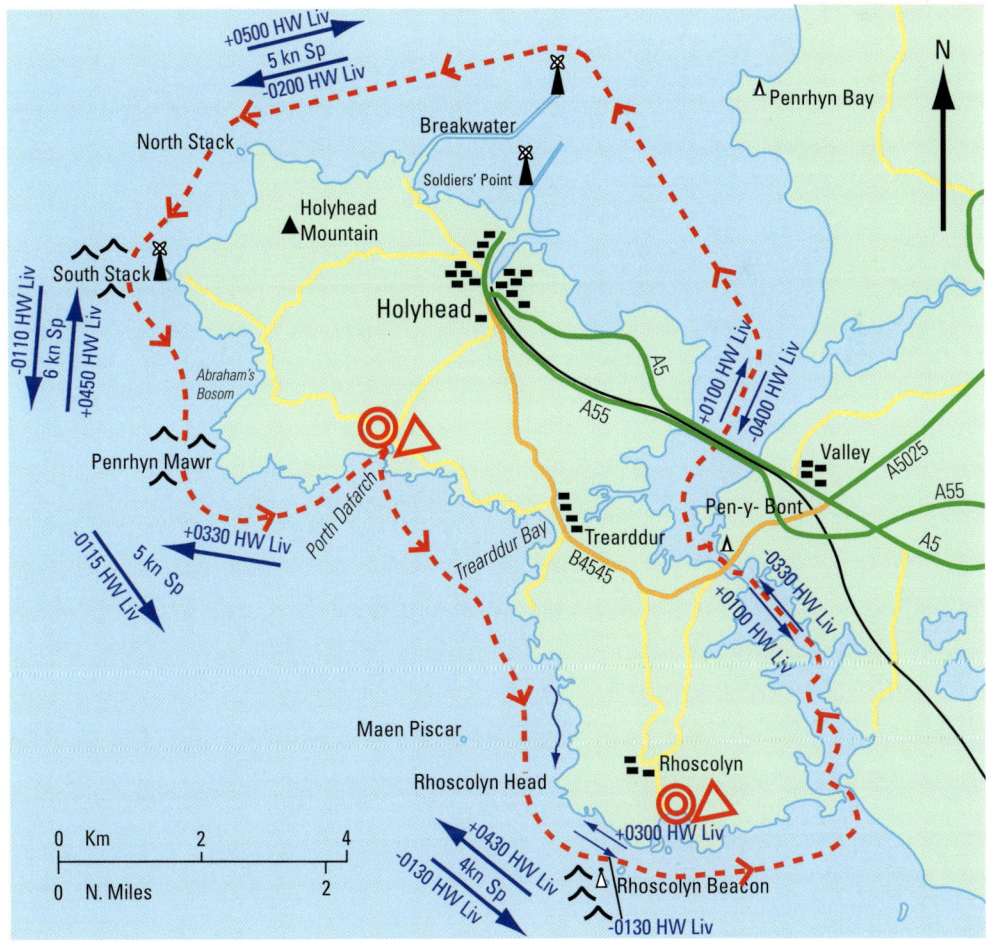

first 30 minutes of the flood it would become impossible to make progress against the flow. As the flow increases a standing wave forms where water exits the tunnel and enters the Inland Sea. This wave has been popular with playboaters for many years and can become crowded on summer weekends. Playboaters will want to arrive around 3 ½ hours before HW Liverpool in order to spend time warming up as the wave builds. As the flood dies away and the flow decreases it becomes possible to paddle through the tunnel from the Inland Sea towards Holyhead Harbour. The ebbing waters from the Inland Sea offer less excitement to playboaters and are generally of more interest to anglers.

A Tale of Two Stoppers - A Cautionary Note

During the middle hours of the flood, when the height difference between the water in Holyhead Bay and the Inland Sea is at its greatest, a dangerous stopper forms inside the tunnel. The stopper presents no danger to those playing on the wave that forms at the southern side but passage from Holyhead Bay through the tunnel during these hours presents a real and potentially fatal danger and should not be considered.

After local high water and as the level drops in Holyhead Bay, the north-going flow increases and a stopper forms at the north exit of the tunnel. This stopper forms very suddenly and is just as dangerous as the one mentioned above.

The area to the north and west of Stanley Embankment is known as Beddmanarch Bay. There is a nature reserve and a car park with easy access to the sea. The northern end of Beddmanarch Bay is marked by a headland called Gorsedd y Penrhyn. As you clear the shallow waters beyond the headland the port of Holyhead will come into view. This is a good time to call Holyhead Port Control to let them know your intentions.

Crossing Holyhead Harbour poses an unfamiliar hazard to kayakers. We regularly and happily learn about the natural dangers of tide races, inclement weather and rocky shores, but we are usually ill-prepared to deal with the close proximity of large shipping. There are frequent car ferry services to Ireland from Holyhead, some of which operate at alarming speeds. In order to get from Stanley Embankment to the end of the harbour breakwater, you must cross the main route that car ferries and other large vessels use to get in and out of the harbour. In order to complete this section of the journey safely, it is vital you contact Holyhead Coastguard and Holyhead Port Control and follow any advice they give to you.

Paddling along the shores of Penrhyn Bay will keep you to the east of the main harbour area but adds about 2km to your journey. There is also a campsite at Penrhyn Bay.

As you pass the end of the breakwater North Stack and its associated headland will come into view 4km to the west. In deteriorating weather conditions Soldiers' Point can provide a good escape route with the centre of Holyhead a short walk away. Porth Namarch provides the last opportunity to land and stretch your legs before committing yourself to paddling round 'The Stacks' with the west-going ebb stream. In fine weather the overfalls at North Stack will provide a good roller-coaster ride and, provided you stay well offshore, the strong tidal stream will assist your passage swiftly to South Stack. A passage close to shore, under the cliffs of Gogarth Bay, offers

Stanley Embankment | Trevor Shepherd

more shelter from winds with a southerly component, but will provide nothing in the way of tidal assistance. Staying offshore after passing South Stack will keep you in the flow, which begins to run in a more southerly direction and assist your passage towards Penrhyn Mawr.

Between South Stack and Penrhyn Mawr is Abraham's Bosom, which is the first useful beach landing since Porth Namarch. There are a set of steep steps and a footpath leading to the coast road, but using this as an escape route would take some desperate determination. The ebb stream runs south-east at Penrhyn Mawr. The seas tend to be far less impressive than during the hours in which the flood stream generates overfalls with fearsome reputation. Porth Dafarch and the end of this circumnavigation is a little over 2km to the east.

Variation (Clockwise) from Borthwen

Borthwen is the bay to the south of Rhoscolyn village. Driving on the narrow winding road to the beach requires patience, especially on a busy summer's day. Leaving Borthwen 4 hours before HW Liverpool will bring the benefits and assistance of the NW going stream. Rhoscolyn Head will be reached quickly and from there you can head directly across to Penrhyn Mawr. As you approach Penryhn Mawr the overfalls will be in fine voice. If you prefer a quieter passage, it is possible to make your way through some narrow channels immediately beneath the cliffs. Once you have passed the lively waters, the north-going stream will provide swift passage round South Stack, across Gogarth Bay and on to North Stack. As you clear North Stack you will be able to see the higher parts of Holyhead Harbour. This is a good time to contact Holyhead Port Control and advise them of your intentions.

A hazard to be taken seriously! | Mark Rainsley

If the harbour is busy with heavy traffic it may be better to cross from the end of the harbour breakwater to the shores of Penrhyn Bay before heading south towards Stanley Embankment. It is important to arrive at Stanley Embankment before water from the Inland Sea begins to flow north through the tunnel, but after the stopper inside the tunnel has dissipated. There will be plenty of time to rest by the shores of the Inland Sea before carrying on through Four Mile Bridge and south down the Cymyran Strait. The south-going ebb stream in the Cymyran Strait will assist your passage to more open waters and Cymyran Bay.

As you leave the confines of the strait you can turn west and follow the rugged coastline back to Borthwen.

Tide & Weather

The point of departure will depend on the tidal times on the day. The direction taken may be determined by the prevailing winds. Doing this trip anticlockwise is generally better on neap tides and with winds of a northerly component. A clockwise circumnavigation will always work better on spring tides and southerly winds.

Additional Information

Apart from the campsites mentioned in No. 7 and 8 there is a campsite with direct access to the sea at Penrhyn Bay, Tel. 01407 730496, www.penrhynbay.com, (SH 282 847 / LL65 4YG), across the water from Holyhead Harbour.

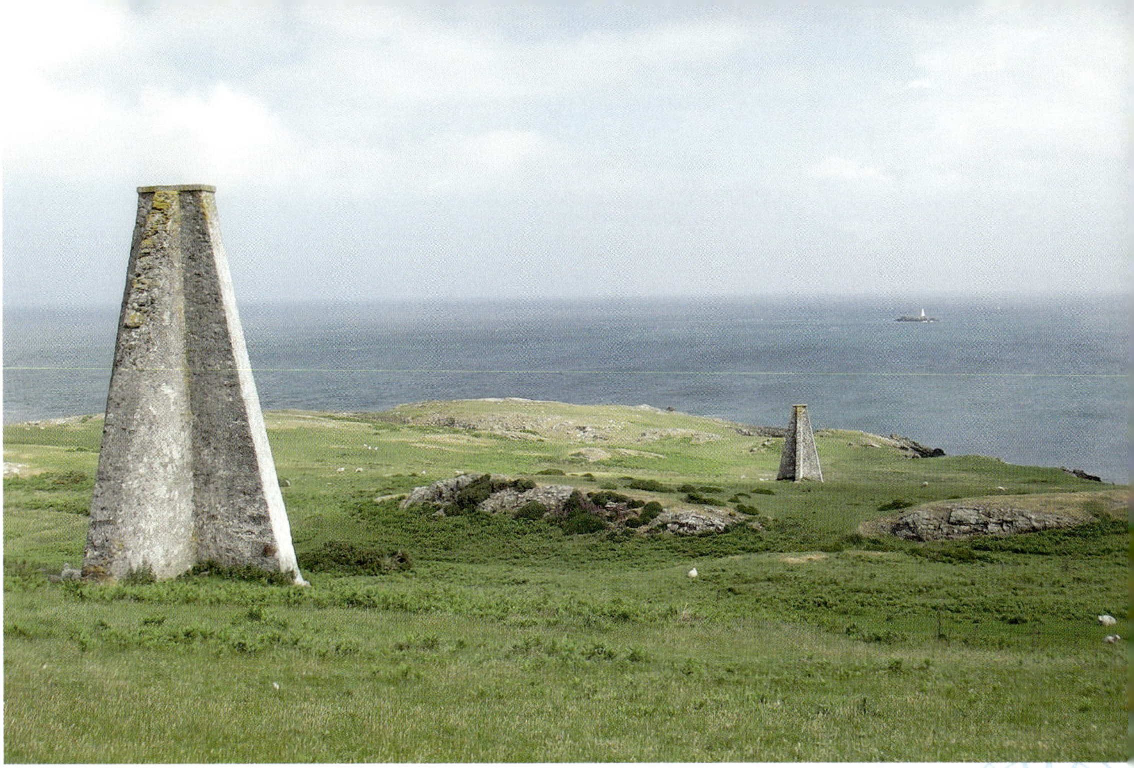

The 'White Ladies' – beacons on Carmel Head

Carmel Head

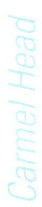

No. 11 | Grade B | 15km | OS Sheet 114 | Tidal Port Liverpool

Start	△ Porth Tywyn Mawr (Sandy Beach) SH 288 850 / LL65 4YH
Finish	◎ Cemlyn Bay SH 335 931 / LL67 0EA
HW / LW	at Holyhead are 48 minutes before Liverpool.
Tidal times	The NE going stream (flood) starts around 5 hours 15 minutes after HW Liverpool. The SW going stream (ebb) starts around 45 minutes before HW Liverpool.
Tidal rates	Around Carmel Head spring tides can run up to 6 knots.
Coastguard	Holyhead, Tel. 01407 762051, VHF 0150 UT repeated every 3 hours

Introduction

Carmel Head forms the north-west corner of Anglesey. Despite the proximity of Holyhead Harbour this coastline takes on a wild feel from the outset. During the summer months you will often see terns from the nearby breeding colonies of the Skerries and Cemlyn.

Description

Porth Tywyn Mawr can be difficult to find without prior knowledge of the narrow lanes or an Ordnance Survey map. About 1km north of Llanfachraeth on the main A5025 there is a road that leads west through the village of Llanfwrog to Porth Tywyn Mawr and the Sandy Beach Caravan and Camping Site. Although the lane is narrow there is room for a number of considerately parked cars. If there is no room at the side of the road, parking is sometimes available, for a fee, on the campsite. The beach is broad and sandy, and gently shelving. At low water the sea can be over 200m away from the high water mark.

As you make your way north from the bay you will find yourself in amongst some good exploring and rockhopping territory. The shores from here to Porth Swtan / Church Bay are made up of semi-submerged rocky reefs with small beaches, some of which have road access. The coastline is gentle at first with grassy slopes but as you venture further north the scenery becomes gradually steeper.

Church Bay can be identified from as far away as Holyhead by its distinctive yellow cliffs. The beach is sandy and gently shelving at mid to low tide. At high water landing can be tricky in rough conditions as there is only steep shingle or a concrete slipway to land on. The Welsh name for Church Bay is Porth Swtan. This name follows the tradition in Wales of naming bays after the type of fish landed in them. 'Swtan' is an old Welsh word for whiting. A steep winding track leads up the cliff to a small café and car park beside a campsite. 'Swtan', the cottage beside the car park

Carmel Head

A Little Gem

This is a little gem that few have found. Generally, we launch from either Penrhyn or Sandy Beach; both spots give easy access and cars can be parked safely for a nominal fee.

Set off a couple of hours before high water, paddling along the coastline to Church Bay; there's plenty of gentle scenery and rockhopping on the way that's often kept our group amused. Aim to reach Church Bay at the top of the tide. A word of warning - the dancing waves from the 'Sea Cats' now reach this beach so make sure that kayaks are well above the water line or up the slipway. There is a café at the top and the cakes and ice creams are great.

Heading across Church Bay in the direction of Carmel Head, hug the shoreline. There's some great scenery with caves and rock formations on the way. 2km from Church Bay you come to a bay with a plantation to its rear and huge caves, all backed by a pleasant secluded beach; this is Ynys y Fydlyn. Break out the barbie and get yer kit off, for this is a sheltered sun spot. The whole area is surrounded by huge magnificent caves; these can be explored by kayak though for a truly surrealist feeling you will want to explore them more closely. There's a myriad of narrow passages that interlink many of the caves… this is aquatic potholing so expect to get wet. It's a mystical experience traversing the long narrow passages and a head torch would be useful; often it's dark then suddenly there's a faint shaft of light that leads to safety. This is a special place and an experience not to be missed. If dark damp passages do not appeal to you then a short walk to the top of the headlands will reward you with fine views over Carmel Head and the Skerries, and a great photo opportunity.

Peter Hatt

is thought to be the last thatched cottage on Anglesey and has been restored as a folk museum by local enthusiasts. It is open to the public from April to September and is well worth a visit.

The scenery north of Church Bay becomes steadily more interesting with higher cliffs riddled with caves.

As you approach Carmel Head, the tidal stream will get stronger and no doubt you will be able to see the overfalls. If you stay offshore you will have a quick roller-coaster ride to the entrance of Cemlyn Bay. If the rough stuff off the headland is enough for one day, a more gentle passage close inshore will be slower but nearer to the many pools and lagoons in amongst the rocky shoreline. Once you enter the sheltered waters of Cemlyn Bay you may well wonder what all the fuss was about, although there will be the best part of a kilometre to the beach by the car park.

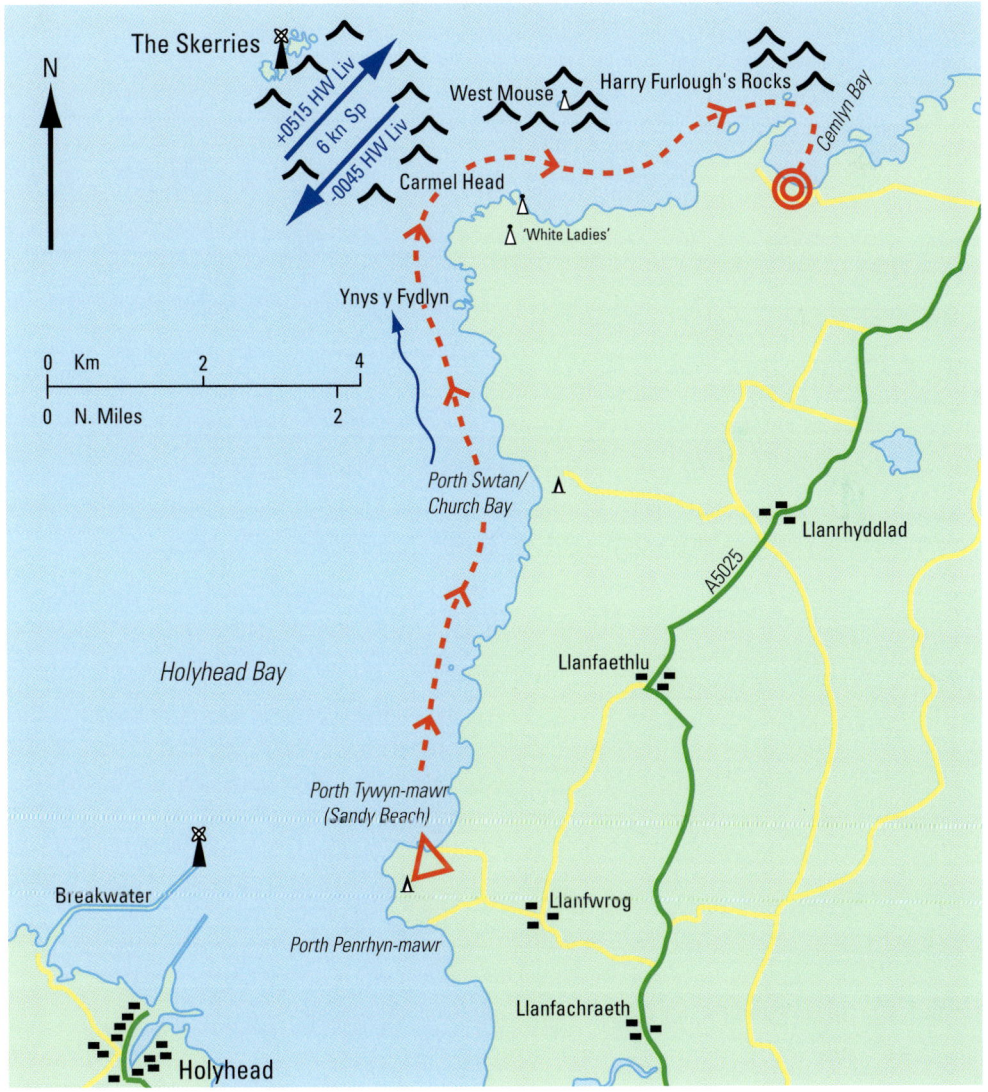

© Ynys y Fydlyn

Carmel Head

Tide & Weather

There are strong tidal streams round Carmel Head and offshore for all of this section, but close to the shore away from Carmel Head the effects of the tide are much reduced.

During the strength of the NE going stream (flood) a localised but strong back eddy runs west, close to the shore as far as 2km east of Carmel Head.

During the strength of the SW going stream (ebb) an extensive back eddy runs north, close to the west-facing shore of Holyhead Bay and is felt most between Church Bay and Carmel Head.

Additional Information

Penrhyn Bay Caravan Park at Llanfwrog (282847), Tel. 01407 730496, has direct access to the sea via a sheltered slipway to Porth Tywyn-mawr, but can be a little awkward close to low water.

Church Bay Cottages Camping and Touring site is fairly basic, quiet and is a short walk from the beach, Tel. 01407 730060. There is a charming seafood restaurant called The Lobster Pot just across the road and the Church Bay Inn is 1km up the road.

Variations

This trip can be done in the opposite direction using the SW going ebb stream round Carmel Head. Shorter less committing trips can be done from Porth Tywyn-mawr, Church Bay or Cemlyn.

Approaching The Skerries from the south

The Skerries

No. 12 | **Grade C** | **16km** | **OS Sheet 114** | **Tidal Port Liverpool**

Start	△ Cemlyn Bay SH 335 931 / LL67 0EA
Finish	◎ Cemlyn Bay SH 335 931 / LL67 0EA
HW / LW	are around 45 minutes before Liverpool.
Tidal times	The SW going stream (ebb) starts around 45 minutes before HW Liverpool. The NE going stream (flood) starts around 5 hours 15 minutes after HW Liverpool.
Tidal rates	The spring rates can reach 6 knots around the Skerries and in the vicinity of Carmel Head.
Coastguard	Holyhead, Tel. 01407 762051, VHF 0150 UT repeated every 3 hours

Introduction

The Skerries / Ynysoedd y Moelrhoniaid lie no more than 3km from Carmel Head and 13km north of Holyhead. There can be no doubt that the journey to the Skerries and back from Cemlyn Bay is a serious undertaking. This trip ensures a good test of navigation skills. On both the outward and return journey you will be ferry gliding across the strong tidal streams and overfalls of the exposed north-west corner of Anglesey. The crossing and arrival at the Skerries affords wonderful

Holyhead viewed from The Skerries | Mark Rainsley

views of the Anglesey coast from Wylfa Head to the east, through to Carmel Head, and 'The Stacks' to the south. The name of the Skerries in Welsh is 'Ynysoedd y Moelrhoniaid', which translates as the islands of the bald-headed grey seals. Your arrival will be carefully observed from the rocks above, and almost certainly from within the waters below by the many Atlantic grey seals for which the Skerries are home. There is also a bustling colony of Arctic terns on the islands, which makes this place incredibly noisy during the spring and summer months.

Description

Cemlyn is signposted from Tregele and Caerdegog Uchaf on the A5025 between Valley and Amlwch. There is a car park at each end of the bay, but the one at the east is closer to the water. Cemlyn has a steep shingle beach, almost 1km long, between low rocky headlands.

You should begin your journey in the last 2 hours of the ebb so that you arrive at the Skerries shortly before the stream dies away. You will feel the effect of the south-west going ebb stream as soon as you pass Trwyn Cemlyn at the western entrance to the bay. There will almost certainly be some rough water as you pass to the west of the green buoy that marks the seaward extremity of Harry Furlough's Rocks. From here onwards you should get used to paddling with the bow of your kayak pointing well to the right of your destination. You should pass close to the south of the north cardinal buoy at Victoria Bank and around 1km to the north of West Mouse. West Mouse is a small rocky islet and has a conspicuous white beacon on the top. You will have completed half of the crossing when the 2 beacons or 'White Ladies' on the hill to the east of Carmel Head line up with the beacon on West Mouse. As you get closer to the Skerries the direction of the tidal stream becomes more south-westerly. If you keep an eye to the south towards Holyhead you will see South Stack appear beyond North Stack. At this point there will be less than a third of the crossing to go and you should keep the northernmost tip of the Skerries to your west. Once you get round the north of the islands you will find the west shores are more sheltered from the tidal stream. With relief you can paddle into a lagoon and land on the pebbly isthmus beach that links the largest island with the smaller Ynys Arw (rough island).

There has been a light on the Skerries since 1717, which at that time was probably no more than a well-fuelled open fire in a brazier. Over the years the light was improved and by 1804 had taken a more traditional shape of a masonry tower with an oil-burning lamp. Trinity House took over the responsibility of maintaining the light in 1841 and further improvements were made. The light was converted to run on electricity in 1927 and automated in 1987. Since automation

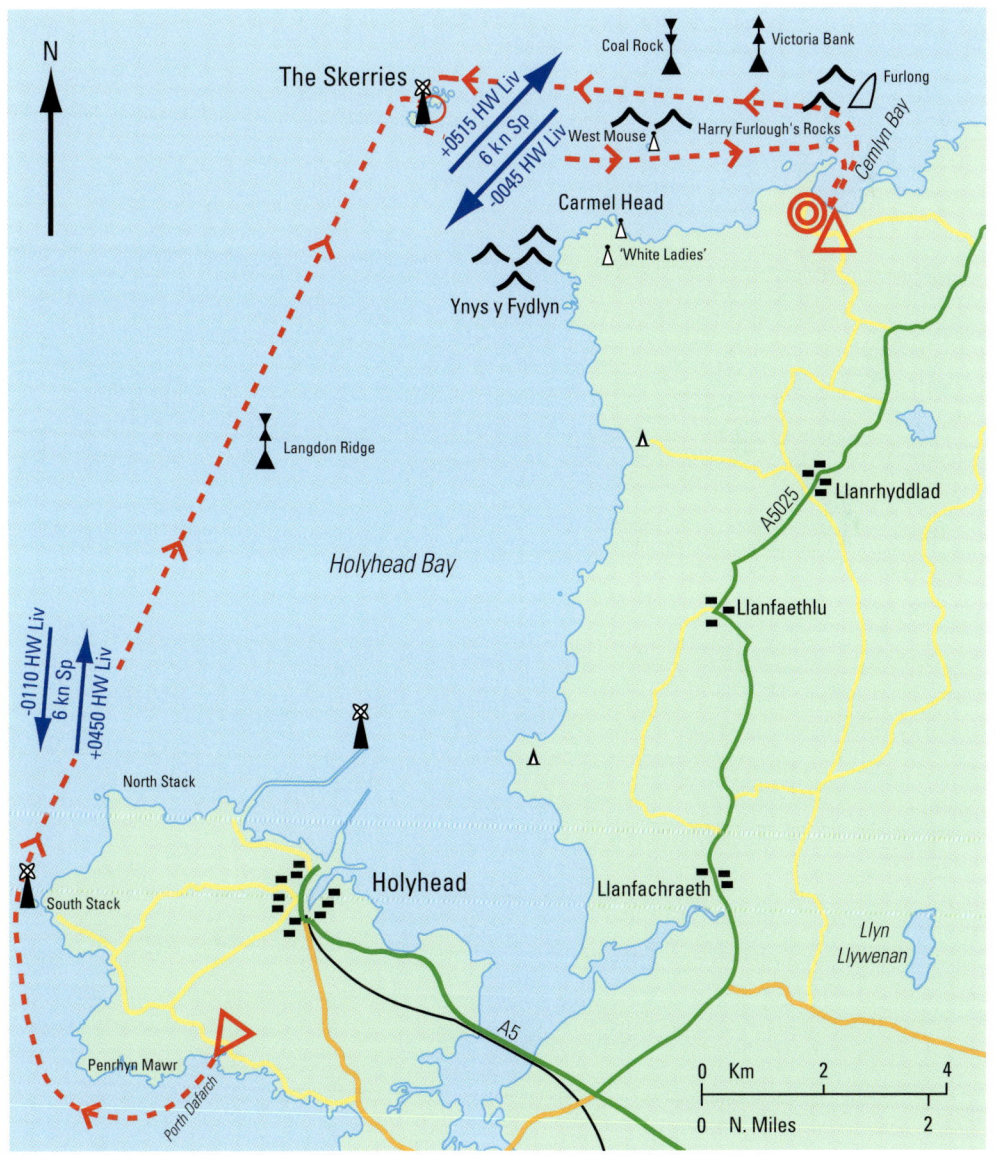

the only permanent inhabitants of the islands are hundreds of feral rabbits and the grey seals. The only minor interruption occurs when lighthouse maintenance crews visit the islands about once a month. During the spring, common and Arctic terns come to nest on the Skerries and the old lighthouse keepers' quarters are used by the enthusiastic volunteers who monitor the tern colony until the birds leave in late summer.

Timing the return is a matter of choice. Once the flood stream has begun, the sooner you leave the smoother the passage will be. In the early stages of the flood it is possible to paddle west from the lagoon and round the south-western shores before beginning the return crossing via West Mouse. Although there is no place to land, the eddy to the east of West Mouse can provide a welcome respite from the increasingly fast-moving tidal waters. The mainland shores to the west of Cemlyn are of great interest. There are wave-cut platforms with gullies and shallow kelp-infested lagoons that can provide some entertaining rockhopping within the last 2km of the journey back.

Tide & Weather

The Skerries are exposed to winds from any direction and lie in the midst of some of the most powerful tidal streams in the UK. There are numerous overfalls around the islands and, as both ebb and flood streams are used for this trip, wind is likely to oppose tide at some point.

Additional Information

Church Bay Cottages Camping and Touring site, Tel. 01407 730496, has direct access to the sea via a sheltered slipway to Porth Tywyn-mawr, but can be a little awkward close to low water.

Ty Newydd campsite at Church Bay, Tel. 01407 730060, is fairly basic and quiet and is a short walk from the beach. There is a charming seafood restaurant called The Lobster Pot just across the road and the Church Bay Inn is 1km up the road.

Variations

Another popular route to the Skerries is from Porth Dafarch on the south shore of Holy Island. This route is nearly 20km in each direction, and is a far more exciting and committing prospect. The major headlands at Penrhyn Mawr, South Stack and North Stack must be passed before crossing over 12km of open sea. After you pass South Stack your route should be around 1km offshore west of North Stack. This is a good time to call Holyhead Port Control for advice regarding traffic in and out of the harbour. It is vitally important that they know your plans when you are between North Stack and Langdon Ridge.

As you get closer to the Skerries the north-going flood stream becomes more north-westerly and you should pass the west cardinal mark at Langdon Ridge (SH 242 901) at least 500m to its west and keeping the Skerries well to the right of your bow. South Stack should always be visible, well out from behind North Stack.

As you approach the lagoon from the west on the last of the flood, the isthmus beach will almost certainly be submerged but there is a small rocky landing beneath the lighthouse. You may wish to paddle back to 'The Stacks', aiming to pass to the east of the Langdon Ridge cardinal mark as the south-west going ebb stream will tend to push you offshore.

View from Porth Wen towards Cemlyn | www.pixaerial.com

Porth Wen

No. 13	**Grade B**	**12km**	**OS Sheet 114**	**Tidal Port Liverpool**
Start	△ Cemlyn Bay SH 335 931 / LL67 0EA
Finish	◉ Bull Bay slipway SH 426 943 / LL68 9SW
HW / LW	are 35 minutes before Liverpool.
Tidal times	The east-going stream (flood) starts around 5 hours 15 minutes after HW Liverpool, the west-going stream (ebb) starts around 45 minutes before HW Liverpool.
Tidal rates	The tidal streams in this area run up to 5 knots during spring tides in open offshore waters. Closer in to the shore this is greatly reduced and there are numerous back eddies.
Coastguard	Holyhead, Tel. 01407 762051, VHF 0150 UT repeated every 3 hours

Introduction

This section introduces a stunning contrast of industry, ancient and modern, divided both by time and bold headlands. The nuclear power station at Wylfa Head is conveniently out of sight for much of this section. On the hills beyond, a modern wind farm generates electricity of a more

© Porth Llanlleiana

eco-friendly kind. The old china clay works at Porth Llanlleiana and the ruined brickworks at Porth Wen are hidden gems, and add to the diversity of the adventure to be experienced along Anglesey's north coast. The lack of road access to much of this coastline brings an eerie quietness to this wild and remote area.

Description

Cemlyn is signposted from Tregele and Caerdegog Uchaf on the A5025 between Valley and Amlwch. There is a car park at each end of the bay, but the one at the east is closer to the water. Cemlyn has a steep shingle beach, almost 1km long, between low rocky headlands. An interesting feature is the freshwater lagoon behind the beach which was created by Captain Vivian Hewitt in the 1930's. Hewitt's love for wildlife moved him to buy much of the surrounding land and run it as a wildfowl refuge. After he died the area was bought by the National Trust and has been managed by the North Wales Wildlife Trust since 1971. During the spring and early summer months, this is the best place in Wales to see Arctic, common and sandwich terns.

As you paddle out of the east side of the bay, the imposing hulk of the Wylfa Head Nuclear Power Station looms into view. This unfortunate blot on the coastline was opened in 1971 and remained in service until 2015. The power station used sea water as a coolant. This raised the sea temperature locally by several degrees. This rise in temperature contributed to an unusually high population of sand eels and other small fish upon which terns feed. It will be interesting to see what effect the decommissioning will have on the fish populations and in turn the seabirds. Paddling swiftly on will take you past Wylfa Head and into Cemaes Bay. The south-east corner of the bay has a picturesque harbour and a sandy beach. All of this makes Cemaes another good start or finish for a trip. There are two car parks with public toilets close to the beach and the town has plenty in the way of shops, cafes and local services. Just inside the eastern entrance of Cemaes Bay there is another small bay called Porth Padrig. The name literally translates as Patrick's Bay. The 'Patrick' to whom this refers is the patron saint of Ireland, who is said to have been shipwrecked upon these shores. In giving thanks for his survival, St Patrick built a church on the headland. Parts of the original structure date from AD 440.

As you paddle east from Cemaes the coast becomes rocky with steep cliffs rising to more than 30m. After 2km there is a small bay with a shingle beach and the stone ruin of an old factory on the land beyond. The bay is called Porth Llanlleiana and the ruin was once a china clay works. This is an excellent lunch spot with good shelter on a breezy day. From the beach there is an excellent view of Middle Mouse / Ynys Badrig. During early summer you will be able to hear the chaotic clamour from the razorbills, guillemots and cormorants that both populate and decorate this small rocky islet.

As you carry on to the east, the cliffs become higher and steeper. The north facing aspect of this area makes for a dark and foreboding feel on any but the sunniest days. No wonder the English name for the small gully, Porth Cynfor, is Hell's Mouth.

Porth Wen is a deep north-facing bay only 1km from Porth Cynfor. There are cliffs and high ground giving excellent shelter in all but northerly winds. The rocky shores with small pebbly beaches make this bay a perfect habitat for oystercatchers. The abandoned brickworks dominate the west side of Porth Wen. This small ghost town is a must to explore. It is possible to land on the pebbly beach beside a two storey building which housed the main workshop and accommodation. Other parts of the works are in varying states of decay but the 'beehive' kilns, where the bricks were fired, are in remarkably good condition.

The cliffs between Porth Wen and Bull Bay become steep and rocky once more. There is plenty in the way of rockhopping as well as a cave that can be paddled in one entrance and out of another when there is enough water. Bull Bay appears, less than 2km from Porth Wen, and the easiest

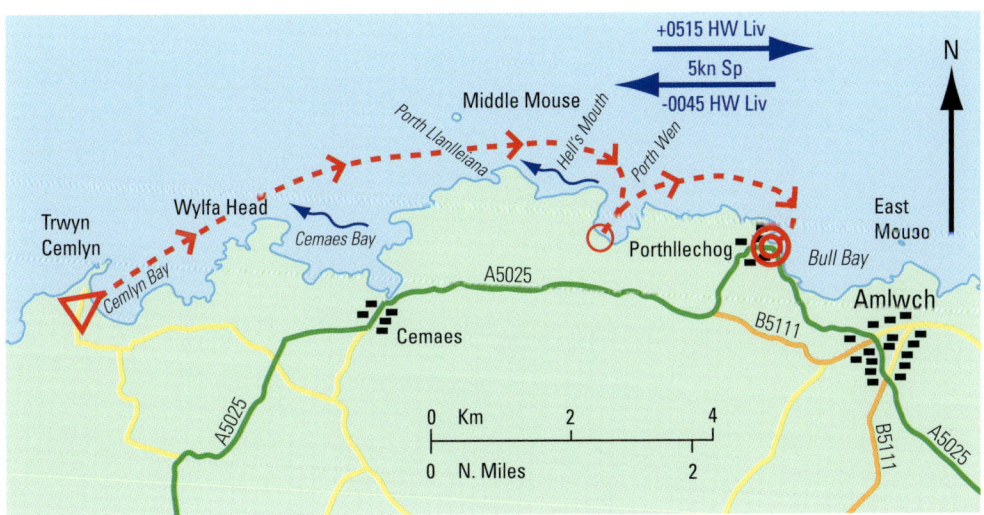

Arctic tern

Terns

Nothing can be more beautiful or distracting than the aerial display exhibited by a group of terns diving for small fish, the delicate 'lighter than air' look to their flight as they search and hover for food, changing to a dart-like dive into the water.

Common, Arctic and sandwich terns breed in great numbers along the northern shores of Anglesey. Common and Arctic terns are notoriously difficult to tell apart other than at close quarters. The Arctic tern has a deep red bill and short legs. The common tern has noticeably longer legs and a paler, shorter bill that has a black tip.

The Arctic tern undergoes an astonishing and seemingly exhausting migration cycle (surely an inspiration to all seafarers). From their breeding grounds in northern and sub-arctic Europe they fly to Antarctica for the winter, effectively enjoying a lifetime of summers. This extraordinary migratory pattern is unique to this bird and ensures that Arctic terns see more daylight in a year than any other living creature.

Sandwich terns are the largest terns to visit Welsh shores and are easier to distinguish from Arctic and common terns. They have a noticeably longer, almost crest-like black cap, a black bill and black legs.

landing is on a pebbly beach with a slipway just inside the western entrance to the bay. There is limited parking on the road beside the slipway but there is an additional public car park on the street opposite.

Natural arch and Brick kilns at Porth Wen | Eurion Brown

The Brick kilns at Porth Wen | Mark Rainsley

Exploring a sea cave near Bull Bay

Tide & Weather

High cliffs along the coast between Cemaes and Bull Bay can offer excellent shelter in strong southerly winds, but downdraughts can be a problem in places especially at Porth Cynfor / Hell's Mouth. Winds with a northerly component can give rise to tricky conditions with clapotis close to steep cliffs and headlands.

Tidal streams are strong in this area and can run up to 5 knots. Wind against tide conditions can produce difficult conditions with large breaking seas.

Back eddies form during the strength of the east-going flood stream across the entrances of Cemaes Bay and Porth Wen. This can hinder your approach to Porth Wen during the hours of the flood. The flood stream runs east, whilst the eddy stream runs west and can reach 3 knots. Progress against this eddy stream can be slow and difficult. To avoid the eddy and keep with the main tidal stream you will need to be 500m offshore until you can see right into the bay.

Variations

Cemaes Bay makes a wonderful alternative start / finish to a trip in this area. There are two car parks by the main beach, with shops and public toilets close by.

This trip can easily be done in reverse, making use of the ebb stream instead of the flood. A return trip to the brickworks at Porth Wen from Bull Bay can be as little as 4–6km in total but can be an excellent short paddle packed with interest.

Point Lynas

No. 14	**Grade B** **17km** **OS Sheet 114** **Tidal Port Liverpool**
Start	△ Bull Bay slipway SH 426 943 / LL68 9SW
Finish	◎ Moelfre Beach SH 512 863 / LL72 8HP
HW / LW	are around 30 minutes before Liverpool.
Tidal times	The SE going stream (flood) starts around 5 hours 30 minutes after HW Liverpool. The NW going stream (ebb) starts around 30 minutes before HW Liverpool.
Tidal rates	Around Point Lynas the spring rate can reach 6 knots but is more typically 2-3 knots for the rest of this section.
Coastguard	Holyhead, Tel. 01407 762051, VHF 0150 UT repeated every 3 hours

Introduction

The north-east corner of Anglesey is a bleak and inhospitable place. Strong tidal flows along the northern part of this section give rise to races and overfalls. In the southern part of this section the scenery and tides are gentler. There is a small island with a colony of seals and there are bays with sandy beaches. Journey's end is at Moelfre, a small town steeped in maritime history, which is celebrated in the nearby Seawatch Centre.

© Bull Bay

Description

Bull Bay is on the A5025 north coast road between Cemaes and Amlwch. The name in Welsh is Porth Llechog which translates as 'well sheltered bay'. There is limited parking beside a slipway that leads to a gently shelving, pebbly beach. There are public toilets opposite a small public car park in the street opposite.

As you leave the beach at Bull Bay, it is worth spending a little time exploring the rocky shore and caves before heading out to East Mouse. East Mouse / Ynys Amlwch is a small rocky islet to which cormorants and seals seem to have exclusive access. The tidal stream is swift around the islet and overfalls develop during the middle hours of the tide, especially when wind opposes the direction of the stream. The nearby town of Amlwch grew up in the 1800's as a port exporting copper and other minerals mined from the nearby Parys Mountain. Amlwch also gained a reputation for shipbuilding of the highest quality and at least 28 vessels were built in the late 1700's and 1800's.

Amlwch Port provides little in the way of interest to sea kayakers other than a general store, pub and a fish and chip shop (open lunchtimes). All are within easy walking distance from the inner harbour. The Amlwch Heritage Centre is of more general interest and can be found in the Sail Loft building beside the port.

The coast to the east of Amlwch becomes greener but the shore is still rocky and steep with no opportunity for landing until the sheltered bay at Porth Eilian is reached. Porth Eilian is west of Point Lynas and is sometimes referred to as Lynas Cove. There is a sheltered shingle beach and a slipway, making this an ideal lunch spot, especially as there is often a tea van parked here. There are also public toilets just 100m up the hill and a pleasant campsite just a little further. It is only the lack of car parking close to the beach that prevents Porth Eilian from being a good start or finish for a paddling trip.

Point Lynas / Trwyn Eilian is the northern spur that stretches more than 500m into the sea from the coastline beneath the slopes of Mynydd Eilian. This forms the north-eastern extremity of Anglesey. The Mersey Docks and Harbour Company built the lighthouse in 1835, replacing a more primitive light that had been in operation since 1779. The jetty to the south-east was used by pilots guiding ships across the notoriously difficult waters to Liverpool.

The overfalls that form to the east of the headland extend between 1-2km offshore and can give rise to big seas in wind against tide conditions. It is sometimes possible to avoid the biggest water by keeping close in to the headland. During the hours of the flood the main tidal race rushes east, then south-east, initially leading offshore, then running parallel to the coast. The waters to the south of the overfalls begin to eddy in the opposite direction, north-west towards the end of Point Lynas. This eddy effect can seriously hamper any progress towards Moelfre. There are two routes possible: either stay with the fast-moving water in the main tidal race offshore, or cross the rough water as quickly as possible and paddle close to the shore. The effect of the north-west going eddy stream is much reduced close in under the cliffs. At times you will need to be no more than 2-3m from the shore. The good thing about choosing the inshore route is that you will be better placed to explore the craggy cliffs and blocky shoreline of Fresh Water Bay, Porthygwichiaid and Penrhyn Glas in relatively peaceful waters.

Ynys Dulas is little more than a narrow rocky ledge less than 500m long and lies 1km off the northern entrance of Dulas Bay. The islet and its surrounding waters support a thriving population

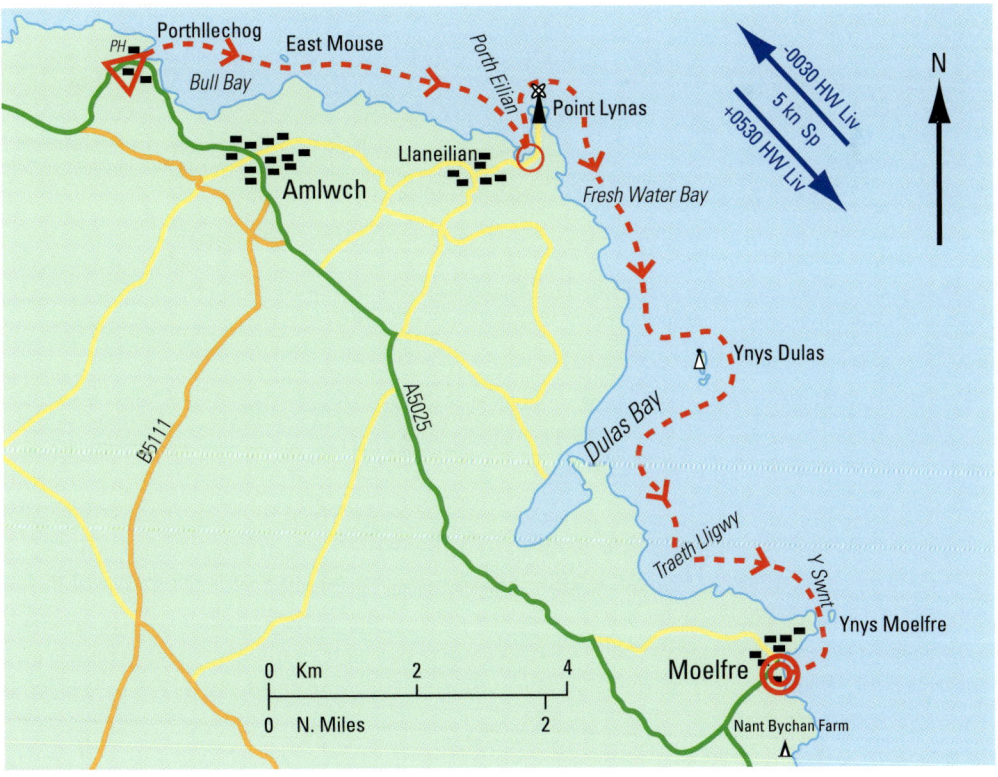

The Royal Charter

It was on these rocks that the biggest maritime disaster to happen in peacetime ended in the loss of 454 lives. On the 26th October 1859 the ship 'Royal Charter' was on the final leg of a voyage from Melbourne in Australia to Liverpool. As the vessel entered the Irish Sea the storm of the century blew up. The weather was too bad for the pilot from Point Lynas to board the vessel, so the decision was made to wait for better weather in the bay off Moelfre. Through the night the wind gained strength and changed direction. The force of the wind on the ship was so great that the anchor chains broke, leaving the Royal Charter to be swept onto the rocks where she began to break up. Many of the lives were lost in attempts to clamber up the slippery limestone cliffs to safety. Some accounts tell of bodies of drowned men from the wreck having been found laden with gold.

Fresh Water Bay

of cormorants, herring gulls and grey seals. The tower in the middle is hollow and was built to serve firstly as a beacon to mark the position of the rocks and secondly as a shelter for shipwrecked seamen, should its primary function prove unsuccessful.

To the south of Dulas Bay there is a more gently rolling landscape. There are the sandy beaches of Traeth Dulas, Traeth yr Ora and the most popular Traeth Lligwy. Traeth Lligwy has an extensive car park, toilets and a beach shop, making this a good place to base a short seal-watching trip to Ynys Dulas, although you will be presented with a long walk with your kayak at low water.

Between Lligwy Beach and Moelfre there is an area of low cliffs and a headland made of limestone. This is the beginning of the band of limestone, which characterises the rest of the east coast of Anglesey and continues across the water to the Ormes at Llandudno and onwards across Flintshire into Clwyd.

Less than 200m from the headland lies Ynys Moelfre, a low rocky stack often adorned with cormorants. The stretch of water that separates Ynys Moelfre from the headland is known as 'Y Swnt' and is popular with anglers who cast their many lines from the headland. The steep shingle beach beneath the Kinmel Arms brings this section to a close with spectacular views across Anglesey to the mountains of Snowdonia and across the water to the Great Orme on the coast of North Wales.

Tide & Weather

Tidal streams along this section are strong and there are overfalls in the vicinity of East Mouse and Point Lynas. In wind against tide conditions seas can build up, and steep confused water can

become very challenging. In these conditions the overfalls at Point Lynas extend from the rocky shore, well out to sea. However, this section of coastline can be one of the few paddling options open to you in a strong south-westerly wind.

The east coast of Anglesey has the weakest tidal streams and is best sheltered from the prevailing south-westerly winds.

Additional Information

The town of Amlwch has a petrol station and local shops.

There is camping at Nant Bychan Farm (SH 514 855), Tel. 01248 410269, with direct access to the sea less than a mile away at Moelfre. There is the added advantage of a fish and chip shop, bakery and the Kinmel Arms close by.

Variations

This trip can be done in either direction. If you intend to start at Moelfre use the ebb stream for assistance.

Lynas Cove / Porth Eilian can be a pleasant and well sheltered alternative start or finish for a trip along this section of coastline.

A short trip from Moelfre or Traeth Lligwy, round Ynys Dulas to look at the seals, avoids any major tidal problems.

Approaching the Isle of Man from the south | Barry Shaw

Bull Bay to Isle of Man

No. 15 | Grade C | 76km | OS Sheet 114 & 95 | Tidal Port Liverpool

Start	△ Bull Bay slipway SH 426 943 / LL68 9SW
Finish	◎ Port St Mary SC 210 676 / IM9 5EB
HW / LW	High and low water at Bull Bay are around 35 minutes before Liverpool. High and low water at Port St Mary are similar to Liverpool.
Tidal times	For Bull Bay see No.13. Offshore and off the Isle of Man's south coast the ENE going stream (flood) starts around 6 hours before HW Liverpool, the WSW going stream (ebb) starts around HW Liverpool. In Calf Sound the SE going stream starts around 3 hours after HW Liverpool, the NW going stream starts around 2 hours before HW Liverpool.
Tidal rates	Within 2-3km of the coast at Bull Bay the spring rate can reach 4 knots. In the vicinity of the Calf of Man tidal streams can reach 5 knots. The effect of tidal streams in the open sea is considerably less and normally reaches 2-3 knots.
Coastguard	Holyhead, Tel. 01407 762051, VHF Holyhead (A) 0150 UT repeated every 3 hours; Holyhead, Tel. 01407 762051, VHF Holyhead (B) 0130 UT repeated every 3 hours; Isle of Man, Tel. 01624 686612

© Port Erin, Isle of Man | Keirron Tastagh

Introduction

This open crossing is significantly shorter than the crossing from Porth Dafarch to Dun Laoghaire, but the distance and tidal streams still pose many problems for even the most experienced and hardy paddlers.

Destination or Journey

I lie awake, the darkness
Holding many questions
The time for leaving draws inevitably closer
Sleep evades me

Acute excitement mixed with dread
My senses razor sharp
Absolute self belief crosses swords with knowledge of risk
And the biggest question… What if?

Success enhanced self confidence leads the way

Ego follows just behind
Is this a dangerous combination?
Or the key to this adventurous undertaking

Keirron Tastagh – www.adventurousexperiences.com

Description

It is best to start around 5 hours after HW Liverpool in order to make the best of any advantage that the ENE going flood may provide. The highest point on the Isle of Man is the summit of Snaefell and it provides a target to aim for. The height of Snaefell, when compared to the mountains of Snowdonia or Wicklow, is relatively modest at 621m. However, cumulus clouds often build around the summit during fair weather, providing a good visual target. The strong tidal streams close to the southern shores of the Isle of Man can present difficulties on the final part of this voyage. If you end up too far to the west to arrive at Port St Mary, Port Erin makes a suitable second choice landing. Both Port St Mary and Port Erin have good harbour facilities.

Tide & Weather

There are strong tidal streams on the approach to the Calf of Man. Before embarking upon a long exposed open crossing you should have an accurate weather forecast for the area.

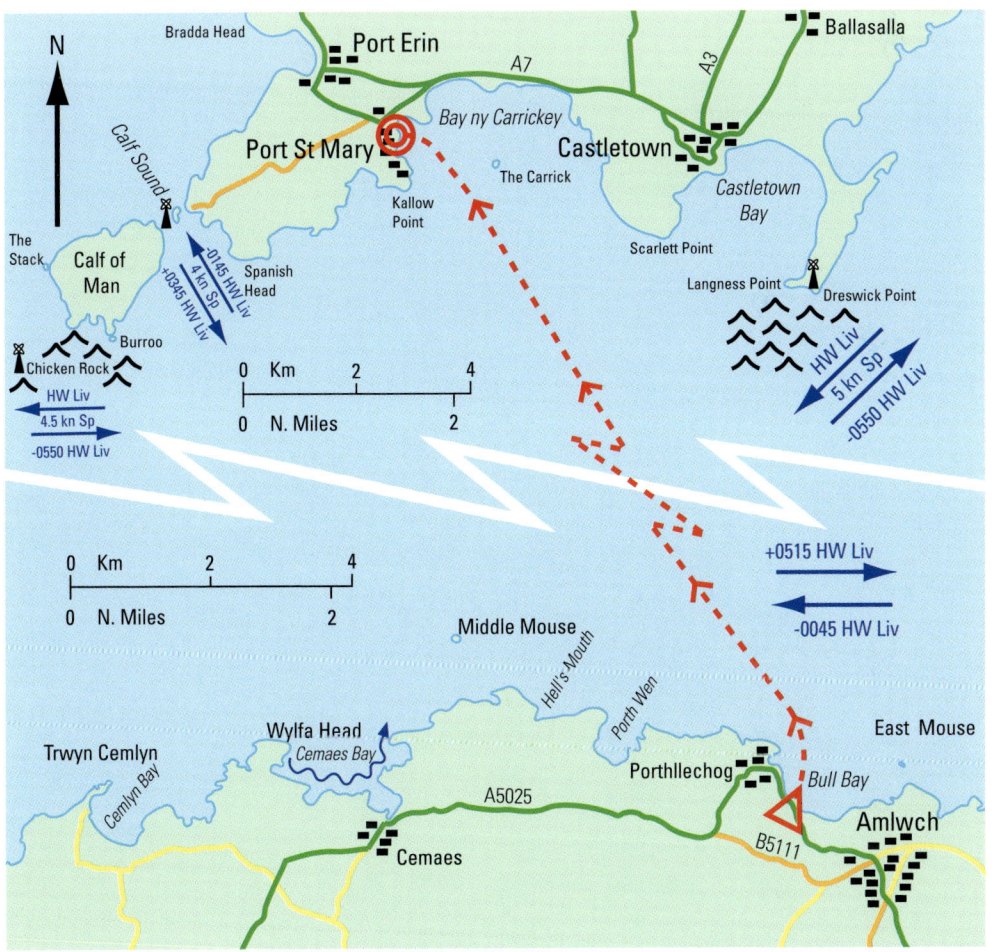

Quotes from the Kayak

"Here we are at 6 in the morning and I've still absolutely no sight of land, and no idea where I am… I've been hallucinating… Not sure if it's the chocolate that I ate or what. Maybe lack of sleep."

"3 hours on and I've still absolutely no idea where I am….A bit more worried now.

I guess the only thing I might have maybe done….I might have gone out west. So I've just paddled due north for an hour….And there's still no sight of land.

I'm going to do another hour or two and see what happens."

"Here we are again. I think I can see what appears to be a hill over there, but I've been seeing houses and trees and people and cars for the last 4 hours….I don't know what it is, so I'll carry on paddling and see."

"I just feel like I might be out here all week… It's horrendous!"

"Such a good start early on, paddled out through the races… The moon coming up… Shooting stars. It looked liked the perfect evening. Now it looks like the perfect disaster!

I'm not sure which hurts more; my ego or my pride… Probably both."

Taken from my video diary, on my second crossing from Holyhead to the Isle of Man. Unlike my first time, completed mostly in daylight, I chose to undertake this one through the night. Open crossings are for me, an aspect of sea kayaking almost conflicting with my main motivations to paddle.

The joys and contentment of the coastline, bird and marine life, desire to improve and introduce others to this life, sharing with them experiences, thoughts and happiness. This continuous, acute stimulation of the senses is sacrificed for a deeper, more powerful feeling, personal, and centred on achievement and the final goal. A demanding journey, where the smallest inner doubt or fear can escalate out of control. Following my first successful crossing home to the Isle of Man, (young bravado attitude making me oblivious to negative feelings), I looked forward to repeating the trip. It was an educational experience.

Keirron Tastagh – www.adventurousexperiences.com

Additional Information

Port St Mary Harbour Office, Tel. 01624 833205, 9am - 4pm.
Toilets and showers are available by calling the harbour office in advance.

Port St Mary Yacht Club, Tel. 01624 832088, toilets and showers.

Port Erin Harbour Office, Tel. 01624 833206, 9am - 4pm.
Toilets and showers are available by calling the harbour office in advance.

Adventurous Experiences (Sea Kayaking Centre) 01624 843034.
www.adventurousexperiences.com

The Lleyn Peninsula

An Introduction

The Lleyn Peninsula is the part of north-west Wales which juts out into the Irish Sea, just to the south of Anglesey. The word 'Peninsula' quite literally means 'almost an island' and, like an island, the Lleyn has a unique and insular flavour all of its own. Some of the earliest travellers to this ancient wilderness were pilgrims and saints who trudged their way along the rugged, north coast trail towards Aberdaron. Their quests to reach Bardsey Island are well documented in local churches, especially the church of St Beuno at Pistyll, which had a reputation as a centre for healing. The pilgrims also found shelter and replenishment at Cwrt, by Aberdaron, whilst waiting for favourable conditions to cross the treacherous waters of Bardsey Sound.

The next few chapters run parallel to the pilgrims' footsteps along the rugged north coast, and across the sea to the holy and mystical island of Bardsey. The north coast of the Lleyn Peninsula is one of the wildest areas covered by this book. Towering cliffs swarming with seabirds, sandy beaches and a feeling of being at the extremity of a great land, greet all who visit these impressive shores. Despite the wild qualities of this coastline there are a good number of escape routes, footpaths and lanes leading to main roads with bus routes. Civilisation is never all that far away.

In contrast, the coastline of the southern Lleyn offers trips of a gentler nature. The paddling experience on the south side may be more relaxed, but the opportunity for adventure is by no means dissipated. Rolling hills descend to the sea to become broad sandy beaches, slung between bold headlands with off-lying islands. The comparative calmness of the waters here make it easier to appreciate wildlife and the inspiring scenery it occupies.

The Lleyn has plenty of paddling for everyone, from short afternoon or sunset paddles to longer and even multi-day trips. The 75km trip from Trefor to Pwllheli is a true classic. It is often dwarfed in importance and popularity by the circumnavigation of Anglesey but, with fewer towns en route, offers a greater sense of wilderness. The direction taken is less important in terms of tides than around Anglesey, but campsites in the Trefor area offer a safer place to leave your car. The journey can be completed in 3 or 4 days and a frequent bus service makes it easy to collect your car at the end of the trip. There is an hourly service between Pwllheli and Caernarfon, which also calls in at Trefor. Most other towns and villages on the Lleyn have buses 3-6 times daily. . If you pass close to the town of Llanberis on your way to the Lleyn, there is a good paddlesport shop called Snowdonia Watersports beside Llyn Padarn.

Background Reading

Cruising Anglesey and Adjoining Waters, Ralph Morris, Imray, 2021, ISBN 9781786791825
www.rhiw.com a website depicting the cultural heritage of the Lleyn.

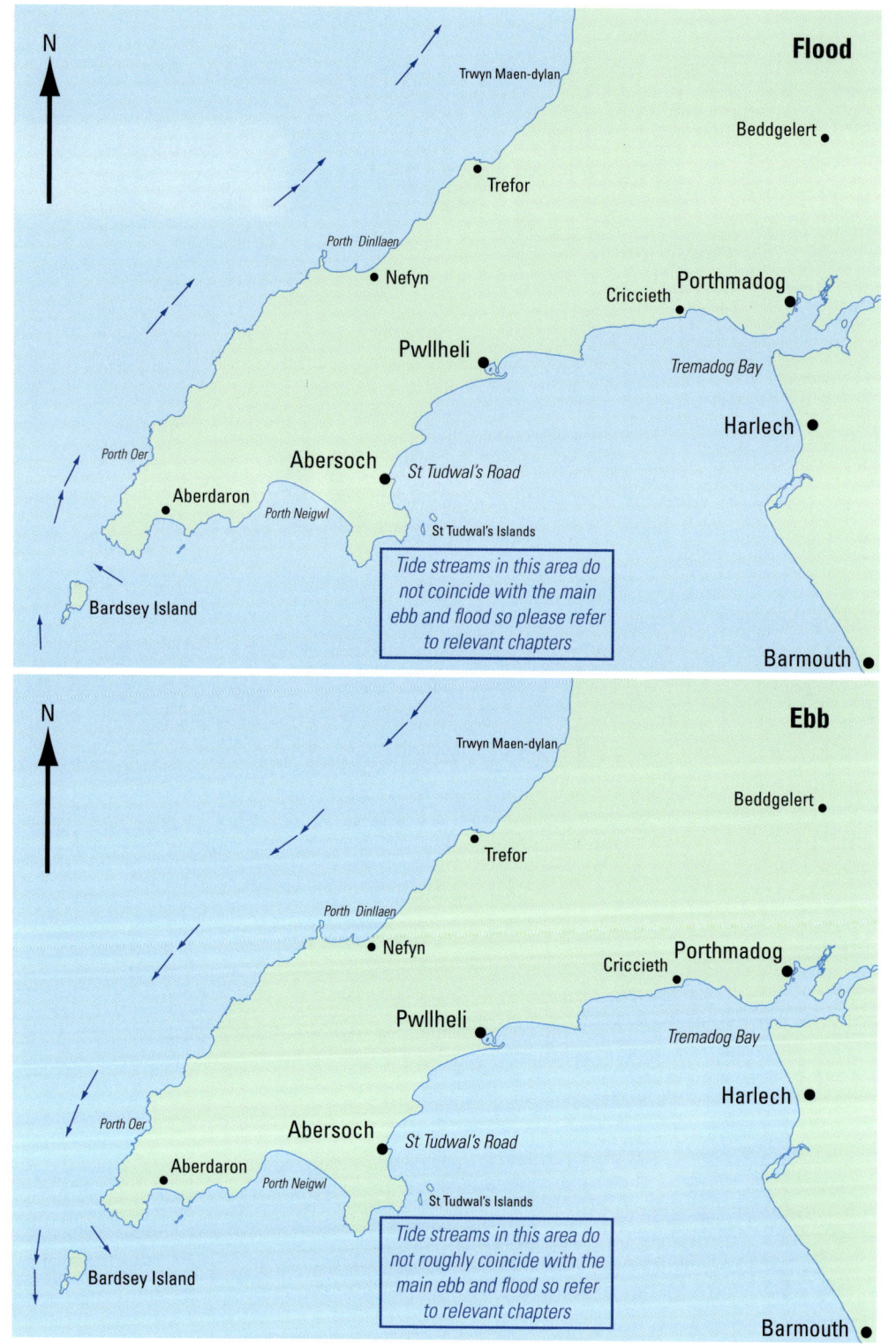

The above charts are intended to give a general overview. Consult the relevant chapters and other sources for more precise information.

The west-facing slopes of Yr Eifl

Trefor to Porth Dinllaen

No. 16 | Grade A | 12km | OS Sheet 123 | Tidal Port Liverpool

Start	△ Trefor beach SH 376 472 / LL54 5LB or Aberafon Campsite SH 400 484 / LL54 5PL
Finish	◎ Lon Bridin, Morfa Nefyn SH 282 408 / LL53 6BY, via Tŷ Coch SH 276 416 / LL53 6DB
HW / LW	are around 2 hours before Liverpool.
Tidal times	The SW stream starts 2 hours before HW Liverpool. NE stream starts 4 hours after HW Liverpool.
Tidal rates	The spring rate for most of this section is no more than 2 knots.
Coastguard	Holyhead, Tel. 01407 762051, VHF 0150 UT repeated every 3 hours

Introduction

A range of three bold peaks called Yr Eifl dominates this spectacular coastal scenery. The west-facing slopes drop dramatically into the Irish Sea forming some impressive cliffs. As if the scenery itself were not enough to take your breath away, these cliffs are home to thousands of nesting seabirds such as guillemots, razorbills and fulmars during their breeding season in spring and early summer. The coastline beyond the mountains becomes gradually more relaxed with pleasant beaches and

© Gyrn Goch, Gyrn Ddu, and Yr Eifl Quarry | Mark Rainsley

Trefor to Porth Dinllaen

smaller headlands, until you reach Porth Dinllaen, where you can relax with a refreshing drink outside a charming pub beside the beach.

Description

There is a large car park at Trefor and the harbour beach is generally well sheltered. Paddling west from Trefor you will find yourself beneath some impressive cliffs where there are several small stacks, caves and inlets to explore. The coastline soon turns south-west and the cliffs give way to easier views of Yr Eifl, the largest of three peaks which dominate the northern coast of the Lleyn Peninsula. The western edge of Yr Eifl crashes dramatically into the sea and forms a steep headland, Trwyn y Gorlech. This and the next headland, Penrhyn Glas, have seabird breeding colonies; this is a good place to see guillemots, razorbills and fulmars during the late spring and early summer.

Between these headlands is Porth y Nant; the beach here is steep and mostly made up of large pebbles making landing tricky in all but calm conditions. Landing is a little easier beside the remains of an old pier at the foot of Nant Gwrtheyrn, a wooded valley and abandoned, even haunted, mining settlement. Nowadays, Nant Gwrtheyrn is home to the National Welsh Language and Heritage Centre.

Once round Penrhyn Glas, white buildings at Porth Dinllaen will be in sight, the coastline is less steep and beaches become increasingly sandy. Don't be too tempted to make a dash across the bay, instead stay close to the shore, as the small headlands at Penrhyn Bodeilas and Nefyn can provide some pleasant rockhopping fun. From Penrhyn Nefyn, the charming Tŷ Coch public house is 2km to the west across Porth Dinllaen. Tŷ Coch can provide a fine range of hot drinks, snacks and meals as well as the expected alcoholic refreshment. There is no public road access to Tŷ Coch so there remains a 1km paddle to reach the point where the road, Lon Bridin, meets the shore close to Morfa Nefyn.

Rhys and Meinir

Rhys and his childhood sweetheart, Meinir, were orphaned children living in the proud, but poverty-stricken village of Nant Gwrtheyrn. As they became teenagers they fell in love and plans were soon made for their wedding. On the big day, Rhys went to the church as his friends went to Meinir's home to collect her. It was traditional for the bride to hide from the groom's entourage, so she ran into the woods and hid in the hollow trunk of an old oak tree, where she and Rhys often met at sunset. Rhys's friends couldn't find her, and assuming she had made her own way to church, they went to see if she was there. Meinir was not to be found anywhere in the village, and in the following days everyone was involved in looking for her. As the days passed less and less people searched for her. It was assumed that she had strayed too close to the cliffs and fallen to her death into the sea. In fact Meinir had become trapped in the hollow oak and had perished in her vain attempts to escape. Rhys went insane with grief but never gave up looking for his bride. Each day he would wander thorough the woods calling out, "Meinir, Meinir!" One stormy day Rhys took shelter beside the old oak where they had met in the past. Lightning struck the tree, splitting the trunk open and revealing the skeleton of Meinir, still in her wedding dress. Rhys is said to have died on the spot from a broken heart.

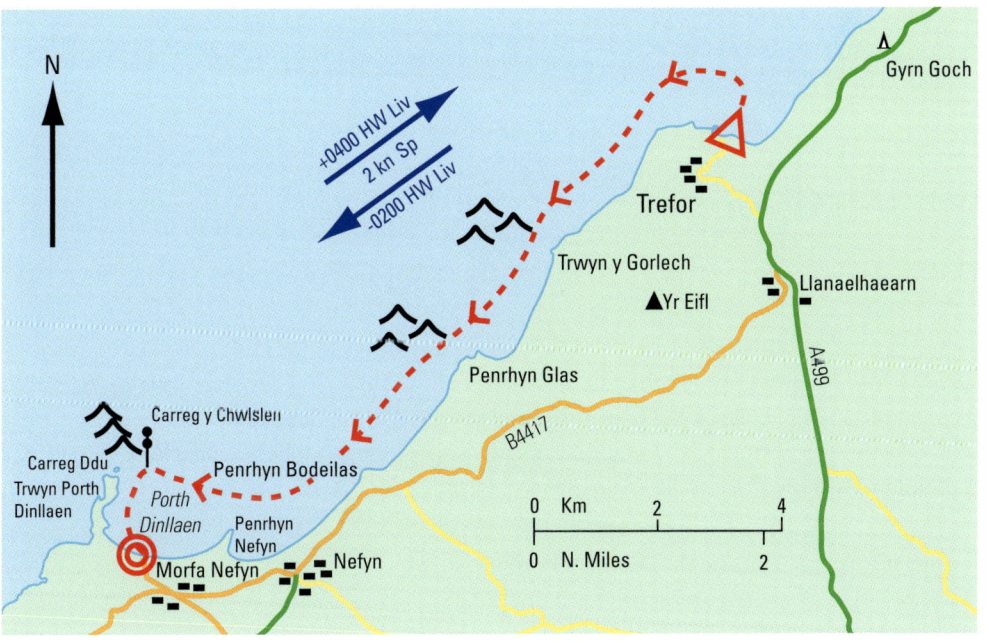

Looking north over Porth Dinllaen

Tide & Weather

The north part of the Lleyn Peninsula is exposed to any winds with a westerly or northerly component but is generally well sheltered in south-easterlies. Leaving Trefor within an hour of local high water is best so as to take advantage of the south-west running ebb stream. There are stronger currents with overfalls beyond and to the north of Trwyn Porth Dinllaen.

Additional Information

Aberafon Campsite has direct access to the sea 2km north-east of Trefor, Tel. 01286 660295, www.aberafon.co.uk. Parsal Campsite, Tel. 01286 660222, is a little closer to Trefor, but direct access to the sea is less convenient. The petrol station at Clynnog Fawr also has a well-stocked general store for last minute goodies.

Variations

This trip can be done in the reverse; care should be taken if ending the trip on the beach at Aberafon Campsite. This beach is made up of large pebbles and boulders and from mid to low water would make for a difficult or possibly dangerous carry up the beach to the campsite. Winds and swell from the west or north-west can also produce dumping surf here. If in doubt a sheltered landing can be made beside the pier at Trefor.

Morfa Nefyn beach

Porth Dinllaen to Porth Oer

No. 17 | **Grade B** | **19km** | **OS Sheet 123** | **Tidal Port Liverpool**	
Start	△ Lon Bridin, Morfa Nefyn SH 282 408 / LL53 6BY
Finish	◎ Porth Oer (Whistling Sands) SH 165 298 / LL53 8LH
HW / LW	at Porth Dinllaen are 2 hours before Liverpool and at Porth Oer are around 2 hours 30 minutes before Liverpool.
Tidal times	The SW stream starts 2 hours before HW Liverpool. NE stream starts 4 hours after HW Liverpool.
Tidal rates	The maximum rate at springs is 3 knots, these are usually strongest around headlands causing small overfalls.
Coastguard	Holyhead, Tel. 01407 762051, VHF U150 UT repeated every 3 hours

Introduction

This section of coastline is steeped in seafaring history. During the 18th Century fishing, shipbuilding and goods trading maintained a thriving maritime community which competed with that of Holyhead. Evidence of this bustling past has been mostly swept away by years of storms but the atmosphere of a maritime past remains strong.

97

© Porth Oer

Looking beyond Trwyn Porth Dinllaen, the north coast of the Lleyn beckons you away to the south-west, headland after headland, stretching away into the distance. When paddling this section as part of a longer trip, it may be tempting to rush past, taking advantage of the tidal streams, which can reach 3 knots. It is far better to take a little time to have a closer look. The shores here are a mixture of small rocky cliffs, wave-cut platforms and small inlets infested with kelp. Remember to have your rockhopping head on, but be prepared for a close encounter with a startled seal.

Description

Porth Dinllaen is signposted as you pass through Morfa Nefyn on the B4417. The road down to the wide sandy beach is called Lon Bridin. There is no parking at the end of Lon Bridin but there

Porth Dinllaen Harbour

In 1804 some 700 ships sought shelter in the harbour at Porth Dinllaen and in one month alone 100 ships came there to escape storms. These were the days when Porth Dinllaen was considered to have claims of becoming a first rate harbour and, up to 1873 when Holyhead harbour was opened, many thought the former might obtain that honour. In later years traffic grew so brisk that locals talked about a railway being constructed to Porth Dinllaen but it never materialized, for which many of us are thankful today.

Rhiw.com

is a large car park on the cliffs above the beach. Kayak and kit can be unloaded at the end of the road and the car park is back up the hill, first right onto Lon Golff and first right again.

The headland, Trwyn Porth Dinllaen, forms the western end of the bay and provides good shelter from prevailing west and south-westerly winds. The Tŷ Coch pub and the surrounding cottages have a homely and comforting look, nestled together beneath the cliff. There are few buildings to be seen along the rest of this sparsely populated coastline.

If you are starting this trip during the middle hours of the ebb you can have a fun ride out of the bay through the overfalls to the north of Trwyn Porth Dinllaen. If, however you prefer the comforts of a smoother passage, the rough water can be avoided by staying close into the shore. With Porth Dinllaen and the headland behind you a series of low cliffs, with wave-cut platforms at the base, make happy playgrounds for seals. The coves and gullies throw up many challenges for those keen on rockhopping. Shortly after the sandy beaches of Porth Towyn a distinctive ruin, the remnants of a limekiln, upon a low rocky headland marks the entrance of Porth Ysgaden. There is a small shingle beach and a steep track to a small car park. A short walk inland from here would bring you to a couple of campsites not far from the village of Tudweiliog, which has a pub and a post office. 4km further along the coast lies a bay with a sandy beach nearly 2km long. At its southern end Porth Colmon provides an alternative start or finish point. There is a slipway, parking for 4-6 cars and a campsite very close by.

If you stay close into shore after Porth Colmon you will arrive at the scene of the Lleyn's very own 'Whisky Galore' story.

The Wreck of 'The Stuart'

On the morning of the 6th of April 1901 a trading ship called 'The Stuart' ran aground in misty conditions at Porth Ty Mawr. 'The Stuart' had been carrying porcelain goods, pianos, cotton and whisky for export to New Zealand. The crew made it ashore unharmed but it wasn't long before local people began to take advantage of 'The Stuart's' misfortune. When news of the accident reached Caernarfon, Customs and Excise officers hurried to secure the valuable cargo, but it was too late! The party had already begun. Some local people wishing to keep their new-found treasure from the customs men resorted to hiding bottles of whisky down rabbit burrows. The problem with thinking up a clever hiding place whilst drunk is that you invariably forget all about it by morning. Rumour has it that ancient bottles are still occasionally being unearthed, intact! The keel and some plating from 'The Stuart' can be seen at Porth Ty Mawr at low water on a spring tide.

Rhiw.com

From Porth Tŷ Mawr the end of this section, Porth Oer, is another 4km round Penrhyn Mawr. Not to be confused with its reputable namesake on Anglesey this headland does produce overfalls during the middle hours of the tide, but on a relatively small scale. Landing is easiest at the south end of the beach at Porth Oer, as it is more sheltered from prevailing wind and swell; this is also where the beach café and access road to the National Trust car park are.

Tide & Weather

The north part of the Lleyn Peninsula is exposed to any winds with a westerly or northerly component but is generally well sheltered in south-easterlies. Leaving Porth Dinllaen within an hour or two of local high water is best so as to take advantage of the south-west running ebb stream. During the middle hours of the tide, overfalls form off Trwyn Porth Dinllaen and Penrhyn Mawr. Wind against tide conditions can produce large breaking seas around these and other smaller headlands.

Additional Information

There is a well-stocked general grocers shop at Nefyn. There are also shops at Morfa Nefyn as well as a petrol station. Tudweiliog has little more than a pub and a post office. There is camping at Llechyn, close to Porth Colmon, Tel. 01758 770347, and Porth Ysgaden, Tel. 01758 770206, neither of which has direct access to the sea, but both are very close.

Variations

This trip can easily be done in reverse by starting at Porth Oer early in the flood. Shorter trips along this section can be started or finished at Porth Colmon and Porth Ysgaden.

Looking across Bardsey Sound to Bardsey Island / Ynys Enlli

Bardsey Sound

No. 18 | Grade C | 14km | OS Sheet 123 | Tidal Port Liverpool

Start	△ Porth Oer (Whistling Sands) SH 165 298 / LL53 8LH
Finish	◎ Aberdaron Beach SH 171 264 / LL53 8BE
HW / LW	at Porth Oer are around 2 hours, 30 minutes before Liverpool, and at Aberdaron are about 3 hours before Liverpool.
Tidal times	Lleyn north coast: The SW going stream begins around 2 hours before HW Liverpool, the NE going stream begins around 4 hours after HW Liverpool.
	Bardsey Sound: The SE going stream begins around 1 hour 15 minutes before HW Liverpool, the NW going stream begins around 4 hours 45 minutes after HW Liverpool.
	Bardsey Sound close inshore: A 'young flood' stream begins around 3 hours, 30 minutes after HW Liverpool and runs along the west side of Aberdaron Bay, then NW, close to the mainland shore of Bardsey Sound.
Tidal rates	Between Porth Oer and Braich Anelog the spring rates can reach 4 knots. On the approach to Braich y Pwll tidal streams become much stronger causing substantial overfalls. The maximum rate at springs is 6 knots here, through Bardsey Sound to Pen y Cil.
Coastguard	Holyhead, Tel. 01407-762-051, VHF 0150 UT repeated every 3 hours

101

Porth Oer

18 Bardsey Sound

Introduction

This is a committing paddle with strong tidal streams, few landings and no escape routes. The start and finish are in quiet, sheltered bays frequented by holidaymakers during the summer months where the bucket and spade are the tools of choice in the soft sands. The scenery on the journey between could not be more in contrast. The end of the Lleyn is the most westerly point in North Wales; the bold, rocky headlands bear the might of winter storms year after year. The views of Bardsey Island, as you make your way round Braich y Pwll, are awe-inspiring. The terrific reputation of Bardsey Sound alone is enough to get your heart racing. The sheer might of this mountainous headland will feed your imagination and inspire your paddling adventures for years to come. The exposed nature and strong tidal streams of this area require respect. If you get your tidal planning just right, on a fine day this trip can be a real dream, but wind against tide conditions can produce huge waves in confused seas. A good weather forecast and accurate tidal planning are just as essential as excellent paddling and navigation skills.

Description

Porth Oer is signposted from the B4413 just to the west of Pen y Groeslon. The surrounding land is managed by the National Trust; there are basic toilet facilities and plenty of car parking space in the fields above the beach. A steep, narrow track leads from the car park down to the beach where there is enough space to unload kayaks and kit; there is also a charming little beach shop where you can buy ice creams, hot drinks and snacks.

The beach at Porth Oer is made up from fine and uniquely soft sand. If you shuffle or stub your toes through a dry patch the sand squeaks or whistles beneath your feet, hence its anglicised name of 'Whistling Sands'. As you paddle from the beach there is entertaining scenery almost immediately. The grassy slopes to the west drop steeply down to a rocky shore riddled with gullies and pools bristling with anemonies and small fish. Make the most of this opportunity because as you pass the two stacks, Dinas Fach and Dinas Fawr, the coastline rapidly steepens to imposing cliffs over 100m high. Despite the height of these cliffs they are almost devoid of bird life. On a still morning with only the occasional cry of a chough from above, a relative stillness reinforces the isolated and lonely feeling of this place. As you approach the final headland, Braich y Pwll, the stark mass of Bardsey Island rapidly comes into view. Even during the final hour of the south-going ebb there can be overfalls here known as the 'Tripods'. There will almost certainly be overfalls at Braich Y Pwll also, but calmer waters should greet you as you turn to the south to enter Bardsey Sound.

The cliffs in the sound are broken up by a series of small bays, gullies and caves, all waiting to be explored. In one such bay, to the east of Trwyn Maen Melyn, is St Mary's Well (SH 139 251). Miraculously this pool contains fresh water despite being below the level of the highest Spring tides. The view of Bardsey Island to the south is a persistent but welcome distraction and may even prevent you from getting a cricked neck! As you pass Carreg Ddu you will be less than 1km from Pen y Cil and the entrance to Aberdaron Bay. Once round Pen y Cil, the beach and Ty Newydd Hotel will be clearly visible along the western edge of the bay.

The tide can go out as far as 200m on Aberdaron beach; landing at low water will give you a laborious carry. The village of Aberdaron is a picture postcard scene, narrow streets with tiny, whitewashed cottages made of stone. Access to the beach from the village is via a slipway between the Ty Newydd Hotel and the Church of St Hywyn. There is ample parking space and beach access in the village car-park beside the bridge over the River Daron.

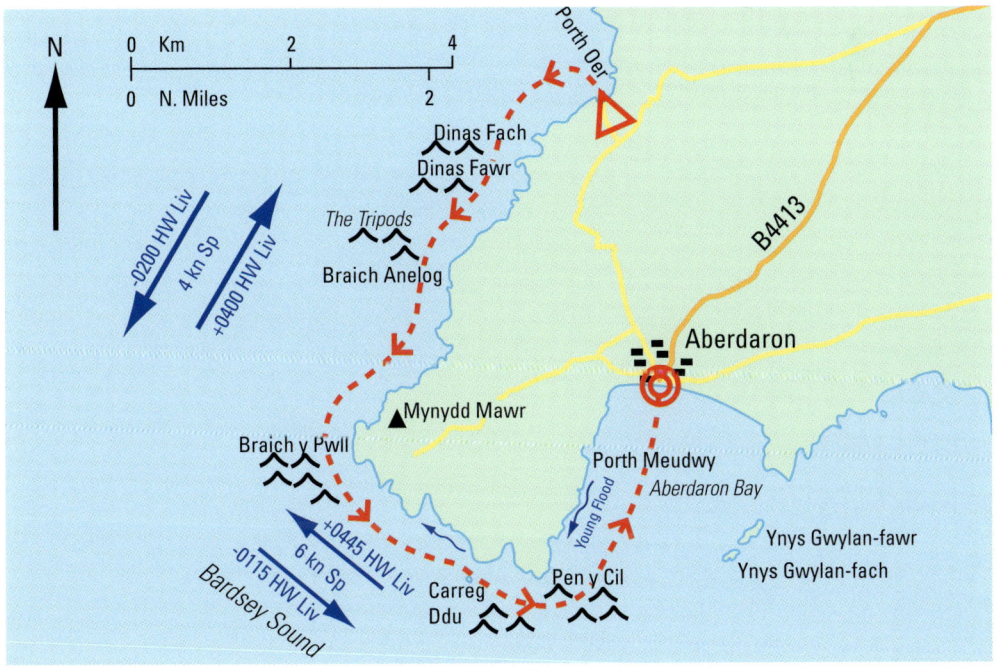

Choughs

The Chough (Pyrrhocorax pyrrhocorax)

Pronounced "chuff", the name of this bird is derived from its startling 'cheeow' call which is often heard above cliff tops and craggy headlands. The glossy black plumage and fiery red bill and feet of the chough give it a striking appearance. It should come as no surprise that these most regal members of the crow family have associations with the legend of King Arthur.

Some believe that Bardsey Island is the Isle of Avalon, the final resting place of King Arthur. One legend says that after being fatally wounded during his last battle, King Arthur was brought to Avalon where he was reincarnated as a chough.

To this day the spectacular aerial antics of the chough can be seen around the shores of Bardsey, the craggy headlands of the Lleyn and other remote headlands along the Welsh coast.

Tide & Weather

This section takes you around the most exposed coast of the North Wales mainland and is exposed to winds from almost any direction at some point. Be certain of the weather forecast before committing yourself. Ideally, for a smooth trip, your timing should mean that you pass Pen y Cil at around slack water. During the middle hours of the tide large overfalls form off Braich Anelog, Braich y Pwll, Carreg Ddu and Pen y Cil. These overfalls cannot always be avoided by keeping close in to shore.

◎ *Approaching Bardsey Sound*

◎ *Aberdaron*

Tide race off Braich y Pwll

Additional Information

There are a couple of campsites on the road from Pen y Groeslon to Porth Oer and over half a dozen in and around Aberdaron. One site of note is called Mynydd Mawr to the east of the hill of the same name (SH 143 255 / LL53 8BY), Tel. 01758 760223. This campsite is the closest to the end of the Lleyn and provides excellent views over the sea. From here you can see, hear and capture the mood of the racing currents of Bardsey Sound.

Just a few hundred metres away from Mynydd Mawr Campsite is a highly recommended licensed seafood restaurant. There are two wonderful cafés in Aberdaron, both with their individual charm. There are also two hotels, which serve food and drink to non-residents. There are a couple of well-stocked local shops and a bakery, and the 'Spar' shop has a good local butcher incorporated.

Variations

If you only have one car and do not wish to return to Porth Oer by sea, the walk back is only just over 4km along pleasant country lanes.

Doing this trip in reverse poses no additional problems. It is best to leave Aberdaron around 5 hours after HW Liverpool to leave the bay with the 'young flood' stream.

Bardsey viewed from Pen y Cil

Bardsey Island

No. 19 | Grade C | 17km | OS Sheet 123 | Tidal Port Liverpool

Start	△ Aberdaron Beach SH 171 264 / LL53 8BE
Finish	◎ Aberdaron Beach SH 171 264 / LL53 8BE
HW / LW	at Aberdaron occur around 3 hours 15 minutes before Liverpool and at Bardsey occur around 3 hours 20 minutes before Liverpool.
Tidal times	Lleyn north coast and west side of Bardsey: The SW going stream begins around 2 hours before HW Liverpool, the NE going stream begins around 4 hours after HW Liverpool.
	Bardsey Sound: The SE going stream begins around 1 hour 15 minutes before HW Liverpool, the NW going stream begins around 4 hours 45 minutes after HW Liverpool.
	Bardsey Sound close inshore: A 'young flood' stream begins around 3 hours, 30 minutes after HW Liverpool and runs along the west side of Aberdaron Bay, then NW, close to the mainland shore of Bardsey Sound.
Tidal rates	The spring rate in Bardsey Sound can reach 6 knots in places. Impressive overfalls form off Pen y Cil and Carreg Ddu during the middle hours of the tide.
Coastguard	Holyhead, Tel. 01407 762051, VHF 0150 UT repeated every 3 hours

© Henllwyn and Bardsey lighthouse

Bardsey Island — 19

Introduction

The Welsh name for Bardsey is Ynys Enlli, which translates as 'Isle of the Currents'. It is not the 3km from the mainland that makes this island so remote and tricky to get to, it is the strong tidal streams that run up to 6 knots in its surrounding waters. These are the waters that claimed many of the lives of those 20,000 saints to whom a memorial cross stands on the site of the old abbey on the island.

In the days of the Celtic saints and their travels, three pilgrimages to Bardsey Island held the same merit as one to Rome. To the present day Ynys Enlli / Bardsey Island retains its small time 'Holy Grail' status amongst sea kayakers. A trip to Bardsey is a serious undertaking in any weather. Careful tidal planning and a good weather forecast are essential, as well as the appropriate navigation and paddling skills.

The ancient pilgrims were not alone in their travels; Bardsey and the Lleyn are where many of Britain's migrating birds such as wheatear, sand martin and redwing stop for a rest before continuing to their final destinations. More significantly this is one of the few places where the rare and unusual Manx shearwater breed. Peregrine falcons and, oddly enough, long-eared owls have been breeding here now for a number of years.

Description

Paddle from Aberdaron about 4 hours after HW Liverpool in order to reach Pen y Cil and begin the crossing to Bardsey during the last hour of the ebb. Just over 1km south-west from Aberdaron is Porth Meudwy, a small sheltered bay nestled in amongst the steep cliffs. Porth Meudwy has served as a small, natural harbour and departure point for Bardsey since ancient times, a role which has changed very little to this day as tourist trips depart from here during the summer months.

Paddling on towards Pen y Cil you can see some of the disused mining quays wedged tightly into tiny bays and gullies. As you get closer to the headland you will begin to gain the assistance of the 'young flood' eddy stream. Pen y Cil will greet you with its might, splendour and reputation; the rock here stands firm in spite of tide and storm. From here you will have your first breathtaking view of Bardsey. The north-eastern slopes, forbidding and inhospitable, are all that can be seen at first.

Once away from Pen y Cil and its associated confused waters, you will tend to drift SE on the dying ebb stream and Pen Diban, the southernmost tip of Bardsey, will slowly come into view. Use Pen Diban, or even the lighthouse in line with Pen Cristin, as a transit. Slack water will greet you close to Henllwyn and Cafn Enlli. Henllwyn has a shingle beach at high water but dries to reveal jagged rocks and pools with kelp. It is easy to while away an hour or so watching the seals basking in the afternoon sunshine here. Landing is easiest by the slipway at the north end of the bay in the narrow gully called Cafn Enlli.

If you plan to paddle round Bardsey it is best done anticlockwise before landing so that the northern extremity, Trwyn y Gorlech, is passed as close as possible to slack water. The western shore is rugged. Low gnarly cliffs topped with heather and rough pasture give the feeling that this is a shore regularly battered by the prevailing south-westerly winds. On a pleasant day this is a wonderful place for watching seals at play. Landing is easy at Porth Solfach but at high water only! Beware of staying on this beach too long with a falling tide. As the water recedes, a steep

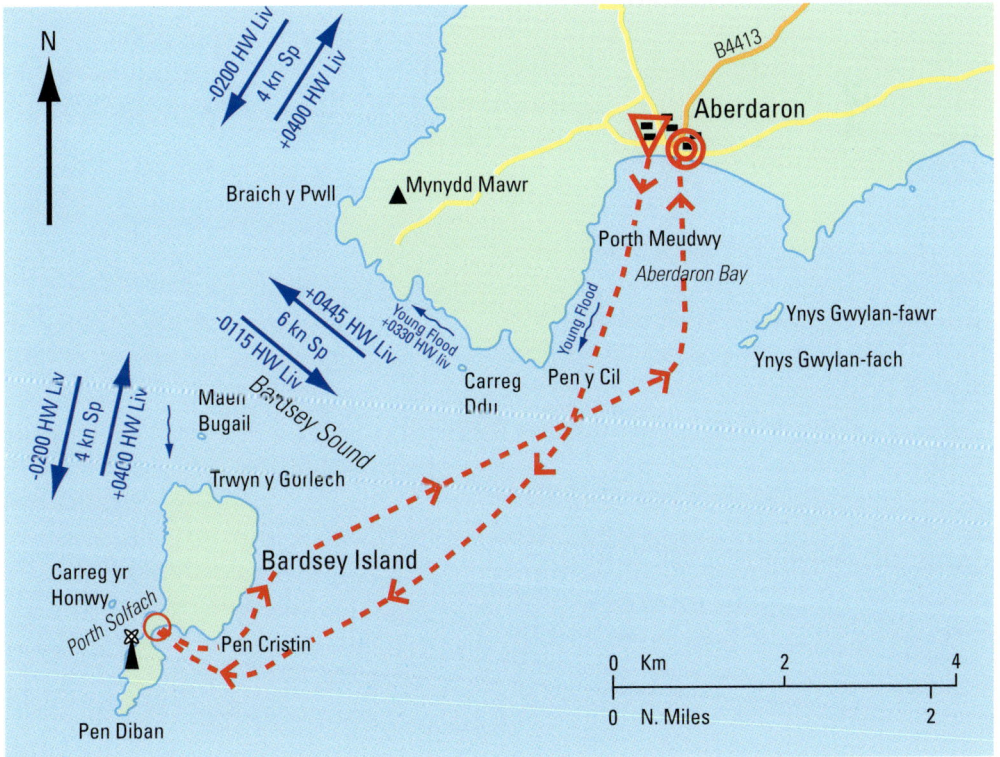

The north-west tip of Bardsey, Mynydd Mawr and Braich y Pwll beyond.

seaweed-infested boulder field is exposed; carrying boats across this is difficult and carries a real risk of injury. An alternative to battling with the boulders could be to portage 300m across the island to the slipway at Cafn Enlli. The southernmost point on Bardsey is Pen Diban. There are two caves and plenty more seals for company right round the headland, and across Henllwyn Bay to the slipway at Cafn Enlli.

Landing upon the shores of Bardsey deserves some self-congratulation, but remember you are only halfway through your trip. This is a good moment to check plans for your return. There is little point in getting back on the water more than an hour before the next slack water, so take your time to explore the island. The lighthouse is close to the southern tip of the island and is accompanied by several impressive buildings. The uniquely square tower, which stands 30m tall, was built in 1877. The lighthouse was automated in 1987 but unfortunately the buildings remain closed to the public.

The top of Mynydd Enlli can be most easily reached by walking to the farmhouse of Ty Pellaf. As you approach the farmhouse there is a marked path on the left. This leads you to the ridge on the skyline; the ridge can then be followed north to the summit. Mynydd Enlli stands a mere 167m above sea level, but from its summit it is possible to see most of the major peaks of Snowdonia to the north, the Preseli Mountains and Pembrokeshire to the south and even the Wicklow Mountains of Ireland to the west. If you cast your eyes down to the sea it is quite easy to become mesmerized by the movement and patterns created by strong tidal currents. A path leads steeply down the north-west slopes through heather and gorse towards the 13th Century ruins of St Mary's Abbey. On the way back along the rough track that leads towards Cafn Enlli is

© Bardsey Lighthouse

'Cristin' where the Bardsey Bird and Field Observatory is located and surprisingly souvenirs can be purchased. Payment is usually made by the use of an honesty box.

Begin your return as the flood stream dies out. As you paddle out from Cafn Enlli, Pen y Cil will appear beyond Pen Cristin and can then be used as a transit with buildings or hillside features beyond Aberdaron Bay. The beginnings of the new ebb stream will tend to push you east in the late stages of the crossing. As you pass Pen y Cil, Aberdaron and the Ty Newdd Hotel come into view, standing bold and bright beyond the shore, a welcoming sight, yet still almost 3km away.

Tide & Weather

The crossing to Bardsey Island combines all the exposure of an open sea crossing with fast tidal streams. It is possible to paddle from Aberdaron to Pen y Cil and base your decision to cross the sound upon the conditions you find there. If you don't like what you see, you can always turn back. Be confident of your weather forecast because once you land on Bardsey fast tidal streams will prevent a safe return for around 5 hours.

Variations

The description above is a crossing based around HW slack. To do the same route around LW slack, leave Aberdaron around 2 hours before HW Liverpool. In this case you would do well to begin your return crossing earlier and give Pen y Cil and its 'young flood' stream a wide berth.

Memorial cross and the remains of St Mary's Abbey

A longer and more exciting trip can be done in the last couple of hours of the ebb from Porth Oer / Whistling Sands (SH 165 298 / LL53 8LH). This is a good way to see the west of the island. From Braich y Pwll, make your crossing to Maen Bugail, a small rock 500m from Bardsey's north shore. Determined paddling may be required to reach the main shore and creep round to the west of the island if the ebb is still running. Once you are round to the east side, a return to Porth Oer can then be made on the north-going flood stream.

Additional Information

There is no shortage of accommodation in and around Aberdaron. A campsite mentioned in the previous chapter called Mynydd Mawr (SH 143 255 / LL53 8BY) holds a very special position, Tel. 01758 760223. A short walk from your tent up Mynydd y Gwyddel or Mynydd Mawr will provide excellent views across Bardsey Sound.

Camping on Bardsey is not permitted but there are cottages available for rent from the Bardsey Island Trust, www.bardsey.org and there is a small hostel run by the Bardsey Bird Observatory www.bbfo.org.uk. The crossing to Bardsey is essentially weather dependant, which makes booking a long way in advance impractical.

Looking across Porth Neigwl / Hell's Mouth towards Trwyn Cilan

South-west Lleyn

No. 20 | Grade C | 29km | OS Sheet 123 | Tidal Port Liverpool

Start	△ Aberdaron Beach SH 171 264 / LL53 8BE
Finish	◎ Llanbedrog Beach SH 331 313 / LL53 7TR
HW / LW	at Aberdaron occur around 3 hours before Liverpool, and at Abersoch are around 3 hours 15 minutes before Liverpool.
Tidal times	In St Tudwal's Sound the south-going stream starts around 3 hours before HW Liverpool. The north-going stream starts around 3 hours after HW Liverpool. Between Aberdaron Bay and Trwyn Cilan the west-going stream begins 3 hours after HW Liverpool. The east-going stream begins 3 hours before HW Liverpool.
Tidal rates	The tidal rates for this section are generally weak but can reach 2–3 knots at the eastern entrance to Aberdaron Bay, Trwyn Talfarach, and Trwyn Cilan and in St Tudwal's Sound.
Coastguard	Holyhead, Tel. 01407-762-051, VHF 0150 UT repeated every 3 hours

Introduction

This is one of the longer coastal trips described in this book, and the distance is well worth it, for this is the south facing, sunshine coast of the Lleyn. It would not be difficult to complete this trip in a day but combining the journey with an overnight camp at Hell's Mouth makes more time to explore the many delights en route.

Bouldering at Porth Ysgo

Bouldering at Porth Ysgo - Graham Desroy

To boulder on a beach is always a bonus; to boulder on perfect sea-washed gabbro surrounded by shimmering seas, hazy headlands and inquisitive seals is something special. Porth Ysgo is a unique venue. It is blessed with a micro-climate akin to Cornwall, cursed with the worst landings imaginable and provides the best bouldering in Wales. The rock texture and architecture is diverse, giving rise to the names of boulder problems such as Popcorn Party, Welsh Anvil, Black Krispy Traverse, Jaw Breaker and Belly Flop. For half a kilometre or so the boulder beach throws up irresistible challenges, where the boulderer can excel and enjoy, brave and fear, chill and relax. Rusting and rotting amongst this playground lie the remains of an ancient pier, axles and winding gear - relics of a long-lost era mining for manganese. Porth Ysgo is a special place. Discover it and enjoy it.

Description

Aberdaron lies at the end of the Lleyn peninsula and can be reached by driving along the B4417 to Pen y Groeslon; Aberdaron is then signposted along the B4413. There are also signs for Aberdaron along the A499 at Llanbedrog and Abersoch.

The wide, sandy beach at Aberdaron is popular with holidaymakers but rarely gets awfully busy. There is a slipway which gives direct access to the beach in the narrow street beside the Church of St Hywyn but be wary of driving onto the sand as cars and boat trailers can easily get stuck. The cliffs at the eastern end of the bay provide a pleasant rockhopping experience around low to mid tide. Closer to high water there is less general interest, but there is an interesting cave, which can be paddled all the way through.

As you paddle out of the bay, the two islands stand guard over the eastern entrance. The islands Ynys Gwylan Fawr (the big one) and Ynys Gwylan Fach (the little one) are a little under 2km offshore. There are no beaches or easy landings on these islands but they are swarming with bird life, and the waters teeming with seals. The theme continues further round into the next bay with a series of coves and rocky islets.

Porth Ysgo is 4km to the east of Aberdaron. The waters are generally more sheltered than those of the north coast and Bardsey Sound and there are no major tidal problems.

The western part of Porth Ysgo has a beach of sand and shingle and is a wonderful place to chill out in the sunshine and break out the picnic. Along to the east, the beach is locally known as Porth Alwm, and is packed with large boulders amidst rock pools. Upon closer inspection some of the drier boulders display the tell-tale chalky marks left by climbers. This area is becoming well loved by the North Wales rock climbing and bouldering community.

Trwyn Talfarach is the bold blocky headland leading to Porth Neigwl / Hell's Mouth. Eventually, over the next 3-4km the rocky drama relents and the shore becomes more gentle. There are steep slopes with bracken and heather, beyond boulder beaches. Above half tide there is a sheltered

Caves and rock strata, Trwyn Cilan

landing close to a small ruined building in the north-west corner of the bay. A small number of local fishermen maintain the site. There is a loose gravel slipway leading to an inlet amongst the boulders described locally as 'Winkle Pond'. From here you will be able to see the campsite at Treheli Farm. The main part of the site is over 30m above sea level, which will give you a short but steep hike with your camping gear.

If you intend to spend the night at Treheli Campsite you should time your arrival and departure as close as possible to high tide so as to avoid landing in amongst boulders. Treheli is a wonderful place to while away the hours. Plas yn Rhiw is nearby, where there is a small manor house with ornamental gardens managed by the National Trust, which is well worth a visit. A half hour walk up the hill will bring you to the village of Rhiw. There are little in the way of shops and amenities but a walk to the top of Mynydd y Graig will be rewarded with stunning views, especially at sunset.

Hell's Mouth / Porth Neigwl has a broad sandy beach that stretches over 5km south-east towards Trwyn Cilan. This beach enjoys the reputation of being the best surf beach in North Wales. The surf is usually at its best at the south-eastern end, and on weekends when conditions are good there will be plenty of riders competing for the best of the break. The north-western end of the beach, close to Treheli, is a little more sheltered and the break is usually smaller and therefore less popular. In spite of this the Treheli part of the beach can still provide hours of kayak surfing fun. Unfortunately, the access to the beach is via a steep footpath beside the campsite that descends over 30m from the road. The 'West Coast Surf' shop in Abersoch has a website that provides regularly updated information about conditions at Hell's Mouth, www.westcoastsurf.co.uk.

Porth Ysgo

Trwyn Cilan is the major headland that forms the centrepiece for the view to the east, from Treheli. It is nearly 6km paddling but the immense scale of the 100m cliffs is not realised until you get really close. The many ledges and caves make Cilan ideal for the many seabirds that nest here during the spring and summer months. As you pass Trwyn Cilan, the St Tudwal's Islands and Porth Ceiriad will come into view. Porth Ceiriad is a smaller version of Hell's Mouth. The rocky headlands and shallow beach pick up the surf well after stormy weather and there can often be good surf here when there is none at Hell's Mouth. Care should be taken when landing here because waves dump heavily on the pebbly areas of the beach at high tide. There is a campsite high above the beach called Nant y Big but the steep walk from the beach makes this a labour intensive place to spend the night. Paddling north from Porth Ceiriad will bring you to St Tudwal's Sound and towards Abersoch. The wild and remote feel of the Lleyn will quickly melt away as you enter the world of jet skis, motorboats and sailing dinghies.

Abersoch is a bustling holiday town with all the amenities and pleasures you would expect. At high water it is possible to paddle right into the little harbour where there is road access and shops close by. At low water it is best to land on the beach beside the sailing club where there is a car park and a café. The town has two good grocers shops, a chandler's and several cafes. Abersoch also has a regular bus service to Pwllheli. If the hustle and bustle of Abersoch is too much for you then perhaps it would be better to stay offshore and keep heading north towards the distinctive headland of Trwyn Llanbedrog. Beyond the headland lies Llanbedrog beach. The beach dries out to more than 200m at low tide so make plans to arrive above half tide. There is an excellent café beside the beach and a large car park close by. The main A499 is a short walk up the hill where there is a grocery store, pub and regular bus service to Pwllheli.

Towering cliffs, Trwyn Cilan

Tide & Weather

The tidal streams for this section are generally weak. They tend to be stronger round headlands where their effects tend to be localised. In most cases, with some determination, these headlands can be paddled around against the tide. Any exposed headlands can produce clapotis in onshore winds. Porth Ceiriad and Hell's Mouth have reputations for good surf. In fact most of the beaches in this section can give tricky landing conditions with wind and / or swell from the south. Abersoch and Llanbedrog are exceptions to this as they both have good shelter from the south and west.

Additional Information

It is possible to paddle a further 6km on from Llanbedrog to the promenade beach at Pwllheli, which is less than 1km from the bus station. The scenery is nothing to shout about, but neither is the inside of a Gwynedd bus! Paddling through the Marina would take you even closer to the bus station. There is a frequent service from Pwllheli bus station to Caernarfon and regular buses to other parts of the Lleyn.

The Tourist Information Offices at Pwllheli and Abersoch can provide useful information on accommodation and buses.

Variations

This trip can easily be done in reverse but the tides will not work quite as well. A return trip to Porth Ysgo from Aberdaron is perfect for those with an interest in bouldering. A return trip to Trwyn Cilan from Abersoch is recommended for those with an interest in seabirds and wildlife.

St Tudwal's Island West

St Tudwal's Islands

No. 21 | Grade A | 10km | OS Sheet 123 | Tidal Port Liverpool

Start	△ Abersoch Beach SH 314 277 / LL53 7EF
Finish	◯ Abersoch Beach SH 314 277 / LL53 7EF
HW / LW	are around 3 hours 20 minutes before Liverpool.
Tidal times	The south-going stream starts around 3 hours before HW Liverpool. The north-going stream starts around 3 hours after HW Liverpool.
Tidal rates	Tidal streams are generally weak, less than 2 knots maximum at springs.
Coastguard	Holyhead, Tel. 01407-762-051, VHF 0150 UT repeated every 3 hours

Introduction

The St Tudwal's Islands are two small rugged islands situated 3km to the south-west of Abersoch. The islands dominate the view from the beach beside the South Caernarvonshire Yacht Club. Abersoch has gained a reputation as a centre for a variety of water sports with good reason. The main beaches at Abersoch face east, and are well sheltered from the prevailing winds, whereas the nearby beaches at Porth Ceiriad and Hell's Mouth face south and south-west respectively and are renowned for good surfing conditions. There is plenty of good accommodation plus shops,

Abersoch and Penbennar

and travel to the area is relatively easy by the A499 road. Access to the sea is also easy with two car parks by the main beach. After paddling a relatively short distance from Abersoch you will find yourself in a truly wild place. Considering the proximity of these islands to the hustle and bustle of the Lleyn's premier holiday resort, there is a surprising amount of wildlife and potential for adventure.

Description

The main beach car park is signposted from the centre of Abersoch. Drive south down the busy main street and take the first left after the shops onto Lon Golff. The St Tudwal's Islands are around 3km paddling from the beach.

St Tudwal's Island West is less than 1km long; the shore is steep and rocky making landing almost impossible. Along the west shore, sparse and barren grassland descends to extensive, smooth rock slabs which dip steeply into the water. The southern end has a forbidding shore of rock fragments, broken from the high cliffs above. Seals often bask in the morning sun on the eastern ledges and these ever-curious mammals will closely scrutinize your progress along this shore. The lighthouse and its associated buildings were built by Trinity House in 1877. Following automation in the late 1980s the buildings were sold as private accommodation. There is a small jetty at the north end of the island where a large sign says, "Private, No Landing!" and, "Beware of Snakes!" This is more likely to be an indication that visitors are not welcome rather than an indication that the island is riddled with vindictive serpents.

Adders (Vipera Berus)

The adder is one of 3 snakes that live in the British Isles but the only one with a poisonous venom. These snakes are often seen basking in the sun at the edge of footpaths on the heather and gorse moorland so typical of the southern Lleyn Peninsula.

Most adders show a distinctive zigzag marking running the entire length of the back. Males are usually whitish or pale grey with black markings. Females are usually light brown and the zigzag pattern is more dark brown. Marking and patterns vary greatly amongst adders, and occasionally these zigzag markings are so bold that the snake appears to be almost entirely black.

Encounters with adders are usually brief, as once spotted they will slither away into the undergrowth in a flash. Although these snakes are poisonous we have little to fear from them, you are unlikely to be bitten unless you accidentally tread on one or try to handle one.

St Tudwal's Island East is a similar size to its western neighbour. The shores are also steep and rocky but more interestingly riddled with caves, which ring to the boisterous clamour of countless kittiwakes and fulmars. The only buildings on this island are an abandoned shelter beside the remains of an ancient monastic settlement. This is where Prince Tudwal is said to have lived as a hermit in around AD 550 before emigrating to Brittany where he became Bishop of Treguier. A little over 500m to the east of St Tudwal's East is a small reef which breaks the surface of the

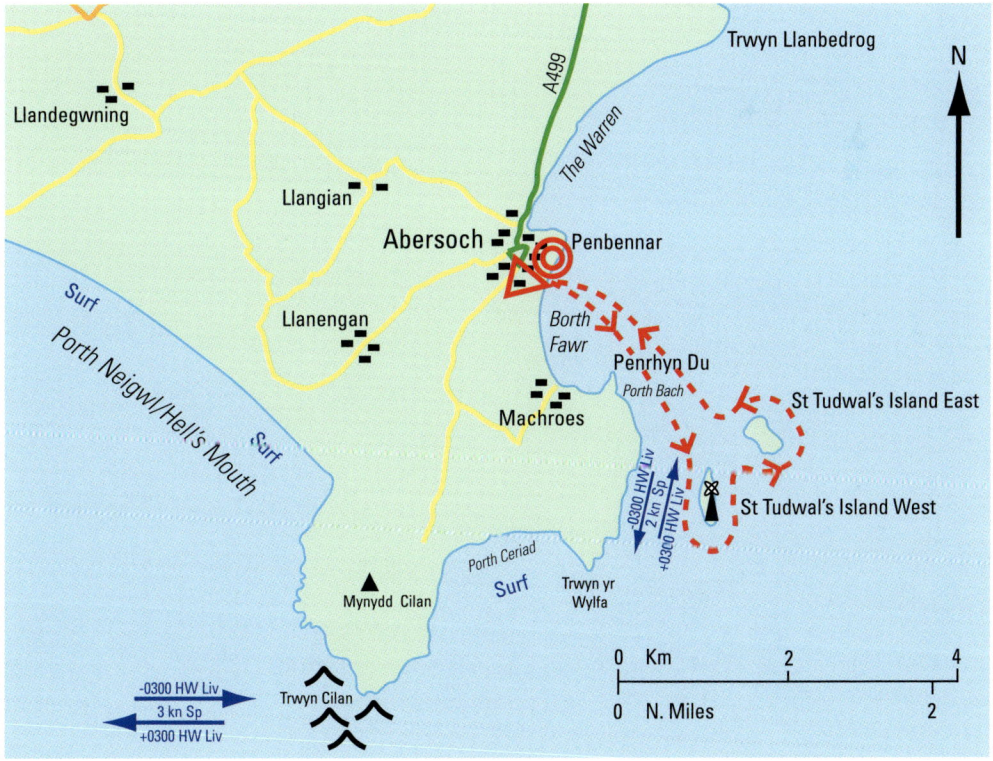

Sea Cave, St Tudwal's Island East

sea below half tide. Carreg y Trai is often heavily laden with basking seals with plenty of seabirds in attendance.

Tide and weather

The strongest tidal flow is in St Tudwal's Sound in the passage between the two islands. The currents rarely exceed 2 knots. Despite the relatively gentle nature of the tidal streams, wind against tide conditions can produce some choppy seas and steep standing waves, especially in strong southerly winds.

Additional information

Abersoch is a busy holiday town with all the amenities you would expect. There are two car parks just outside the town that offer direct access to the beach; these can get a little busy during hectic summer weekends. The campsite at Nant y Big overlooks the bay and popular surfing beach at Porth Ceiriad. Although this is not an easy place to launch a sea kayak, it is a spectacular place to stay whilst exploring the area, Tel. 01758 712686.

Variations

If you have a little more time on your hands, this trip can be extended to include more in the way of wildlife by paddling to Trwyn Cilan. For those wanting an adrenalin rush, a visit to the nearby surf beach at Porth Ceiriad can make a more varied day out.

Pwllheli Marina and Beach – Photo: www.pixaerial.com

Pwllheli to Cricceth

| No. 22 | Grade A | 15km | OS Sheet 123 | Tidal Port Liverpool |

Start	Pwllheli Harbour Beach SH 384 350 / LL53 5YT
Finish	Cricceth Beach SH 502 380 / LL52 0HW
HW / LW	along this stretch of coast are around 3 hours and 5 minutes before Liverpool.
Tidal Streams	The tidal streams in this section are weak and may be considered insignificant.
Coastguard	Holyhead, Tel. 01407-762-051, VHF 0150 UT repeated every 3 hours; Pwllheli Harbourmaster, Tel. 01758-704-081

Introduction

This is an ideal introductory trip for larger groups; this stretch of coastline is far from committing, as there are beaches for much of the way. This trip is as straightforward as they come; there are no significant tidal streams to consider and spontaneous landings for picnics, sunbathing or post rescue re-grouping can be made quite readily along the majority of this section. The hills of southern Snowdonia rise gently from the coastline and form the perfect backdrop to this trip. From less than halfway along, Cricceth's ancient castle ruins and distinctive Victorian seafront beckon you across the water. A rewarding cup of tea or delicious ice cream will make the perfect end to one of the Lleyn's less dramatic, but nonetheless scenic, sea kayaking journeys.

Leatherback Turtles (Dermochelys coriacea)

It is a little-known fact that leatherback turtles are found in the waters around Wales and Ireland. Indeed the largest specimen ever recorded washed up in North Wales in 1998 measuring nearly 3m and weighing 916kg! Despite this our knowledge of this elusive species remains limited to anecdotal sightings and stranding events along the coast. Although such data are invaluable, we are still left with many unanswered questions such as how leatherbacks can live almost entirely on jellyfish that are composed mainly of water! To address such gaps in our knowledge the Irish Sea Leatherback Turtle Project was established in April 2003 as a joint venture between the University of Wales Swansea and the University College Cork. Funded by the European Regional Development Fund, key elements of the project include aerial surveys of the Irish Sea, satellite tracking of the leatherback turtles, shoreline jellyfish surveys, schools workshops and public seminars. Through collaboration with existing conservation bodies they hope to tackle the long unanswered question of whether leatherbacks are merely oceanic wanderers that occasionally find themselves in our waters or whether they form an important part of our natural heritage.

Description

The harbour beach, Glan-y-Mor, is east of the marina and is easily found off the A497 road to the east of Pwllheli. There is a short way to carry your kayak from the public car park to the beach. Glan-y-Mor is sandy, gently shelving and well sheltered. This provides an excellent area in which to practise skills and to build your plans for the day's activities. The beach extends to the east towards the headland Pen-ychain, which lies just under halfway directly between Pwllheli and Criccieth. The land to your left is Morfa Abererch where there is a holiday centre and campsite, unfortunately camping here is available for "Families only".

At the eastern end of the beach at Abererch is Pen-ychain, a low rocky headland that forms the south-western entrance to the bay, Porth Fechan. Porth Fechan is home to a more famous holiday camp, which in its hayday was the pride and joy of the Butlin's empire. The camp started its life as a training centre for the Admiralty and Merchant Navy and was known as HMS Glendower. Following the end of WW2 the camp was sold to Butlin's and, after considerable local opposition, was opened as a holiday camp in 1947. The camp has undergone many changes since but still retains its function and is now known as Hafan-y-Mor.

About 4km to the east the waters of the Afon Dwyfor enter the sea, bringing stones and shingle that form a shallow fan-shaped reef which extends over 100m beyond the low water mark. Keep a keen eye out for larger rocks lurking just beneath the surface close to low water.

The end of the trip approaches with style along 'Marine Beach' beneath the delightful Victorian promenade, and Criccieth's famous 13th century castle. The castle is thought to have been the original stronghold of Llywelyn the Great. His grandson, Llywelyn ap Gruffydd, added further fortifications in the mid to late 1200s but before the end of the century, Criccieth Castle fell to King Edward I of England. It was not until Owain Glyndŵr led the final Welsh rebellion

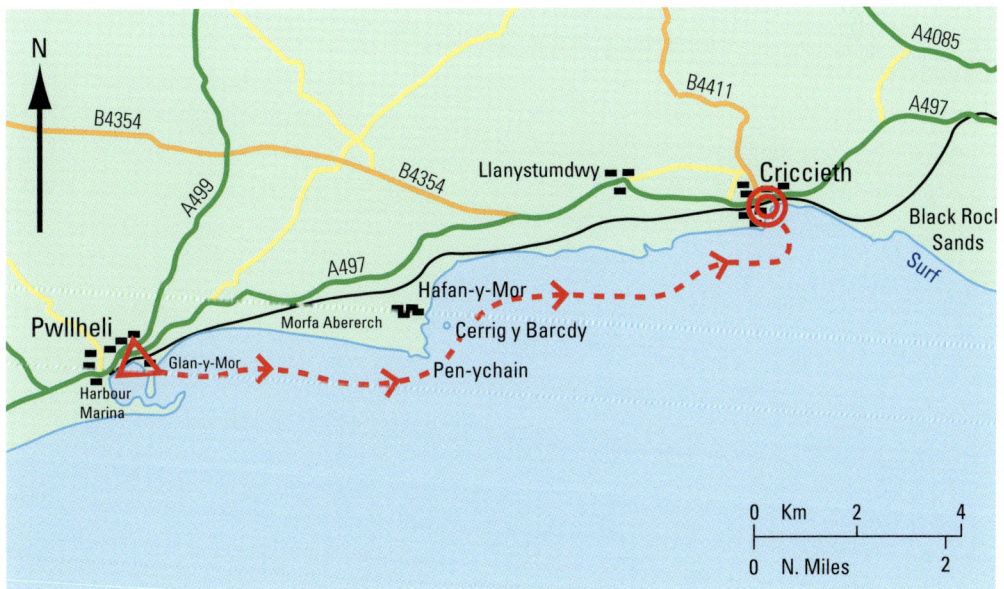

Jellyfish Common to Welsh Waters

Moon jellyfish (Aurelia aurita) are mostly transparent with four distinctive circles visible beneath the bell. They are normally 10–30cm in diameter and are sometimes found washed up on beaches in great numbers during late summer.

Compass jellyfish (Chrysaora hysoscella) are pale yellow in colour with distinctive brown markings that radiate from the centre of the bell. They are normally 15–30cm across the bell. There are normally 24 fine, long tentacles that trail from the edge of the bell and 4 even longer wrinkly arms that trail from the mouth.

Barrel jellyfish (Rhizostoma octopus) are pale yellow or orange in colour and are commonly found measuring over 45cm across the bell and a metre in length.

Lion's mane jellyfish (Cyanea capillata) are yellow, orange through to red in colour. The bell is normally around 15–40cm and the fine tentacles, which can be difficult to see, can be over a metre in length.

The Irish Sea Leatherback Turtle Project is looking for conservation bodies or enthusiastic individuals who would be able to help gather basic information on jellyfish strandings along our shores. If you, or someone you know, might be interested please contact Dr Jonathan Houghton.

Dr Jonathan Houghton, Irish Sea Leatherback Turtle Project, School of Biological Sciences, University of Wales Swansea, Singleton Park, Swansea, Wales. SA2 8PP. E-mail j.d.r.houghton@swansea.ac.uk

against the English in the early 1400s that the walls of Criccieth Castle were finally brought down, bringing an end to Criccieth as a military stronghold. The turbulent history of occupation and construction by Welsh and Edwardian forces gives Criccieth a unique character amongst Welsh castles and it is well worth a visit.

The main beach at Criccieth has a promenade with good car parking and public toilets. Like any good Victorian holiday resort it is difficult to refuse tea and cakes, if not an ice cream.

Tide & Weather

There is reasonably good shelter in winds from the north and, for the most part, west. The waters around Pen-ychain can be surprisingly choppy when there is wind or swell from the south and may catch inexperienced paddlers unawares. Tidal streams are relatively insignificant here but the beaches at Pwllheli and Criccieth dry a long way out, so it is better to plan your trip to start and finish as close as possible to high water.

© Compass Jellyfish

© Barrel Jellyfish | P.G.H Evans, www.seawatchfoundation.org.uk

Criccieth Promenade and Castle

Additional Information

There is a frequent bus service along the A497 coast road, which can be used for the shuttling between the start and finish.

Variations

The trip can be done in reverse to suit the direction of the wind. Black Rock Sands is just over 2km to the east of Criccieth and can provide reasonable surfing conditions although this beach can get very crowded during summer weekends.

Cardigan Bay

An Introduction

Cardigan Bay is a huge expanse of relatively shallow sea. The bay is sheltered from the north by the Lleyn Peninsula and from the south by Pembrokeshire and the Preseli Hills. There is over 170km of coastline between Criccieth and Cardigan. The coast of the northern half is characterised by the three major estuaries of the Dwyryd, Mawddach and Dyfi. These estuaries are fed by the waters from rivers that drain the south-west part of Snowdonia. While giving shelter, these waters afford such scenic delights as the Italianate village at Portmeirion, steep wooded slopes between the Rhinogs and Cadair Idris, and the ever-shifting sandbanks and dunes at Aberdyfi. The sandy beaches at Fairbourne, Towyn and Barmouth are great for surf.

The seabed of Cardigan Bay is broken up by a series of long submarine ridges, which are made up of glacial deposits. These ridges or 'sarns' often break the surface of the sea on low spring tides and are shrouded in myths and legends.

Further south, the underlying geology at Borth and at Newquay has given rise to spectacular cliffs. This dramatic scenery is without the seriousness and exposure found along the western coasts of Anglesey, the Lleyn and Pembrokeshire. The lack of strong tidal streams leaves the mind freer to experience the wildlife for which Cardigan Bay is famous. The abundance of rare species of plants, insects, birds and mammals has prompted the European Union to designate much of this coastline as 'Special Areas for Conservation'. The unique nature of our kayaks enables us to slip almost silently through these habitats, allowing us to experience a special relationship with the creatures that occupy the waters of Cardigan Bay.

Background Reading

Coast - A Celebration of Britain's Coastal Heritage, Christopher Somerville, BBC Books, 2005, ISBN 9780563522799

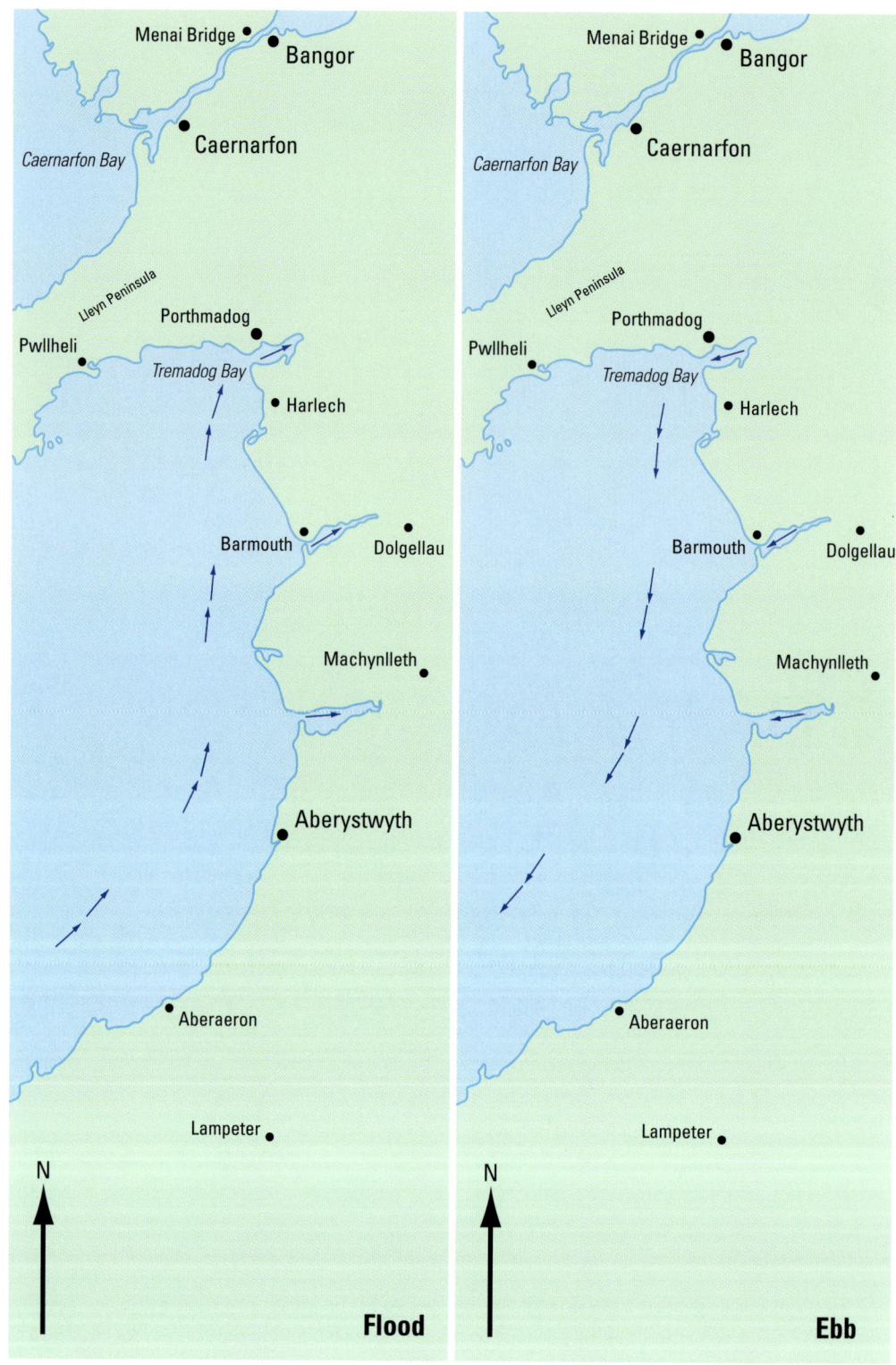

The above charts are intended to give a general overview. Consult the relevant chapters and other sources for more precise information.

Tremadog and Southern Snowdonia

Dwyryd Estuary

No. 23 | Grade A | 15-20km | OS Sheet 124 | Tidal Port Liverpool

Start	△ Borth-y-Gest Harbour SH 565374 / LL49 9TT
Finish	◎ Borth-y-Gest Harbour SH 565374 / LL49 9TT
HW / LW	at Borth-y-Gest are around 2 hours 45 minutes before Liverpool.
Tidal times	The east-flowing stream (flood) begins around 3 hours 15 minutes after HW Liverpool and continues to run for a further hour in the gorge section of the estuary, upstream of Pont Briwet. The west-flowing stream (ebb) begins around 2 hours 45 minutes before HW Liverpool.
Tidal rates	Tidal streams rarely exceed 2 knots in this section.
Coastguard	Holyhead, Tel. 01407 762051, VHF 0150 UT repeated every 3 hours, Porthmadog Harbourmaster, Tel. 01766 512927

Introduction

The Dwyryd Estuary offers a good introductory paddle in the north-east corner of Cardigan Bay. The crags at Tremadog and the hills of southern Snowdonia beyond make the perfect backdrop to a scenic day on the water. The start and finish at Borth-y-Gest has convenient parking and easy

131

📷 *Portmeirion*

Dwyryd Estuary

access to the water. The Dwyryd can be paddled to its tidal limit at Maentwrog, passing the ornate village of Portmeirion and the slate quays from a long gone industrial past, before entering the steep-sided Vale of Ffestiniog. A hasty return will be necessary so as not to become beached on sandbanks. This estuary, like so many others, begins to dry quickly, even in the early stages of the ebb. There should be a tide of at least 8.5m at Liverpool to make this trip worthwhile.

Description

Borth-y-Gest is less than 2km to the south of Porthmadog, and was one of the original crossing points over the tidal sands of the Glaslyn Estuary, until the completion of 'The Cob', in 1813. 'The Cob' is the embankment that spans Traeth Mawr and the Glaslyn Estuary. The engineer, William Alexander Madocks, built it as part of his intended route from London to Dublin via Porth Dinllaen on the north coast of the Lleyn. It was Isambard Kingdom Brunel with his route via Holyhead who eventually beat Madocks to it, but 'The Cob' remains in use today carrying the famous Ffestiniog Railway, as well as the main A487 road.

As Borth-y-Gest was the crossing point in the past it makes an ideal base from which to explore this area by kayak. At the south end of the bay there is a car park and slipway. Access to the water should be easy 2 hours either side of local high water. A pair of binoculars may come in handy to survey the first part of your route. Looking east from the car park, you will be able to see a small white tower, a folly lighthouse, which marks the southernmost point of Portmeirion. Initially, it may be necessary to paddle round to the south of a series of sandbanks. As water floods the estuary and the deeper channel of the Dwyryd is reached, it will be possible to head east and paddle closer to the wooded, rocky shores that herald the famous Italianate village.

Clough Williams-Ellis made Portmeirion his life's work. Much of the construction was done in the 1920's and 30's, but further significant work was done between the 1950's and 1970's, when the area was the setting for the cult television series 'The Prisoner'. Beyond Portmeirion the deep channel lies to the west of Ynys Gifftan. It can be difficult to follow as it winds its way generally north-west towards Pont Briwet, the toll bridge that carries the A487 and the Cambrian Coast Railway line. Once under the bridge, whilst still very much under tidal influence, the river channel is easier to see as you enter a rugged, steep-sided gorge with some dramatic rock formations above. The old stone quays beside the water were built in the mid-1800's for loading slate from nearby quarries and mines onto barges for export. Paddling beyond the gorge leads you to a more open landscape and the Vale of Ffestiniog. Your return should be trouble-free as long as you leave plenty of time and remember not to hang around at Portmeirion for too long. It may be necessary to paddle to the south of the sandbanks south-east of Portmeirion, mentioned earlier in this trip.

Tide & Weather

It is best to plan your trip on the basis that, wherever you get to, you begin your return at the time of HW at Borth-y-Gest. The rising waters, having reached beyond Pont Briwet and the gorge, get held up by these obstructions creating an unusually long period of high water within and upstream of the gorge. By the time the tide turns in the upper reaches, the ebb will be entering its second hour at Borth-y-Gest.

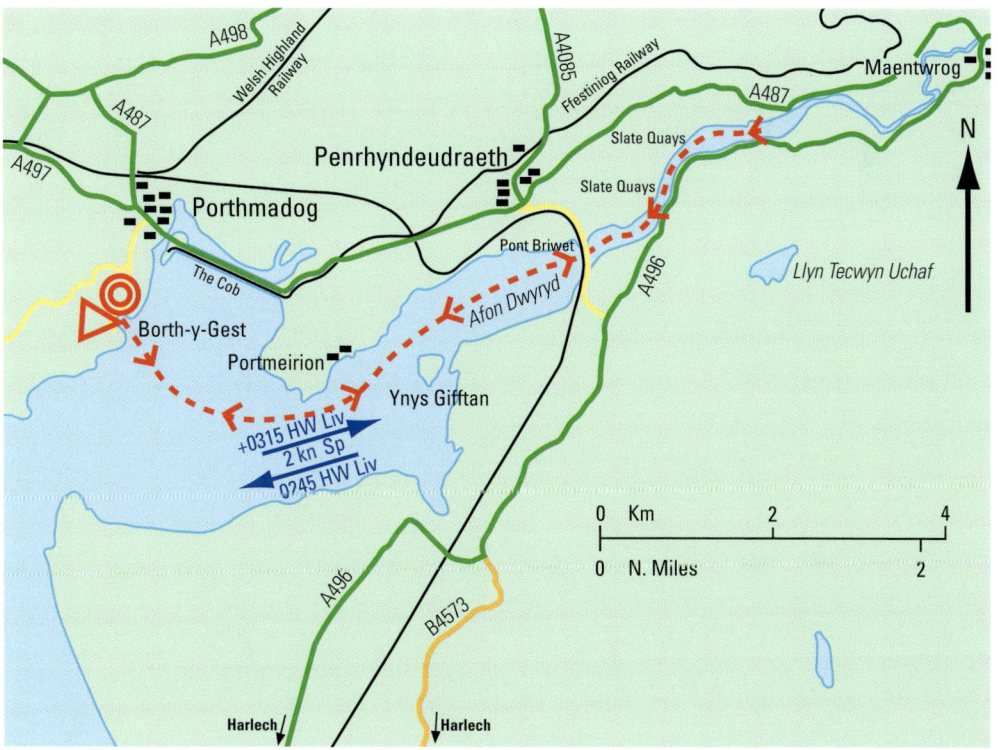

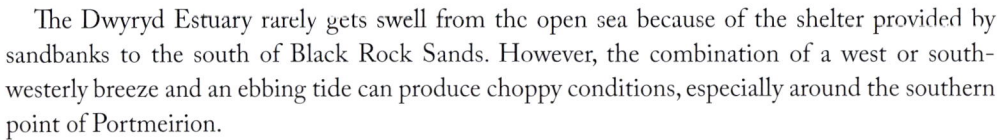

The Dwyryd Estuary rarely gets swell from the open sea because of the shelter provided by sandbanks to the south of Black Rock Sands. However, the combination of a west or south-westerly breeze and an ebbing tide can produce choppy conditions, especially around the southern point of Portmeirion.

Additional Information

Borth-y-Gest not only has a good car park with convenient access to the sea, but there are also public toilets and a licensed café which offers a wide range of hot and cold snacks and drinks.

There is a pleasant campsite on the banks of the Dwyryd, upstream from the tidal limit, close to Maentwrog at Llechrwd Riverside Camping Site, Tel. 01766 590240.

Variations

There is a small car park and slipway to the south of Minffordd (SH 600 370 / LL48 6EH) which can be used as an alternative start / finish.

The Mawddach Estuary

No. 24 | Grade A | 10km | OS Sheet 124 | Liverpool

Start	△ Barmouth SH 614 154 / LL42 1HB
Finish	◎ Penmaenpool SH 694 184 / LL40 1YJ
HW / LW	at Barmouth are around 3 hours before Liverpool. At Penmaenpool are around 2 hours 30 minutes before Liverpool.
Tidal times	The east-going stream (flood) runs up the estuary and begins around 3 hours after HW Liverpool. The west-going stream (ebb) begins around 3 hours before HW Liverpool.
Tidal rates	For most of the estuary tidal streams rarely exceed 3 knots. However, in the vicinity of Barmouth Bridge, water can move up to 6 knots on a spring tide and can create choppy conditions.
Coastguard	Holyhead, Tel. 01407 762051, VHF 0150 UT repeated every 3 hours, Barmouth Harbourmaster, Tel. 01341 280671

Introduction

The Mawddach rises in the southern hills of Snowdonia and along with its tributaries Gain, Eden and Wnion, is perhaps better known for its white-water kayaking. Even in its tidal reaches the

© Penmaenpool

waters are well sheltered by steep, wooded valley sides. Beyond the woods to the south, the 893m summit of Cadair Idris imposes its greatness over the smaller southern slopes of the Rhinogs across the water to the north. Not only does this provide a bad weather kayaking option but also in mid to late October, when the autumn colours are at their best, the outstanding natural beauty of the Mawddach Estuary comes into its own.

Description

The Bath House area was once known as 'The Graveyard' as it was where local fishermen would leave old boats to decay. It is an east-facing, sandy beach at the southern end of the Barmouth promenade. Just across the road from the Harbourmaster's office there is a slipway that leads to the beach; there are also several cafés, public toilets and plenty of car parking very close by. Access to the water is quite easy up to two and a half hours either side of local high tide; at other times you may have a long way to carry your boat. Soon after you leave the beach, water will be flooding into the estuary and racing towards the wider spans at the northern end of Barmouth Bridge, so follow the water beneath one of the wider spans.

After the bridge the tidal stream eases and a new challenge awaits as the deep channel with the best tidal assistance winds its way from one side of the estuary to the other in a seemingly disorganised manner. Two small settlements, Fegla Fach and Fegla Fawr, lie on the southern shore; the latter is visible as a row of terraced houses beside the shore. From here you can see the Mawddach Trail, which follows the route of an old railway line along the southern shore from Dolgellau until it crosses the bridge to Barmouth. The rising water quickly forgives any errors in route finding, but if you intend to return to Barmouth on the ebb, try to remember the best route, as such forgiveness becomes punishment on a falling tide!

Close to the headland of Penrhyn Cregyn on the south shore, just over halfway up, the estuary becomes narrower and the current becomes noticeably quicker. The Afon Gwynant cascades down through the woods and feeds the estuary from the south. Soon after passing the village of Bontddu, the toll bridge, and then the George III Hotel at Penmaenpool comes into view round a right-hand bend. Upstream from Penmaenpool the tidal push fades and the river becomes narrow with reed-beds; this area is of great interest to bird watchers and some locals have occasionally spotted otters here.

The egress at the George III Hotel can be a little tricky because of the steep bank but 150m to the west there is a grassy area from which there is a track to the public car park to the east of the hotel and toll bridge.

Tide & Weather

Tides within narrow river estuaries can be greatly affected by strong winds and extremes of barometric pressure. Strong west or south-westerly winds will add to the height of high water. Conversely, strong east or north-easterly winds will reduce the height of high water. Extremes of low barometric pressure will increase the height of high water, just as extremes of high pressure will reduce the height of high water. In the Mawddach Estuary be aware that a combination of high pressure and a strong north-easterly could reduce the height of high water by as much as half

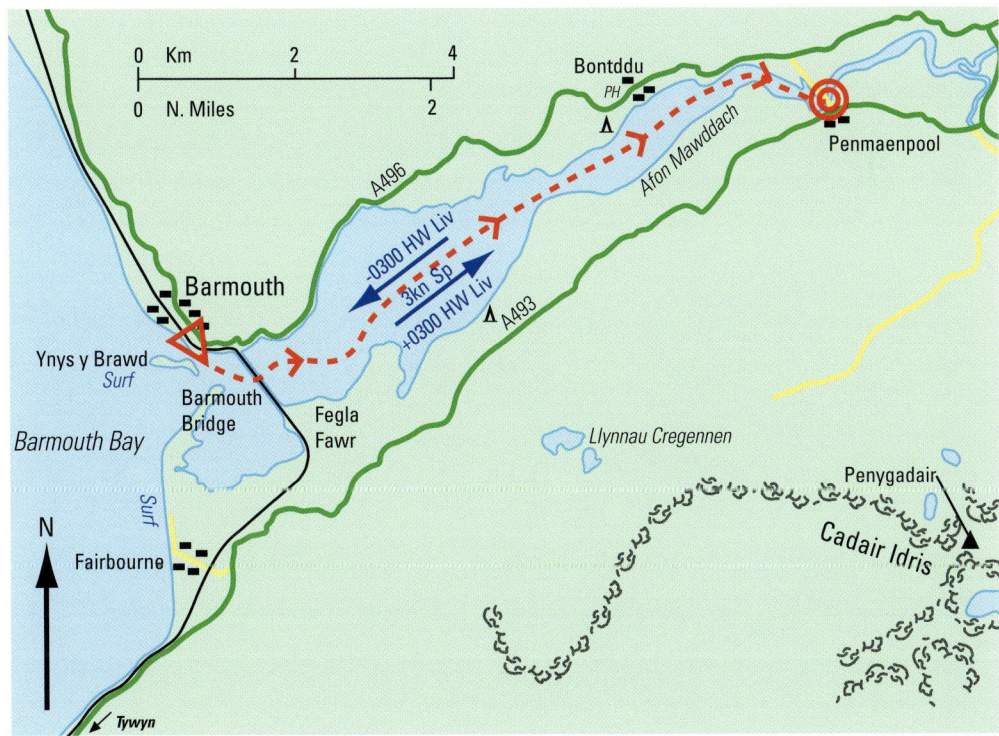

a metre, increasing the risk of becoming stranded on a sandbank whilst paddling on a falling tide. There should be a tide of no less than 8.5m at Liverpool for this trip to be worthwhile.

The sandbanks in the Mawddach Estuary are generally firm and safe to stand on. If you make contact with a sandbank on the flood, rising water will prove quite forgiving. If you get stuck on a falling tide, failing to act quickly can result in having to drag or even carry your kayak for tens or hundreds of metres. The Harbourmaster at Barmouth can provide useful, up-to-date information on the location of deep channels and sandbanks. Alternatively, at low water a stroll along the Precipice Walk, in the hills 2km north of Penmaenpool, gives a bird's eye view of the channels within the estuary.

The tidal stream in the narrows beneath Barmouth Bridge can run up to 6 knots and the complex wooden structure poses a significant hazard to kayakers. It is better to paddle through the wider, unobstructed spans. In wind against tide conditions, there can be standing waves and areas of confused water under Barmouth Bridge and in the narrows close to Penrhyn Cregyn.

Additional Information

The Harbourmaster at Barmouth is a good source of local knowledge and can give good safety advice, Tel. 01341 280671.

There is a basic, sheltered campsite at Bontddu, on the north shore of the estuary called Tyddyndu Farm, Tel. 01341 430644. There is also a campsite on the south shore of the estuary at Graig Wen, (SH 654 157 / LL39 1YP), Tel. 01341 250482.

Variations

Despite the relative shelter provided by Ynys y Brawd, conditions in Barmouth Harbour can be intimidating to paddlers with little experience. Those wishing to avoid these conditions and the strong tidal currents around Barmouth Bridge may wish to use Aberamffra Harbour, which is the old harbour situated 300m NE of the bridge, (SH 622 157 / LL42 1TB). There is a slipway and beach with limited parking across the road.

Should you want to paddle to Barmouth from Penmaenpool be sure to begin as the tide turns at Penmaenpool, this should be around 30 minutes after high water at Barmouth. Don't forget to pack your sense of urgency! Should you become stuck on a sandbank whilst paddling a falling tide here, swift action is required in order to find deep water in the main channel.

South beach and castle, Aberystwyth

Aberdovey to Aberystwyth

No. 25 | Grade A | 15km | OS Sheet 135 | Tidal Port Liverpool

Start	Aberdovey Beach and slipway SN 613 958 / LL35 0EB
Finish	Aberystwyth Harbour SN 580 809 / SY23 1BJ
HW / LW	at Aberdovey are around 3 hours before Liverpool, and at Aberystwyth are around 3 hours 30 minutes before Liverpool.
Tidal times	In the mouth of the Dovey Estuary the west-flowing ebb begins around 2 hours 45 minutes before HW Liverpool, the east-flowing flood begins around 4 hours 30 minutes after HW Liverpool. Along the coast, the south-going stream starts around 1 hour after HW Liverpool, the north-going stream starts around 5 hours before HW Liverpool.
Tidal rates	The maximum rate along most of this section is 2 knots, although in the entrance of the Dovey Estuary the spring rate can be as much as 4 knots.
Coastguard	Milford Haven, Tel. 01646 690909, VHF 0150 UT repeated every 3 hours

Aberdovey / Aberdyfi is a busy seaside town that caters for thousands of holidaymakers each year. The Dovey Yacht Club and nearby Outward Bound Centre have ensured that there is a strong tradition of maritime outdoor pursuits in the area, and the rolling scenery that surrounds the estuary provides a wonderful backdrop to a relaxing day on the water. When the Atlantic swell

Aberdovey, the beach and slipway

runs in from the south-west, the beaches and sandbanks at the mouth of the estuary roar with surf. The tall cliffs and wave-cut platforms between Borth and Aberystwyth will challenge the avid rockhopper and amaze the keen geologist. This scenery is a taste of what is to be found further along the coast in north Pembrokeshire. Unlike the Pembrokeshire and Lleyn Peninsula coasts, tidal streams are weak and so the paddling here tends to be of a less serious nature.

Description

Aberdovey is on the A493 between Dolgellau and Machynlleth. There is a large car park beside the beach, adjacent to the Dovey Yacht Club and slipway. The mouth of the estuary is sheltered by Aberdovey Bar, which extends almost 2km from the north shore. If you are in the mood for some surfing fun in your kayak, Aberdovey Bar may be just the place, especially if the beaches are crowded with swimmers and board surfers. At the southern entrance to the estuary lie the sand dunes and nature reserve of Ynyslas. The main focus of work at the reserve is the conservation of the dune habitat and its insects and wild flowers. The flowers are at their best during late spring when some rare species of orchid can be seen. The reserve extends to the north into the shallow waters of the Dovey that provide rich feeding for thousands of birds including shelduck, ringed plover and curlew. The sandy beaches stretch away over 5km to the south, towards the little town of Borth. Along the beach between Ynyslas and Borth the petrified remains of an ancient forest can be seen when low spring tides reveal tree stumps, branches and even twigs. These ancient remains are of trees that grew here when sea levels were much lower than now, at the end of the last ice age. Some similar remains can be found closer to the town of Borth.

The seafront and sandy beach at Borth are well equipped to serve the needs of tourists. There is a good deal of car parking along the promenade and public toilets. There are also plenty of shops and cafés making this a good alternative start or finish to a shorter trip.

Upper Borth sprawls across the hillside to the south of the seafront. The monument that stands high on the cliffs is a memorial to the local villagers who died in the First and Second World Wars. At one point, the memorial was badly damaged by a lightning strike. It was rebuilt a short distance back from the edge of the decaying cliff to prolong its dominating existence. It is these cliffs beyond the village where this coastline takes on a far more dramatic mood.

The cliffs between Borth and Aberystwyth are a surprise to most who paddle this coastline for the first time. The layers of Llandovery mudstone and sandstone were laid down in the Silurian period around 430 million years ago. Sometime later, these layers of rock were tipped up by massive tectonic forces. The powerful action of the sea has since cut a steep face into the rock, forming a series of smooth slabs that rise to over 60m in places. The base of these cliffs has receded over time leaving almost level wave-cut platforms. These platforms are revealed close to low water and are riddled with shallow lagoons and gullies, which can be exciting places for rockhopping and even snorkelling. After 3km the coastline begins to soften to lower cliffs and

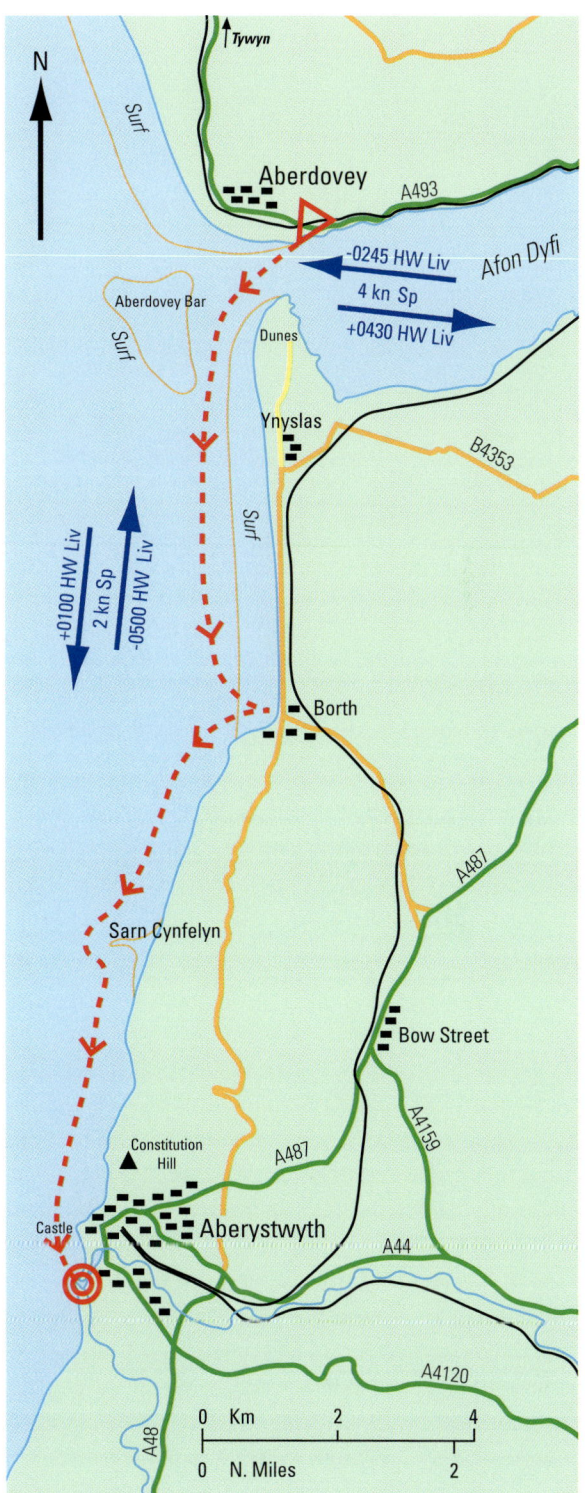

Mudstone slabs near Borth

shingle beaches and a river valley at Wallog. It is here that one of Cardigan Bay's subtler geological features is revealed. Sarn Cwynfelyn is a bank of boulders, pebbles and shingle that extends out to sea for more than 9km from the shore. It is made up of glacial deposits left by receding ice sheets at the end of the last ice age. The Welsh word 'sarn' means 'causeway' and there are other examples such as Sarn y Bwlch close to Tywyn and the largest, Sarn Padrig (St Patrick's Causeway) which extends over 16km south-west from Mochras Point, near Harlech.

Sarn Cwynfelyn is central to the legend of an ancient Welsh kingdom long lost beneath the sea. In times when sea levels were lower, there were huge expanses of low-lying rich pasture that supported the wealthy kingdom known as Cantre'r Gwaelod, meaning 'the bottom hundred'. The whole area was protected from the sea by a series of dykes with sluice gates to let drainage water out to sea at low tide. The man whose job it was to open and close the sluices was a heavy drinker, and one stormy night neglected to close the sluices as the tide rose. Sea water quickly flooded in and Cantre'r Gwaelod was lost forever. The legend says that if you stand on the furthest point of Sarn Cwynfelyn at low water on a quiet Sunday morning, you may be able to hear the ghostly bells of Cantre'r Gwaelod tolling from beneath the sea.

Clarach Bay lies between Sarn Cwynfelyn and Aberystwyth and inflicts an awkward break in the wilderness as the land beyond the beach is packed with static caravans and holiday homes. However, the last kilometre to Aberystwyth is reminiscent of the cliffs and wave-cut platforms close to Borth, with the added excitement of several caves. These cliffs eventually become the seaward side of Constitution Hill, which marks the northern end of Aberystwyth promenade.

In calm conditions the north beach is a pleasant place to land at the end of the day. There is limited parking along the Victorian promenade and there are nearby public toilets and cafés.

Dovey Estuary

In rougher weather, when swell runs in from the west, there can be dumping surf on this steep shingle beach in which case landing will be easier in the harbour 1km to the south. The castle ruins, old university college building and war memorial stand on a low headland, which divides the north beach and promenade from the south beach and harbour entrance. The college building was started in 1865 and was originally intended as a hotel, but before work could be completed the scheme ran out of money. The unfinished structure was bought by the Welsh National University Committee at a fraction of its cost and housed what was to become the first University of Wales.

The entrance to Aberystwyth Harbour lies at the southern end of the south beach and landing is straightforward on the shingle beach or slipway adjacent to the university boathouse. The university boathouse is on the road named Pen yr Angor, which is off the A487, south of the bridge over the Afon Rheidol.

Tide & Weather

The tidal streams in this area are generally weak and can be paddled against, apart from the Dovey Estuary. In the estuary the flood tide can reach 3 knots, the ebb can reach 4 knots especially after periods of heavy rain.

Additional Information

There are shops and cafés along the promenades of Aberdovey, Borth and Aberystwyth. There is also a youth hostel on the promenade at Borth, Tel. 0345 260 2561.

Old boatyard, Frongoch, Dovey Estuary

The Cae Du Campsite is 11km north along the coast from Aberdovey. It commands a marvellous view across Cardigan Bay and has direct access to the beach (SH 566 059 / LL36 9ND), Tel. 01654 711234. However, landing and launching from here can be difficult due to steep shingle banks at high water and boulders at low water.

Variations

The trip along this coastline can be done in either direction to suit prevailing weather conditions. Borth is a good alternative start or finish for a shorter trip.

The sheltered waters of the Dovey Estuary are frequently used by the Dovey Yacht Club and the Aberdovey Outward Bound Centre. A short trip along the north shore of the estuary becomes possible during the hours around local high water. The rolling landscape lacks the drama of the Dwyryd and Mawddach estuaries but the abundant bird life more than makes up for that!

Looking south from Ynys-Lochtyn

Ynys-Lochtyn

No. 26 | Grade B | 18km | OS Sheet 145 | Tidal Port Milford Haven

Start	△ New Quay SN 390 600 / SA45 9NP
Finish	○ Aberporth SN 258 5155 / SA43 2D
HW	at New Quay is 1 hour 40 minutes after HW Milford Haven.
Tidal times	NE going stream starts approximately 2 hours before HW Milford Haven. SW going stream starts 4 hours after Milford Haven.
Tidal rates	The tidal flow is low and normally does not exceed 1 knot.
Coastguard	Milford Haven, Tel. 01646 690909, VHF 0150 UT repeated every 3 hours

Introduction

This trip marks the start of the Ceredigion Marine Heritage Coast. The whole coastline is protected by a code of conduct and kayakers are asked to comply with this agreement. It is also a less frequented stretch of coast and, while the honey pots further south may be crowded, you may find that the only company you have is the abundance of wildlife, including a good chance of seeing bottlenose dolphins and harbour porpoises. The tidal flow in this area is quite low, so it is quite possible to paddle at most times during the day, just watch out as you come round New Quay Head and Ynys-Lochtyn as the tide can be faster at these points.

145

Heading towards Llangrannog

Ynys-Lochtyn

Description

The quiet harbour of New Quay makes an ideal starting place and practice area, as it is well protected except from N or NW winds. Originally New Quay was a fishing and smuggling port, later it became a centre for shipbuilding. The current quay was built in 1835 from local stone, which was conveyed by a small railway through the centre of town, down Rock Street. A small piece of the railway can still be seen near the Tourist Information Centre. Many say that Dylan Thomas' "Under Milk Wood" was based on his experiences of living in New Quay at the end of WW2. It was a play written for radio, a comedy set in an imaginary Welsh seaside town of Llareggub, later changed to Llaregyb. You can find out more about Dylan Thomas's life when you visit the Gower peninsular, as Swansea was his birthplace and there is an excellent centre dedicated to his work. www.dylanthomas.org, Tel. 01792 463980.

Parking close to the shore can become a problem during the height of the summer and the main car park is at the top of the hill, 300m away from the beach. Another option is Little Quay Bay at Llanina which is 2km to the east, where there is a campsite, car park and toilets. However it is a steep carry down to the shore. Setting off from the beach and rounding New Quay Head, a wonderful view of the entire coast opens up and you can make out MOD Aberporth 16km away. The cliffs are steep here and you will see birds circling high above you as they return to their nests.

Cwmtydu is a safe landing place, although it is quite rocky at low tide. There is a car park, toilets and café if you fancy an early break, or it could be used as an alternative launching place. The Tydu Vale campsite, Tel. 01545 560687, is 200m from the beach and would be suitable for those wanting an overnight stopping point. There is a well restored limekiln and the beach was once used by smugglers. Seals can be regularly seen in caves near the beach.

Once you leave the beaches the cliffs will remain high from here, and landing even at low water in an emergency can be a problem but you will be drawn towards the island of Ynys-Lochtyn and the hill fort of Pen Dinas Lochtyn. Originally Ynys-Lochtyn was attached to the mainland by a natural arch, which has long since collapsed. It is quite possible to land here and scramble out to the headland to take some impressive photos of your companions as they pass through the narrow gap that makes Ynys-Lochtyn an island. You can only do this 1 hour either side of high water and coming from the east you will not see the entrance until you are quite close, so it is not recommended in rough conditions. It may be easier to go round the headland and approach the gap from the west. Also amongst the cliffs at the south-west end of this gap is a natural arch that is still standing which you can paddle through. Once past the island and heading south you can soon land on the sandy beach at Llangrannog. This could provide a point of return for those who have left their car in New Quay. Here there is a beach-side café and toilets. It makes a good launching site but arrive early as the narrow roads down to the village can soon become busy. There is a free car park on the edge of the village.

Continuing on towards the end of this section at Aberporth you will soon pass another Iron Age fort above the rocks of Carreg y Ty. You then face the 3km long beach of Traeth Penbryn, where the soft rock that makes up the cliffs behind are slowly being eroded. It is worth stopping at Tresaith to look at the waterfall, caused by the unusual diversion of the River Saith. The Ship Inn up in the village has a good reputation for serving real ale. Soon after leaving the beach you'll follow some low rocky cliffs and turn the corner to land on the small beach at Aberporth.

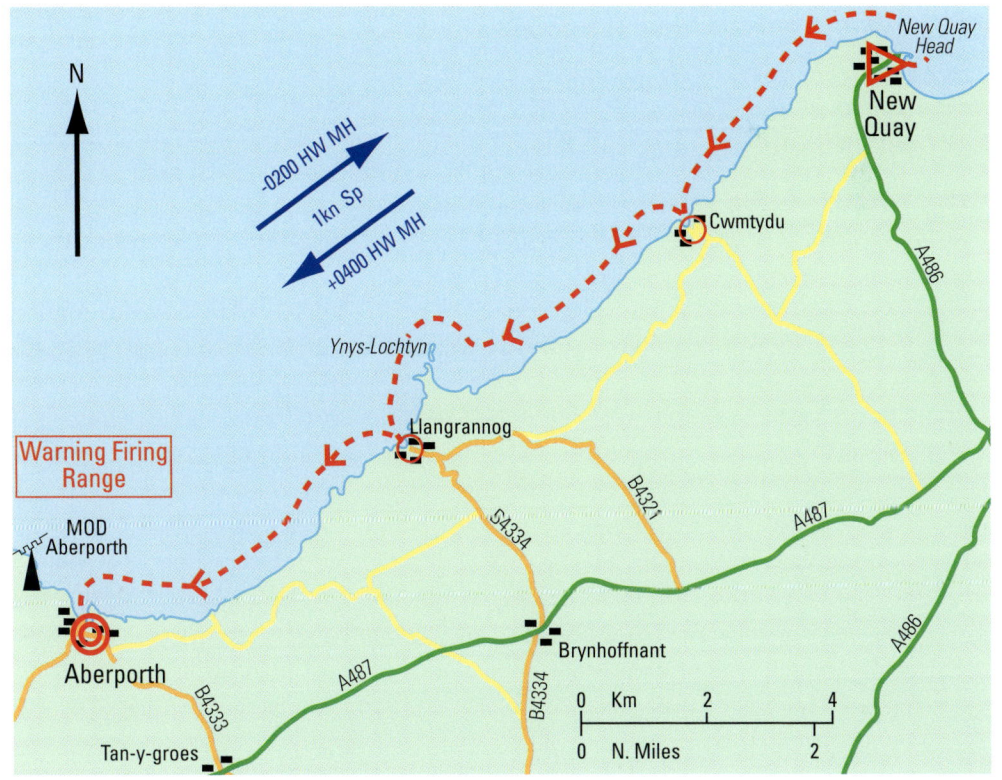

© Launching at Aberporth

Ynys-Lochtyn

This will have been a trip of stopping and exploring, looking at the geology and thoughts about when the coastline was a haven for smugglers.

Tide and weather

A small tide race can form off Ynys-Lochtyn. The tidal information given here is based on Milford Haven. However, be warned that much local information is quite related to HW Aberystwyth, which is 1 hour 40 minutes after Milford Haven. Those wanting accurate information about local offshore weather should look at the Met. Office website. The Marine Automatic Weather Station ID: 62301 Aberporth is 16NM north of Cardigan Island, Position: Latitude 52 ° 24' N Longitude 4 ° 42' W.

http://www.metoffice.gov.uk/research/ocean/goos/maws_pic.html

Ceredigion Marine Heritage Coast

The Ceredigion Marine Heritage Coast is the first such area to be established in British waters and it recognises the natural beauty and wildlife that can be found along the coastline. There is an abundance of wildlife, especially bottlenose dolphins, harbour porpoises and Atlantic grey seals.

Bottlenose dolphins are found worldwide and there are two known populations in UK waters, one in the Moray Firth and the other in Cardigan Bay, where they number about 100. The adults grow to 4m in length and normally live up to 30 years old. They are highly sociable mammals, living together in groups or 'pods' and communicating through high-pitched clicks or whistles.

Atlantic Grey Seal

The grey seal

All along the Welsh coast you will find an abundance of wildlife. However there is one continual companion that will always turn a kayaker's head; the grey seal, sometimes called the Atlantic grey seal. Their scientific name is Halichoeerus Grypus, which means sea pig with a hooked nose. Their characteristic "roman nose" helps distinguish them from the common seal, which is smaller with a mottled coat and more squat face. They are the largest carnivorous mammal in the UK and have a thick layer of blubber that insulates them from the cold. The male grey seal can grow to 3m long and weighs 300kg. During the autumn pupping commences. The fluffy white pups are dependant on their mother's milk and treble their weight in the first three weeks of life. By this time they have lost their white coat, which turns into a greyer hair. Once this happens the mother leaves the pup to fend for itself and she mates again.

Their comical inquisitive nature makes them popular with everyone and it is easy to see why they pull so easily on our heartstrings. The largest populations in Wales are found around Ramsey and Skomer Islands and it is easy to find them in these areas. They are now protected by the Conservation of Seals Act but before this they had been culled because of pressure from the fishing community who accused them of being responsible for falling fish stocks. The UK population is approximately 85,000, which is around half the world's population, with 5,000 found along the Pembrokeshire coast.

Passing Traeth Penbryn

Ynys-Lochtyn

The presence of the dolphins is one of the main reasons for the formation of the Ceredigion Marine Heritage Coast.

The harbour porpoise is a much smaller mammal and grows to less than 2m in length. It has a small triangular fin and unlike the dolphin, it does not jump clear of the water. They are best seen around headlands such as Mwnt and Ynys-Lochtyn where food is swept round by any tidal flow. Their numbers are estimated around 200 in the coastal area near Cardigan.

Stranded marine animals

If you should encounter an injured marine mammal such as a dolphin, porpoise or seal on Ceredigion beaches, please contact the Welsh Strandings Network immediately on 01348 875000 or Live Strandings (RSPCA), Tel. 0345 888999.

Ceredigion Marine Conservation Code of Conduct

Dolphins / porpoises: If these mammals are encountered at sea please: Maintain a steady speed and course, or slow down gradually. Do not chase, manoeuvre erratically, turn towards or attempt to feed or touch them. Take extra care to avoid dolphins with their young. Please do not attempt to swim with these mammals.

Seals: Do not interfere with seals or their pups on the beach. Please leave alone as any attempt to approach may cause distress. Control dogs and keep them away from seals.

Birds: Keep 100m out from cliffs in the breeding season, 1 March to 31 July. Please keep clear of rafts of birds nesting or feeding on the sea and avoid unnecessary noise close to cliffs.

Cardigan Island seen from Mwnt

Mwnt

No. 27	Grade B	14km	OS Sheet 145	Tidal Port Milford Haven
Start		△ Aberporth SN 258 515 / SA43 2DB		
Finish		○ Gwbert SN 163486 / SA43 1PN		
HW / LW		at Aberporth is 1 hour and 35 minutes after Milford Haven.		
Tidal times		The tide starts to flow NE approximately 2 hours before HW Milford Haven and then SW 4 hours after Milford Haven.		
Tidal rates		The tidal flow is low and normally does not exceed 1 knot.		
Coastguard		Milford Haven, Tel. 01646 690909, VHF 0150 UT repeated every 3 hours.		
Range Control		Aberporth Range Control Office Tel. 01239 813489 or 01239 813760 https://www.qinetiq.com/en/aberporth		

Introduction

This section of coast will take you round several small headlands and islands, keeping the interest high. The abundance of wildlife and a military firing range make this a trip for the observant paddler.

151

Surf at Mwnt

Mwnt

Description

There are actually two sandy beaches in Aberporth which are separated by a line of rocks. There is a slipway and a small parking area nearby and toilets, but during the summer it can get busy as the beaches are popular with families. There are lifeguards on duty during peak periods. During the summer there are overspill parking areas on the edge of town.

Head out from the beach and under the cliffs that support DERA Aberporth. This is a missile testing station and you should check their plans for the day prior to departure before they start practising on moving targets. The cliffs remain with you for the next 5km and you may catch a glimpse of Cardigan Island further along the coast.

The beach at Mwnt (pronounced Moont) is hidden from view until you have rounded the headland. It is worth landing here and scrambling up the steps to the chapel, which was built around the 14th century. It was reputedly used by monks stopping off on their way south to St David's. In 1155 a group of 'Flemings' (natives of Flanders) were defeated by a local force and this was celebrated as the festival of "Sul Coch y Mwnt" (the Bloody Sunday of Mwnt) until the 18th century. There is a car park, café and campsite here, but it would not be an easy carry with a loaded boat up a long line of steps.

Leaving Mwnt you'll see Cardigan Island in front of you. This is a popular area to observe seals and you may encounter commercial boat trips that have come out to see them. The tide can reach 2 knots through the narrow gap between the island and Carreg Lydan, so it is worth planning your arrival time accordingly. The SS Hereford was wrecked off the island in 1934 and brown rats from the ship are thought to have destroyed the island's puffin population. The rats have since been removed and attempts have been made to reintroduce puffins to the island. It is now a nature reserve and is home to an important colony of lesser black-backed gulls that nest on the cliff faces. The island is also home to a flock of Soay sheep. Along with the Atlantic grey seals, also keep a look out for bottlenose dolphins.

As you leave the island behind you and head south, keep close to the low rocky cliffs and look out for a large modern white building, which is a hotel. Come round the headland of Craig Y Gwbert, named after St Gwbert who landed here, and continue to follow the estuary; the centre of the channel is marked with a pole that flashes twice every 5 seconds at night. The caravan site on the end of Pen yr Ergyd in front of you unfortunately does not accept tents. You'll need to continue up the estuary, keeping close to the north bank. There is a small slip and roadside parking at (163486). It is possible to launch here at all states of the tide but at low water you will need to float your boat for the first 200m until you reach the Teifi Boat Club slipway. The other option is to cross over to Poppit Sands. However arriving here at low tide can result in a long carry.

Tide and weather

If you do arrive at Gwbert during a strong ebb tide beware that it can become quite rough over the sand bar that stretches north out from Poppit Sands. Keeping close under the cliffs by the hotel should provide a safe if somewhat hard passage as you paddle against the main flow.

Additional information

MOD Aberporth is an active firing range. However if you stay within 2 miles of the coastline you should be out of harm's way but it is advised to check with the range control before you set off. Tel. 01239 813480 or 01239 813760. Firing information is also broadcast on VHF Ch11 or Ch16.

The spacious Blaenwaun Caravan Park near Mwnt also accepts tents and makes an ideal base for exploring this area, www.blaenwaunfarm.com

A coastal bus service called Cardi Bach runs between Cardigan and Newquay and could provide a useful shuttle service.

Limekilns

As well as numerous Iron Age forts, remains of more recent structures can be found in the form of disused limekilns. The Egyptians and Romans used lime for building and developed a waterproof mixture used on aqueducts. It was also used by farmers as a neutralizer of acid soils. To process the lime so that it can be used it must be heated to a high temperature in a kiln. The lime industry around Cardigan started in the 18th century and the only way to move the lime was by ship, therefore kilns were built along the coast and near ports such as New Quay. However with the arrival of the railways which proved more efficient than boats, and the growth in use of other fertilizers, the industry collapsed during the early 1900s. There is a good example of a kiln near the beach at Cwmtydu, which is on trip No. 26. Remains can be seen at Mwnt and Cei-bach, Little Quay Bay.

Pembrokeshire

An Introduction

Pembrokeshire has one of the country's most beautiful coastlines. Dramatic cliffs are interspersed with small secluded sandy beaches. At many locations along the coast you can see wonderful rock formations showing different layers and folds, which were formed over 300 million years ago. There are offshore islands and fast-moving tidal streams. All this amounts to a sea kayaker's paradise. Although it is a national park, formed in 1952 and a popular holiday destination, it is still possible to find some quiet spots. Many of these are accessed via a network of narrow lanes that link the picturesque coastal villages, and your navigation skills may be tested just to find the point of departure. The economic centre for the area is Haverfordwest, with its Georgian architecture and where you will find the county offices, as well as a good range of shops and other services.

There are plenty of options for accommodation, as well as other activities when you or the family want a break from kayaking. For the enthusiastic rock climber there is plenty of scope and it is possible to combine both activities. However there are still military firing ranges along the coast and these need to be taken into consideration when planning a trip.

Although this area is covered by the Milford Haven coastguard, along the north coast you can receive VHF reception from the Holyhead coastguard. The shipping weather forecast areas for Pembroke are Lundy and Irish Sea. Be aware that mobile phone network coverage can be limited in the small harbours and bays that make up the coastline; this can also affect VHF reception.

The Pembrokeshire Coastal Path was opened in 1970 and is designated as a National Trail, so the public may have access along its route. There have been several guides written about the route and these can also provide valuable information for the sea kayaker. The development of the path can be of assistance to the sea paddler as a good range of accommodation and other amenities have built up along its length. One of these is the Pembrokeshire coastal bus service. The service is aimed at walkers who want to complete one stage of the walk and then use public transport to return to their starting point. However it is equally useful to the sea kayaker, as it removes the need to run a shuttle or for a group who want to complete a multi-day trip. There are three buses a day during the summer and a reduced service operates during the winter.

Background Reading

Pembrokeshire Coast Path - National Trail Guides, Brian John, Aurum Press, 2017, ISBN 9781781315729

The Pembrokeshire Coastal Path, Dennis Kelsall, Cicerone Press, 2016, ISBN 9781852848156

Exploring the Pembrokeshire Coast, Phil Carradice, Gomer, 2002, ISBN 9781843231257

Other Useful Contacts

www.visitpembrokeshire.com – www.pembrokeshirecoast.org

Tel. 01437 764551 for information about the Pembrokeshire coastal bus service.

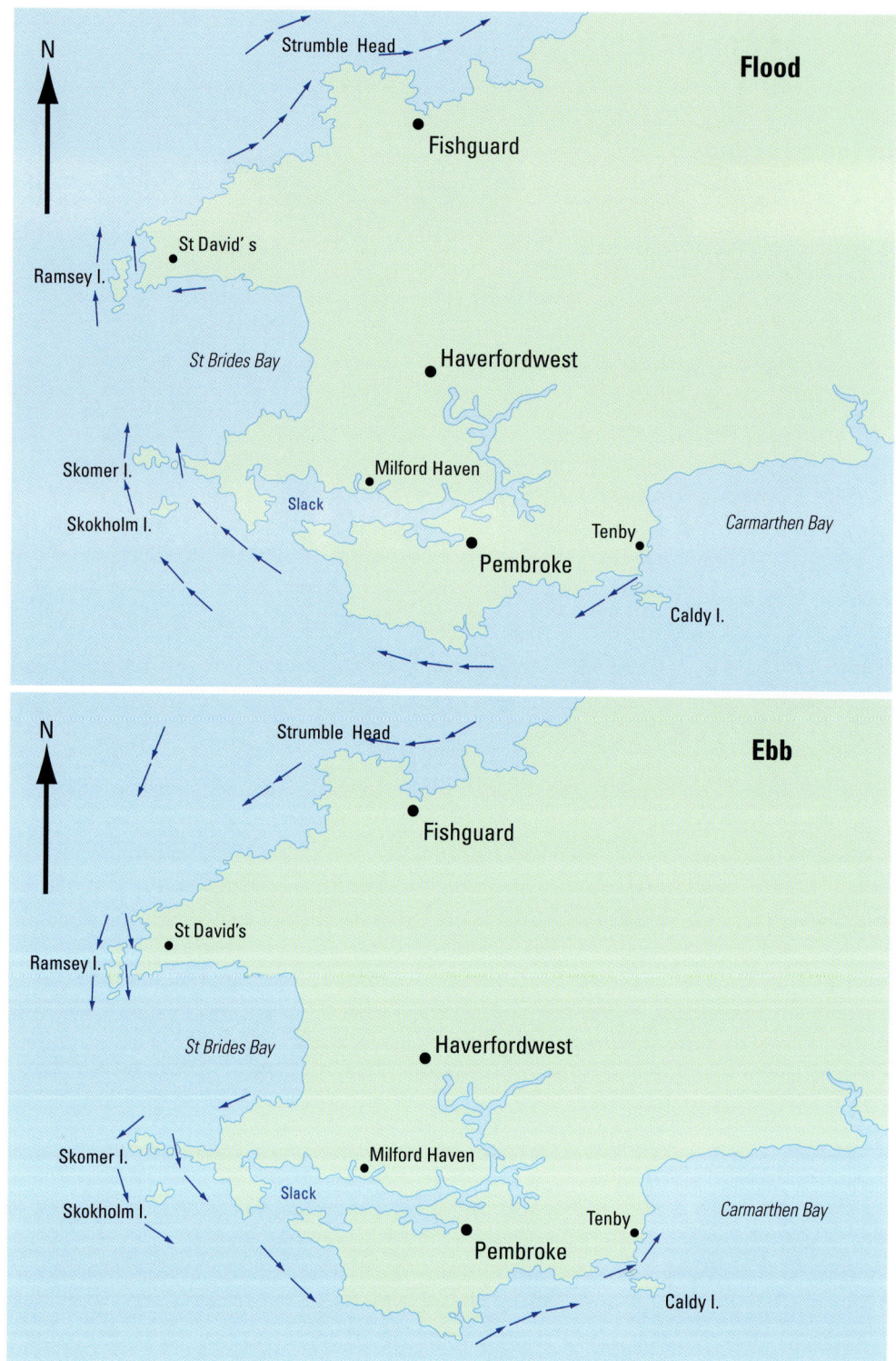

The above charts are intended to give a general overview. Consult the relevant chapters and other sources for more precise information.

Cemaes Head blowhole | Mark Rainsley

Cemaes Head

No. 28 | **Grade B** | **19km** | **OS Sheet 145** | **Tidal Port Milford Haven**

Start	△ Gwbert SN 163 486 / SA43 1PN
Finish	○ Parrog, Newport SN 051 396 / SA42 0RW
HW / LW	at Gwbert is 1 hour and 30 minutes after HW Milford Haven.
Tidal times	The tide starts to flow NE approximately 2 hours before HW Milford Haven and then SW 4 hours after Milford Haven.
Tidal rates	The tidal flow is low and normally does not exceed 1 knot.
Coastguard	Milford Haven, Tel. 01646 690909, VHF 0150 UT repeated every 3 hours

Introduction

This is a committing trip as there are few places to escape because of steep cliffs. This has in turn kept communities and hence the main road well away from the coastline. The cliffs rise to over 170m and are being slowly eroded by the ever-present movement of the sea. Passing 'The Witches Cauldron' you'll see more evidence of this erosion. Your starting point, the Afon Teifi, marks the boundary between Ceredigion and Pembrokeshire; it is also the starting place for the Pembrokeshire Coastal Path. The town of Cardigan has been a port since the Middle

The Witch's Cauldron shower facilities | Mark Rainsley

Ages, and during the 1800s it grew considerably and became one of the country's largest ports for transatlantic emigration. However with the arrival of the railway and silting of the river it declined as a commercial port, finally closing during WW2. The town's history is well documented and effectively displayed at the Cardigan History Centre, which is situated on the south side of the river by the town bridge.

Promontory forts

All along this section of coast you will find evidence, in the form of fortified camps, of previous Iron Age communities that lived here over 2,000 years ago. Built on prominent headlands, these forts gave protection to their inhabitants from tribal feuding. Some are quite small and would have been a place for a last stand, while others are quite large, where communities could have lived inside their protective walls, dykes and embankments. Good examples can be found at Martin's Haven, Westdale Bay, near Dale and on St David's Head.

Castell Henllys is a Scheduled Ancient Monument and one of many prehistoric promontory forts in the National Park dating to around 600 BC. The BBC 1 series 'Surviving the Iron Age' was filmed exclusively at and around Castell Henllys Iron Age fort in Pembrokeshire. It was home to the volunteers for seven weeks as they tried to survive conditions similar to those of over 2000 years ago. It is situated off the A487, 6km east of Newport. http://www.castellhenllys.com/, Tel. 01239 891319.

Description

Poppit Sands is one of the most popular beaches in the area. There is plenty of space for parking, a café, toilets and a summer RNLI station. The area here is important for wildlife and there are projects in place to turn some of the land back to reed-bed. Launching from here does require a long carry; it may therefore be better to launch from the opposite side of the Afon Teifi at (SN 163 486) and park on the side of the road. There is a slipway here and launching 3 hours after HW Milford Haven will see you taken along the river and out into the main stream as it starts to head SW. If you are prepared to walk with your boat for the first 200m until you reach the Teifi Boat Club slipway you can launch at all states of the tide as there is always a small amount of water here. It is also possible to launch further upstream at the north end of St Dogmaels, where there is a slipway that gives easy access at all states of the tide (SN 164 468). However there is limited nearby parking. There are no toilets at either of these slipways.

Cemaes Head stands out in front of you, and makes a clear statement for the start of the Pembrokeshire coastline. There are several caves to explore near the headland. Rounding this and you'll see right down to Dinas Head which is over 15km away, and as you round Pen yr Afr look up; the cliffs above you represent the highest point on the coastal path. The cliffs are made up of alternative layers of sandstone and mudstone, which had been compressed over 400 million years ago as two continents collided and folded into the layers that are visible today. This is a spectacular section of coastline.

In an emergency you could land at Pwllygranant but it is not until Ceibwr Bay could you safely land. The beach is stony here and the surrounding rock formations are wonderful. Fulmars can be

seen nesting on these cliffs and grey seals can be found in the area. Take a rest here because the next time you'll be able to easily get out of your boat will be at Newport and the end of the trip.

Ceibwr Bay is a sheltered spot and therefore makes a good place to launch from. However there is only parking for four cars, so arrive early. A round trip starting from here and heading north past Cardigan Island to Mwnt and back would make a wonderful alternative to the route described here.

Soon after leaving Ceibwr you'll be greeted with the sight of an arch and massive collapsed blowhole called Traeth Bach, "The Witches Cauldron". This was caused by the erosion and collapse of a cave, formed where the sea has been able to wear away the soft rock under the surface. Next to here is Castell Trerufydd, an Iron Age fort. From here the cliffs will remain high for the next 7km and when you finally turn the corner and pass the Carregedrywy rocks, then Newport Sands, your destination will come into view. You have a choice of two places to land, either at the north end of the sands, where there is a large car park and toilets near the golf club or continue parallel to the beach to where the Afon Nyfer enters the sea. You can then use this to paddle up to Parrog, where there is a car park, café, toilets and campsite. By now you will be pleased to get out of the boat and stretch your legs. The trip will have exposed you to some of the geological history of Pembrokeshire and illustrate just how this is still being shaped.

Tide and weather

As there is little actual flow along the coast it is possible to explore this area at most times. However due to the exposed nature and length of this trip it is advised to ensure you have a settled weather forecast before leaving.

Additional information

The campsite at Parrog, Newport (Morawelon Camping and Caravanning, Tel. 01239 820565) is next to the water and could be used for those wanting to link this and trip No. 29 together.

For those wanting accurate information about local offshore weather, you should look at the Met. Office website. The Marine Automatic Weather Station ID: 62301 Aberporth is 16NM north of Cardigan Island. Position: Latitude 52° 24' N, Longitude 4° 42' W.

If the weather forecast is not good or you want to combine some river paddling into your trip to the area, then the River Teifi flows into the sea at Cardigan and is one of the longest rivers to be found in Wales. It is ideal for either open paddling or playboating but is also one of the finest locations for salmon fishing, so please respect the access agreement. With some careful planning it is possible to travel upstream as far as Cilgerran and for those with an open canoe the gorge here and estuary would make an ideal area to explore. It is possible to launch from the car park near Cilgerran Castle and use the downstream flow to take you to the car park and slipway on the north side of the river, between the two bridges (SN 181 459) near the church on the edge of Cardigan where you can egress. While you are in the area take time to visit the Teifi Marshes Nature Reserve, where there are walks and opportunities to explore the nature found on the banks of the Afon Teifi. You can also hire open boats to explore the river from Heritage Canoes, Tel. 01239 613961 if you want a change.

Dinas Head

No. 29 | Grade B | 12km | OS Sheet 145 &157 | Tidal Port Milford Haven

Start	△ Parrog, Newport SN 163 486 / SA43 1PN
Finish	○ Fishguard / Abergwaun, Lower Town Quay SM 962 371 / SA65 9NB
HW / LW	at Newport is approximately 1 hour 15 minutes after Milford Haven.
Tidal times	The tide starts to flow E approximately 2 hours before HW Milford Haven and then W 4 hours after Milford Haven.
Tidal rates	A tide race may form off the NE corner of Dinas Head as the tide flows west out of Newport Bay.
Coastguard	Milford Haven, Tel. 01646 690909, VHF 0150 UT repeated every 3 hours

Introduction

With cliffs along the whole route, small shingle beaches, plenty of opportunities for rockhopping, natural arches and a dramatic headland, this stretch of coastline is an excellent location for an interesting day trip. Departing from either Newport or Fishguard, it can be split into two sections and provides shorter return trips for those who do not want to venture round Dinas Head. During

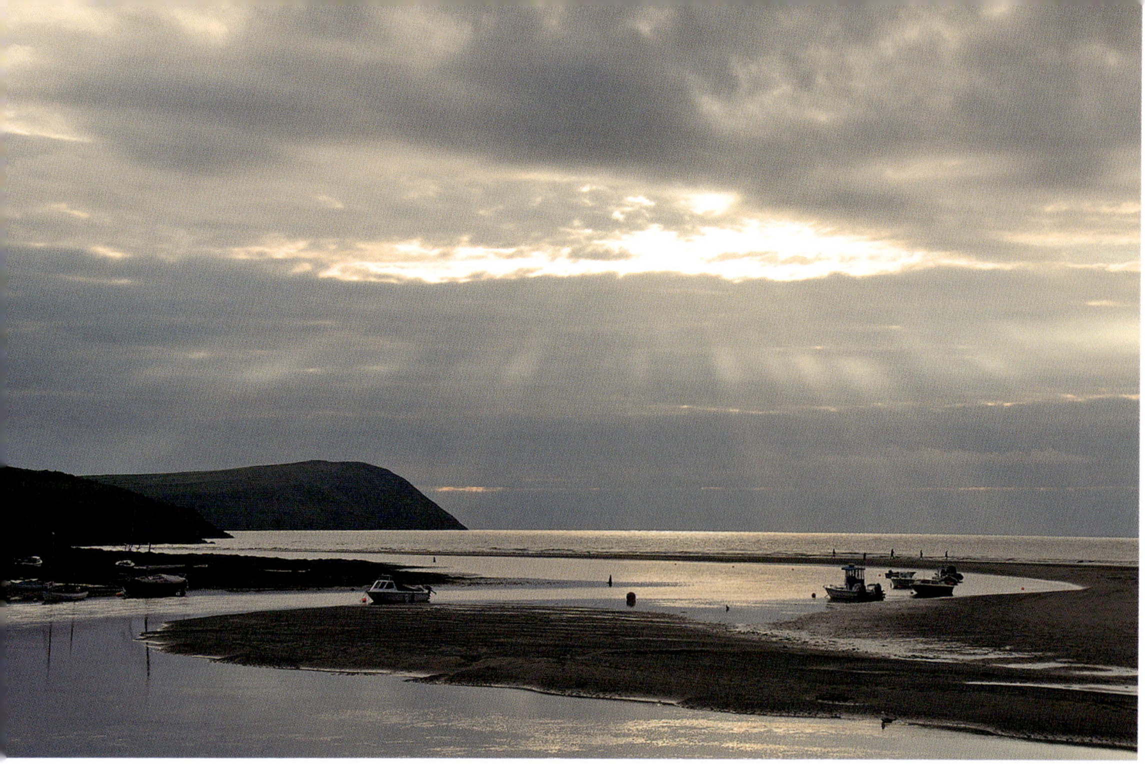

Newport Sands | Mark Rainsley

29

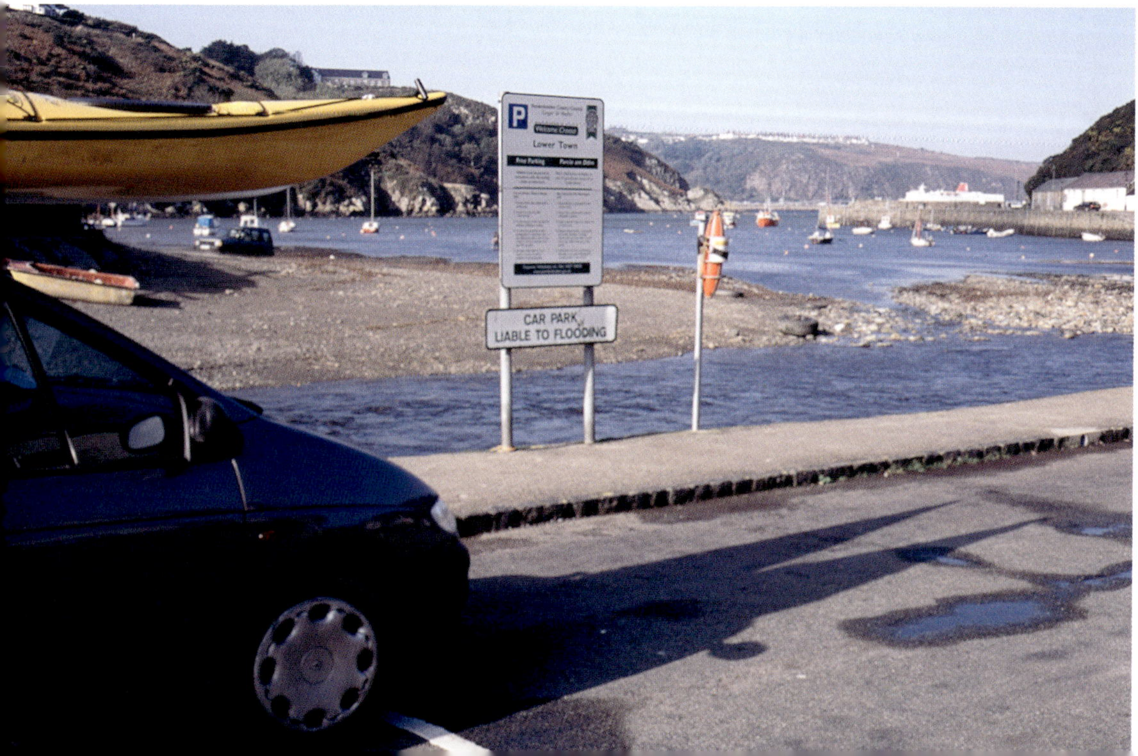

Fishguard Lower Town Quay

strong southerly winds it can provide sheltered paddling and a good place to introduce people to the joys of coastal exploration.

Description

There are good car parks, toilets, a café and easy access to the water at Parrog, as well as the Newport Boat Club (www.newportboatclub.co.uk), which is housed in an old warehouse. This is a reminder of past times, when Newport was a busy port and had a vibrant shipbuilding industry. There is also an example of a limekiln nearby. At low water you will need to walk your boat in places through the shallows. However, if you leave 3 hours after HW Milford Haven you should have enough water and will also pick up the start of the west-flowing ebb tide to take you round Dinas Head and along to Fishguard. During the 19th century and before the estuary silted up, Parrog had been an active port which supported a shipbuilding industry.

Leaving Parrog you will follow a coastline which is made up of low cliffs, submerged rocks and small bays that have been used for quarrying. Arriving at Cwm-yr-Eglwys you will see the remaining west wall of the church of St Brynach, the rest was washed away during a storm in 1859. After that a wall was built to prevent further erosion. You will also find a small sandy beach, car park and toilets. The road down to here is narrow and the car park small so it can become congested during summer months. As you leave the bay and start to go round Dinas Head look for Needle Rock. The tide will start to pick you up by now and take you round the headland, passing several caves on your way to Pwll Gwaelod, where there is another beach and similar facilities including The Old Sailor's Restaurant, which can provide refreshments in its delightful garden. The Pembrokeshire coastal bus service calls here for those wanting to return to Newport. If you don't want to paddle around the headland, this is a good place to walk up to the trig point at Pen y fan and look down on what you have missed.

Further along the coast you will find the small protected bay of Carreg Pen-las which can provide a good, sheltered stopping-off point, but could only be used for an emergency egress as the nearest

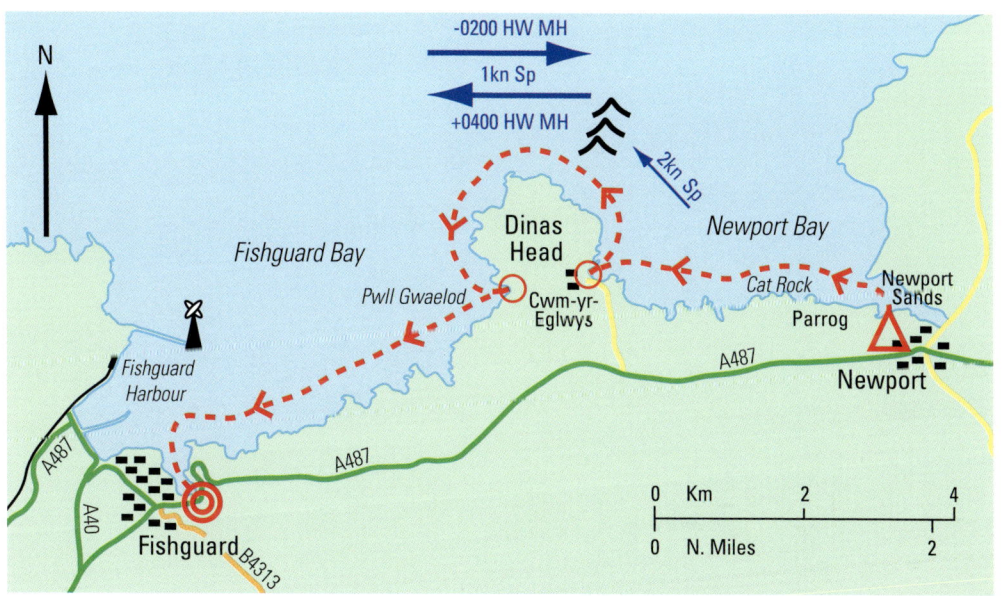

Cliffs south of Newport

Dinas Head

road is 200m away. Further along you will pass under the disused gun emplacement at Penrhyn Ychen and from here you should be able to see the arch of another Needle Rock that you can paddle through in calm weather. Rounding Castle Point into the Lower Town Quay you will see the ruins of Fishguard Fort above you, which was built in 1781 to protect the town from pirates.

By the time you reach Fishguard the water may be low. It is possible to land on the slip at the north end of the delightful Lower Town Quay, where there are toilets and enough space to load the boats. During high spring tides you can literally paddle right into the car park at the south end of the quay, where the Afon Gwaun enters the sea.

Tide & weather

This is generally a safe place to paddle. The tidal flow is small and the only place of risk is off the NE corner of Dinas Head in a strong east-flowing tide, where a tide race can develop. The whole coastline is well protected from any winds coming from a southerly direction.

Additional information

The campsite at Parrog, Newport (Morawelon Camping and Caravanning, Tel. 01239 820565) is next to the water and could be used for those wanting to link this and trip No. 28 together. Slightly further inland is Tycanol Farm Camping, Tel. 01239 820264, which would make an ideal base for exploring the area and is welcoming to sea kayakers. Be warned that the car park by the Lower Town harbour can flood in high tides.

Strumble Head

No. 30 | **Grade C** | **20km** | **OS Sheet 157** | **Tidal Port Milford Haven**

Start	△ Fishguard, Lower Town Quay SN 163 486 / SA43 1PN
Finish	◯ Abercastle SM 852 336 / SA62 5HJ
HW / LW	at Fishguard is approximately 1 hour after Milford Haven.
Tidal times	The east-flowing stream off Strumble Head starts 2 hours before HW Milford Haven. This forms a back eddy in Fishguard Bay, which lasts for 9 hours and starts a west-flowing stream approximately 1 hour after HW Milford Haven along the coast from Pen Anglas towards Strumble Head. The main west-flowing stream starts off Strumble Head 4 hours after HW Milford Haven.
Tidal rates	This can reach 2.5 knots on springs off Strumble Head.
Coastguard	Milford Haven, Tel. 01646 690900, VHF 0150 UT repeated every 3 hours

Introduction

Steep cliffs with few places to escape, an exposed headland with tidal overfalls and a lighthouse make this both a challenging and rewarding trip for an experienced group. You can also re-enact the last invasion of the British mainland, when a 1200 strong French invasion force, under the

165

© Garreg Goffa, where the last invasion of Britain took place in 1797

Strumble Head

leadership of Colonel Tate, landed on Carregwastad Point in 1797. Rumour has it that a group of local women, led by Jemima Nicholas, dressed in local costume including the traditional tall black hats, were mistaken for advancing troops, causing Tate to surrender, in what is now the Royal Oak Inn that can still be found in Fishguard. There is also a monument in St Mary's Church to "Jemima Nicholas, a tall, stout, masculine female" who captured a dozen Frenchmen single-handed and marched them off to the Fishguard guardhouse. A memorial stone high on the cliffs and next to the coastal path commemorates this event.

Description

You can depart from either the Lower Town Quay or from Goodwick. This area has been developed in recent years and there is plenty of parking, toilets, and a café as well as a tourist information centre, Tel. 01348 874737. There is a marine supplier near this complex. The regular ferry service that departs from the quay for Ireland can be observed from either harbour. However arriving boats come round the breakwater and may be unseen. The fast 'Sea Cat' can make a large wake and this could provide an additional hazard. This route, which is only 54 miles, is in fact the shortest route over to Ireland.

Once you have rounded the breakwater, Pen Anglas will be in front of you where there are some interesting rock formations similar to those found on Staffa and the Giant's Causeway. From here a west-flowing eddy will take you along the coast, past Carregwasted Point. All of this coast is made up of high cliffs and gives plenty of opportunity for rockhopping and exploration. As you approach Strumble Head look up at the old WW2 observatory, which is now used by bird watchers; give them a wave. Strumble Head lighthouse was built in 1908 to guide ships into the then new harbour at Goodwick. It is built on the island of Ynys Meicel, and in calm conditions you can paddle close by and look up at the small footbridge which links it to the mainland. The lighthouse was automated in 1980.

Once past the lighthouse you should find some calm water in Carreg Onnen Bay. However expect to eat your lunch afloat, as landing here is not possible. The next headland is Pen Bush, where a tidal race can form. Once past here there are regular opportunities to get out and stretch your legs. At Dinas Mawr there is an Iron Age fort and like much of this coastline you may also encounter seals. This is one of Pembroke's most beautiful spots and the coastline viewed from the Iron Age settlement on Garn Fawr is particularly spectacular. If you pass Pwll Deri near low water, look out for the remains of a shipwreck as you turn SW towards Penbwchdy. This is the remains of the liberty ship Dan Beard, which was launched in 1943 and was torpedoed by U1202 in December 1944.

It is not until Aber Bach and Aber Mawr that there is any road access; even this requires a long carry on a narrow path from the beach to an area of limited parking on the side of the road. Surf can develop at Aber Mawr and on both beaches there are steep stony banks at high water which can make landing difficult. The bay was the scene of a massive storm in 1859, which sank the Charles Holmes with all hands.

Aber Bach had been the initial choice for a ferry port before Goodwick was built. If you walk up the lane to the woods, you can still find remains of the initial construction. Aber Mawr is where the first transatlantic telephone cable was laid via Valentia on the west coast of Ireland. The original small terminus building can still be seen. Look for layers of blue clay in the rocks around Aber Mawr, these were created by sediments being deposited during the end of the last ice age.

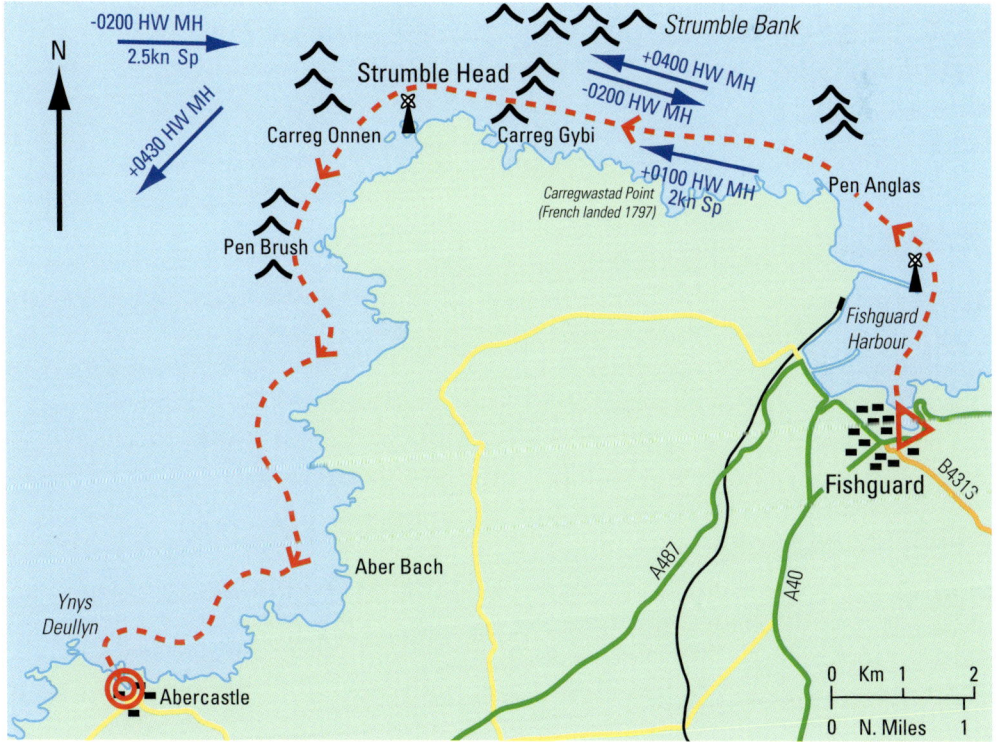

Carreg Samson chambered tomb | Mark Rainsley

It is better to continue to Abercastle where there is a sheltered beach to land on. On the way you will pass Penmorfa and another Iron Age promontory fort. Once you have landed at Abercastle, change your footwear and take a short walk to the west from the beach, which will take you to Carreg Samson, where you will find an impressive burial chamber. Legend has it that St Samson placed the cap stone in place using just his little finger.

Tide and weather

The main westerly flow starts around 4 hours after HW Milford Haven but an earlier eddy starts 1 hour after HW Milford Haven and can form a tide race off Pen Anglas. This allows some flexibility as to when to leave, as long as you arrive at Strumble Head after the main westerly flow has started. If you do reach the headland using this eddy before the main flow has also started to flow west you can expect to find confused water north of the headland. When there is a strong-flowing easterly stream this can cause a north-flowing stream close inshore from Penbwchdy to Pen Brush.

A tide race forms at Pen Brush and Carreg Onnen, west of Strumble Head on the north stream and another race forms at Carreg Gybi to Ynys Meicel on the west-flowing stream.

Additional information

It may be best to obtain ferry arrival times and plan your departure around them. Phone the ferry terminal for current departure times with the operator Stena Line, Tel. 08705 70 70 70 or Tel. 08705 755 755.

Porthgain | Mark Rainsley

Penclegyr

No. 31 | Grade B | 8km | OS Sheet 157 | Tidal Port Milford Haven

Start	△ Abercastle SM 852 336 / SA62 5HJ
Finish	○ Abereiddy Bay SM 797 / 313 SA62 6DT
HW / LW	Abercastle is 1 hour after HM Milford Haven.
Tidal times	NE flow starts 2 hours and 15 minutes before HW Milford Haven and SW flow starts 4 hours after HW Milford Haven.
Tidal rates	2.5 knots at springs.
Coastguard	Milford Haven, Tel. 01646 690909, VHF 0150 UT repeated every 3 hours

Introduction

This is a pleasant day's paddle, with numerous stopping-off points, natural caves, rock formations and plenty of local history to explore. It can easily be completed including a return trip, starting and finishing at either end. There are some points along the route where you will encounter some reasonable tidal streams so it is best to arrange your trip at a time that coincides with a change in the direction of the tidal flow. If you departed from Abercastle 5 hours before HW Milford

Abercastle, where Alfred Johnston landed in 1876

Haven, this would give you time to paddle down to Abereiddy Bay, break for lunch and then return to Abercastle using the start of the NE flow.

Abercastle is a delightful small harbour and village; it is also known as Cwm Badau (Bay of Boats). Looking around you will find plenty of evidence from when it was an active harbour; you can still see the old grain store and a limekiln. In 1876, Alfred Johnston landed here in his 20ft boat 'Centennial' after completing the first solo trans-Atlantic voyage and there is a commemorative plaque near the waterfront. His boat is now on display in the Cape Ann Historical Society museum in Gloucester MA, USA. There is limited roadside parking in Abercastle and the toilets are down near the water but there are no other facilities. Because of this it may be easier to get your timings right with the tide and launch from Abereiddy Bay, using Abercastle as a lunch spot before returning to your starting point.

Description

Ynys Deullyn is a prominent rock that marks the entrance to Abercastle; you can pass between this and the mainland. The coastline from here is a series of small bays and provides plenty of opportunity for exploring. You can experience a number of different eddies in this area.

It is possible to land at Aber Draw (Aber Felin), where there is a disused mill, which inspired the Rev. Crwys Williams to write the poem "Mein Trefin". From here you can walk the 500m into Trefin, where there is a youth hostel, campsite and shop. It is also possible to launch here but there is limited roadside parking and a difficult carry down a narrow path to the beach.

Porthgain is a delightful sheltered harbour, the entrance is marked by two white towers, and will allow you to judge your distance on the approach. There is a good-sized car park but it can soon become full because of the popular Sloop public house, as well as galleries selling locally produced art. There is also 'The Shed' that serves some of the best seafood in the area, but if you are after an evening meal it is best to book in advance. The harbour was originally built to process and transport stone. The remains of the old works can still be seen, these were closed in 1932. If you have time it is worth exploring the harbour and trying to imagine it 100 years ago as a busy port. Soon after leaving Porthgain you will be able to see an old quarry that was linked in the past to the harbour by a tramway. Tidal overfalls can build up at Penclegyr and the rocks of Cerrig Gwylan. From here head SW to Trwyncastell, rounding this you can see a tower high on the headland, and Abereiddy Bay will be in front of you.

At the north end of Abereiddy Bay is the 'Blue Lagoon' but this is no relation to the tourist attraction found in Iceland. Here it is an old quarry that has been opened up to allow the sea to flood in. Its colour is caused by the algae that grows here. The entrance is quite narrow but easy for a kayak. Look out for swimmers diving off the rocks. You'll find remains of some of the quarry buildings, as well as the old tramway line, once you have landed. At low tide there is a wide expanse of sand but look out for dumping surf when the tide is high. There is a large car park, toilets and a mobile café during the summer months.

Tide and weather

You may encounter tidal overfalls at Ynys Deullyn, Penclegyr and Cerrig Gwylan. If it is too rough to paddle, park at Porthgain and use the coastal path to walk over to Abereiddy. You'll be able to see more evidence of the quarrying and remains of the old tramway, as well as being able

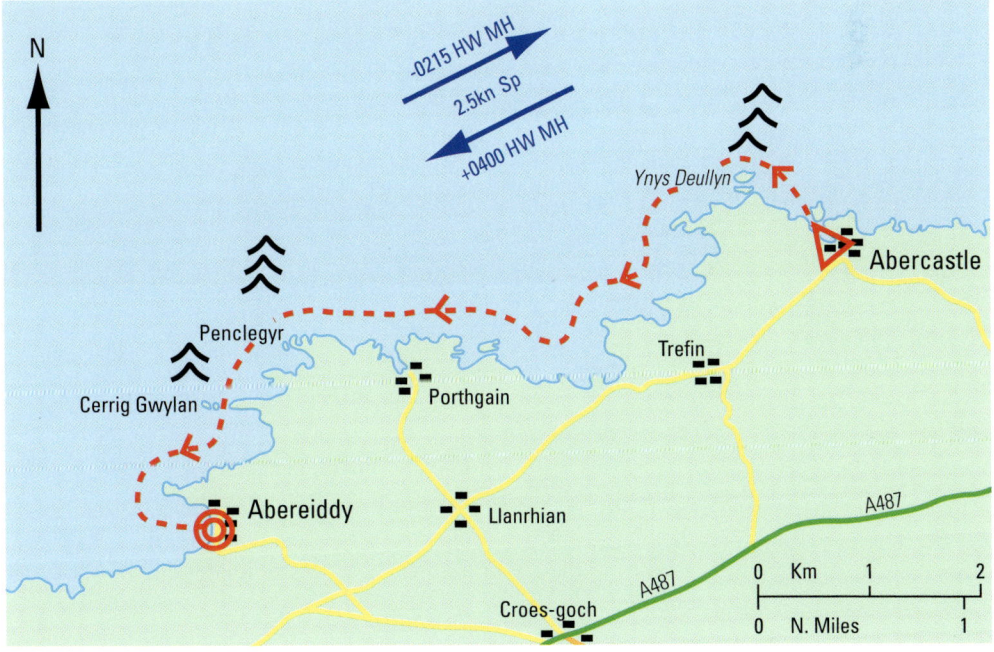

Near Abereiddy | Mark Rainsley

to look out at the tide race at Penclegyr. You'll also be able to look down onto the waters of the Blue Lagoon.

Additional information

This trip is an excellent introduction to the Pembrokeshire coast, providing a variety of places to explore, with an abundance of wildlife, so don't rush it.

St Davids Head | Mark Rainsley

St David's Head

No. 32	**Grade B** **11km** **OS Sheet 157** **Tidal Port Milford Haven**
Start	△ Abereiddy Bay SM 797 313 / SA62 6DT
Finish	○ Whitesands Bay SM 734 271 / SA62 6PS
HW	at Abereiddy is 45 minutes after HW Milford Haven.
HW	at Whitesands is 10 minutes after HW Milford Haven.
Tidal times	NE flow starts 2 hours 15 minutes before HW Milford Haven and SW flow starts 4 hours after HW Milford Haven.
Tidal rates	Maximum rate is 2.5 knots at springs.
Coastguard	Milford Haven, Tel. 01646 690909, VHF 0150 UT repeated every 3 hours

Introduction

This trip takes you round one of the big, well-known corners of the Pembrokeshire coastline. Once you have left Abereiddy there are no easy places to get out until you reach Whitesands and the end of the trip. Leaving Pembroke's industrial past, you'll pass high cliffs, rock formations and tide races, arriving at a golden sandy beach, the contrasts will be clear for all to see.

Description

As you leave the beach you may see the Abereiddy Sledges, which are three rocks about 500m off the coast and are visible at low water. The coast is a series of rocky outcrops, caves and steep cliffs, where seabirds will soar above your head. As you approach St David's Head you will see a series of high rocky tors that have been formed from hard rock, the softer surrounding material being washed away when the sea level was much higher. St David's Head is also a popular climbing area and if you keep in close you should be able to look up for their lines. On top of the headland are the remains of an impressive Iron Age fort. There are remains of several roundhouses and a burial chamber to be seen.

As you arrive at the headland, Ramsey Island will come into view, turn round the final rocks and you will have the feeling that you are going back on yourself. In a north-flowing stream you will experience some confused water as it is swept around the headland and on its way along the coast. In front of you will be the sheltered beach of Porthmelgan and your final destination of Whitesands Bay can be seen to the right.

Whitesands is a popular sandy beach. There is a car park, which soon fills up, as well as toilets, a shop and café. During the summer the beach is managed, separating different water users. Be aware of this if landing during busy periods, especially as it is also popular with surfers. There is a campsite nearby which with the use of a trolley or long carry could provide a suitable stopping-off point on a multi-day trip.

Tide and weather

A NE eddy can form close to St David's Head that will continue to run for an hour after the main stream has turned SW. You may also encounter overfalls during a north-flowing stream off St David's Head and Penllechwen on a south-flowing stream Another place to look out for rough water is around Carreg-gwylan-fach.

Additional information

St David's is the smallest city in the country with a population of less than 2,000. It is named after St David, the patron saint of Wales, who founded a monastic community during the 6th century. The actual cathedral dates back to the 12th century and it was built in a hollow so passing raiders would hopefully not see it. Much of it was destroyed during the Civil War but was later rebuilt under the direction of Sir George Gilbert Scott. There are daily religious services and a music festival during the summer.

See the Cathedral's website for dates and times. http://www.stdavidscathedral.org.uk/

© Whitesands Bay | Mark Rainsley

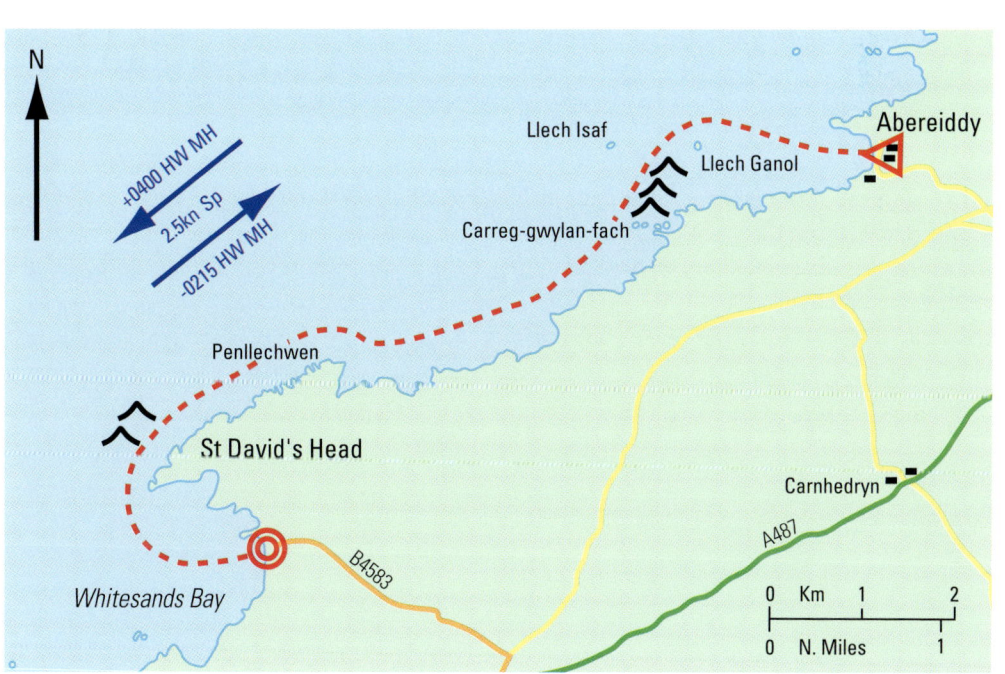

175

The Blue Lagoon at Abereiddy

St David's Head

32

Ramsey Island | Mark Rainsley

Ramsey Island

No. 33 | Grade B | 17km | OS Sheet 157 | Tidal Port Milford Haven

Start	△ Porth Clais SM 740 242 / SA62 6RR
Finish	○ Porth Clais SM 740 242 / SA62 6RR
HW / LW	in Ramsey Sound is 30 minutes after Milford Haven.
Tidal times	The south-flowing stream starts 3 hours after HW Milford Haven. The Bitches cause a north-flowing eddy close to the east coast of Ramsey and can extend around the northern end of the island as far as Trwyn-Sion-Owen. The north-flowing stream starts 3 hours 25 minutes before HW Milford Haven. There isn't really a period of slack, the water just seems to swirl round and then head off in the other direction.
Tidal rates	In Ramsey Sound the tide can flow at 6 knots at springs.
Coastguard	Milford Haven, Tel. 01646 690909, VHF 015U UT repeated every 3 hours

Introduction

A journey around Ramsey Island in a sea kayak has to be one of the best trips to be experienced in this country. You will be surrounded by spectacular rock formations, an abundance of wildlife

Lifeboat station, St Justinian

both above and below the waves, add to this the fact that you will experience some of the fastest moving water to be found, it will be a day to remember. It is possible to complete this trip from St Justinian but car parking can become problematic as you jostle for space with day trippers taking the ferry and playboaters heading out to The Bitches. It is also a difficult carry if you do choose to depart from here. Please be aware of the needs of the lifeboat crew, who may arrive in a hurry and need easy access.

Description

At Porth Clais there is a good-sized car park, toilets and a small café. This is a narrow harbour that dries out as far as the outer quay wall at low water, which makes for a long carry or drag through the shallow stream that flows here. It was created by glacier melt water at the end of the ice age. It had been a busy port and there are restored limekilns on the quay wall. It is suggested to leave here near high water and aim to reach the north end of Ramsey as the tide goes slack and starts to run south, which is 3 hours later.

You can paddle the shore side of Carreg Fran and then move on to explore the caves in Carreg yr Esgob. From here you'll need to ferry glide over to Midland Gap. If there is a strong tidal stream running north be careful not to be swept down into Ramsey Sound and The Bitches. The stream will also flow quickly through the rocks at the south end of the island and you'll experience quite a ride into Bay Dillyn. Here there are numerous caves to explore and this is also a popular area for seals.

Use the end of the north-flowing stream to take you along the west coast of Ramsey, be prepared to meet various eddies running against you. Take time to look for harbour porpoises which frequent these waters. As you round the north end of the island, St David's Head will come into view and if the south-flowing stream has started you may have to paddle a little harder. As you head down Ramsey Sound with a southerly stream look out for Horse Rock, which is normally submerged but can cause eddies and whirlpools that can be dangerous. Also be aware of a northerly eddy that runs close inshore to the island and aim to land near the jetty on the island just north of The Bitches. You can sit here and eat your lunch while watching as the tide builds up behind The Bitches, which causes the north-flowing eddy. There are normally a few mooring buoys just offshore, which will clearly illustrate this effect. There is a natural archway here that will allow you to come inside The Bitches.

Once you decide to leave, use this eddy to take you north before ferry gliding over to the mainland. Do not underestimate the tide's strength, it will soon sweep you down onto The Bitches if you're not careful. Drop into a small eddy that forms just south of Pen Dal-aderyn near Shoe Rock; only now can you relax.

Retrace your course back to Porth Clais, looking for a narrow slot to take you on the shore side of Carreg Fran. The tide will be low by the time you reach Porth Clais and you may have to carry the boat for the last stretch, but it will have been a rewarding day and overcoming this final obstacle will seem a small price to pay.

Tide and weather

At the south end of Ramsey a north-east current, caused by Ynys Eilun, flows through Midland Gap into Bay Dillyn. This can run quite fast and can last for 9 hours making progress from the

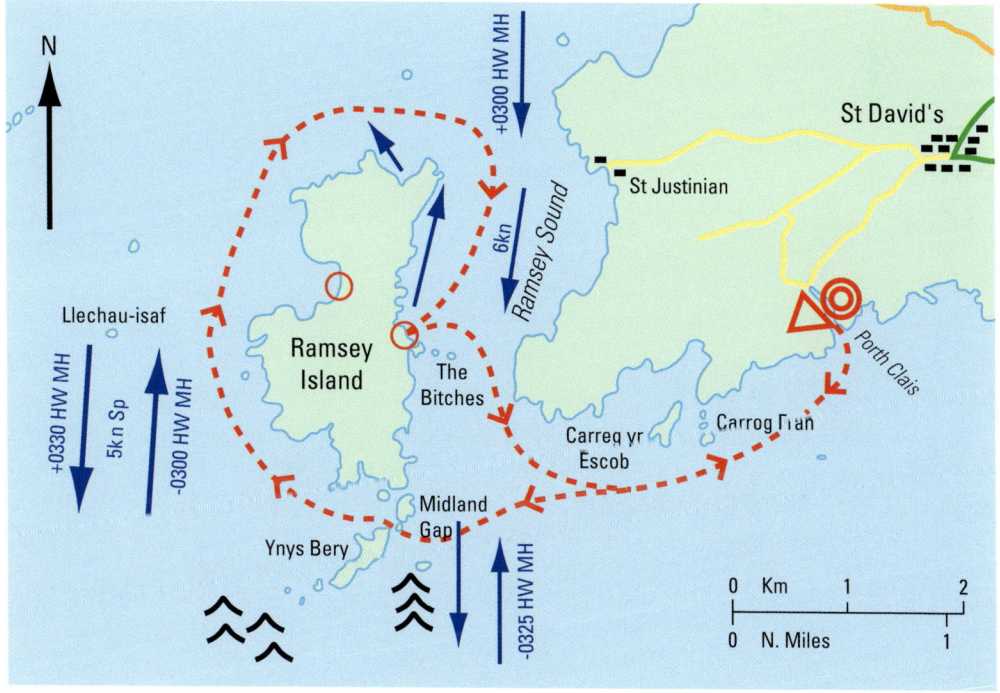

Playing at The Bitches tidal rapid | Mark Rainsley

west difficult. However with a short sprint you can normally get through. This eddy extends up the east coast of Ramsey to Penrhyn Twll. At the height of the south-flowing stream a small race develops off the south end of Carreg Fran.

Additional information

Ramsey Island is an important breeding ground for a wide range of wildlife, including Atlantic grey seals. The island has strong breeding colonies of chough and lapwing, as well as cliff birds on the west coast. The island is managed by the RSPB, who discourage landing anywhere apart from the quay just north of The Bitches. There is a landing fee to pay if you wish to go ashore at the landing jetty on Ramsey.

The name Ramsey comes from the Norse name 'Hrafin'. The Welsh name is Ynys Dewi, which means St David's Island.

Ramsey Island, Tel. 01437 721911 or 0800 854367 (Freephone).

http://www.ramseyisland.co.uk/

Alternative – a circumnavigation from Whitesands Bay

You could complete this trip by departing from Whitesands around Low Water Milford Haven and heading out to St David's Head and using the SW flow to take you around the west side of Ramsey. Pass through Midland Gap and then head SW to complete a circumnavigation of Ynys

Lunch break looking to Ramsey sound | Eurion Brown

The Bitches

The Bitches are a line of rocks that project at right angles to the east coast of Ramsey Island. They cut the width of the sound in half and get their name from the number of ships that have been wrecked on them. The water accelerates to over 15 knots as it rushes through the rocks and this causes massive standing waves of up to 8ft high. They are a playboater's dream and can provide an exhilarating experience but can also be extremely dangerous. Although it has an awesome reputation you can still use it as a good training location, especially during the early stages after slack water. For your first experience use a low neap tide, less than a 6m tide measured at Milford Haven; gain confidence on this before trying a 7m plus high spring tide. The best period to experience the wave is for the 3 hours before high water, when the stream is running north. You'll need to be fit, not just for the playing, but also to have enough energy for the return trip. Ensure your group is well equipped with flares, radio or phone and a towline. To get the most out of the tidal flow, plan to leave St Justinian about 3 and a half hours before HW at Milford Haven and paddle up the mainland coastline before ferry gliding over to The Bitches. It is best to return at about HW Milford Haven. However this can be dangerous, as you may be tired and the tide will still be running fast. Ferry glide over to the end of The Bitches and head back towards the mainland keeping SE of Horse Rock. Allow plenty of space here, as there can be dangerous whirlpools around the rock. If there is a northerly wind blowing, carefully consider if it is wise to go out as the waves will become extreme through the sound. If you want to experience The Bitches for the first time, there are organised events each year you could join or take someone along who has been before.

Whitesands Bay | Mark Rainsley

Bery, before returning back through the gap and heading north. You can pass through the archway at The Bitches and take a break. By now the north-flowing stream will have started; for those feeling brave you could have a play on the waves before heading north back to Whitesands. If you get your timing right and use the eddies well, you'll have the tide with you all day.

South Bishop lighthouse with Daufraich on the right | Eurion Brown

Bishops and Clerks

No. 34 | **Grade C** | **28km** | **OS Sheet 157** | **Tidal Port Milford Haven**

Start	△ Whitesands Bay SM 734 271 / SA62 6PS
Finish	○ Whitesands Bay SM 734 271 / SA62 6PS
HW / LW	in Ramsey Sound is 30 minutes after Milford Haven.
Tidal times	The south-flowing stream starts 3 hours 30 minutes after HW Milford Haven on the west side of Ramsey. The north-flowing stream through Ramsey Sound starts 3 hours 25 minutes before HW; this forms a south-flowing back eddy north of 'The Bitches'.
Tidal rates	In Ramsey Sound the tide can flow at 6 knots at springs. On the west side of Ramsey and around The Bishops the rate is 5 knots at springs. Be warned that the water between Ramsey and The Bishops can become rough.
Coastguard	Milford Haven, Tel. 01646 690900, VHF 01bU UT repeated every 3 hours

Introduction

This is a big trip and should not be undertaken without a good weather forecast and a group of competent paddlers. Getting out of your boat on any of The Bishops or Clerks rocks is not easy, so be prepared to stay in your boat until you get to Ramsey Island. If something does go wrong you are a long way offshore and in the middle of a fast tidal stream. However your sense of achievement as you return safely to the beach will be immense. Whitesands is a popular sandy

© South Bishop lighthouse | Mark Rainsley

beach, where there is a car park which soon fills up, as well as toilets, a shop and café. During the summer the beach is managed, separating different water users, be aware of this when landing.

Description

Plan to leave Whitesands and use a south-flowing stream to take you out to South Bishops, so you reach there towards slack water. Then cross over to the south end of Ramsey as the tide turns and use the start of the northerly flow to return you through Ramsey Sound and back to Whitesands.

Smalls Rock

Lying over 25km from the mainland this would provide an extremely committing trip for any group of kayakers (see Route 35). However the history of the lighthouse, that sits high above this furthest outcrop of Pembrokeshire, is an intriguing one. The first lighthouse was built in 1776 on oak posts that were designed to allow the waves to break between them and therefore not destroying the structure. Remnants of these can still be seen. The current lighthouse was constructed in 1861 and saw one of the most tragic stories connected with the history of Trinity House.

During a stormy period one of the lighthouse keepers died, and with the other unable to obtain assistance he built a coffin, which he then placed outside. This was subsequently damaged, exposing part of the decaying body. The whole experience drove the remaining keeper insane. From then on all manned lighthouses have had three keepers, so if one person became ill or died, the other two could support one another and prevent a reoccurrence of this sad sequence of events.

It is also possible to visit North Bishops as part of this trip but you will need to complete a good ferry glide of 5km from St David's Head.

Head out from Whitesands towards St David's Head to pick up the SW flowing stream and then aim north of the Gwahan rock and out to Carreg Rhoson. Be aware that the tide will take you south so watch your rate of drift and ferry glide as necessary to arrive correctly. At this point look south to see what waves are forming. The water between Ramsey and The Bishops can become very rough. One look at the Imray chart will show why. Rapid changes in water depth cause rolling waves in even quite calm conditions. This is especially the case if there is any SW swell running against a south-flowing stream. If it does look too rough reconsider your plans and spend the day exploring Ramsey Island; this can be a challenging trip in its own right.

Once at Carreg Rhoson it is then easy to use the south-flowing stream to drop down to South Bishop's lighthouse. You can get out but there is always swell here and with no real landing place it is not an easy option. The lighthouse was built in 1839 and has special perches on the lantern for migrating birds; these aim to stop the birds dashing themselves on the light. Look up to where the helipad is and think that this can be awash during storms, so be thankful that you are not out here then.

Leave South Bishop before the tide turns and cross over Bay Dillyn at the south end of Ramsey Island. Here you will find numerous caves to explore, this is also a popular area for seals. This is a long crossing and be prepared, even on calm days if a strong stream is flowing, for rolling breaking water. Think of the marine chart that showed the rapid changes in the depth of water over this area.

Once the tide has started to flow northerly a fast stream will occur through Midland Gap into Bay Dillyn. This will now be against you but some skilful eddy hopping and a final sprint should

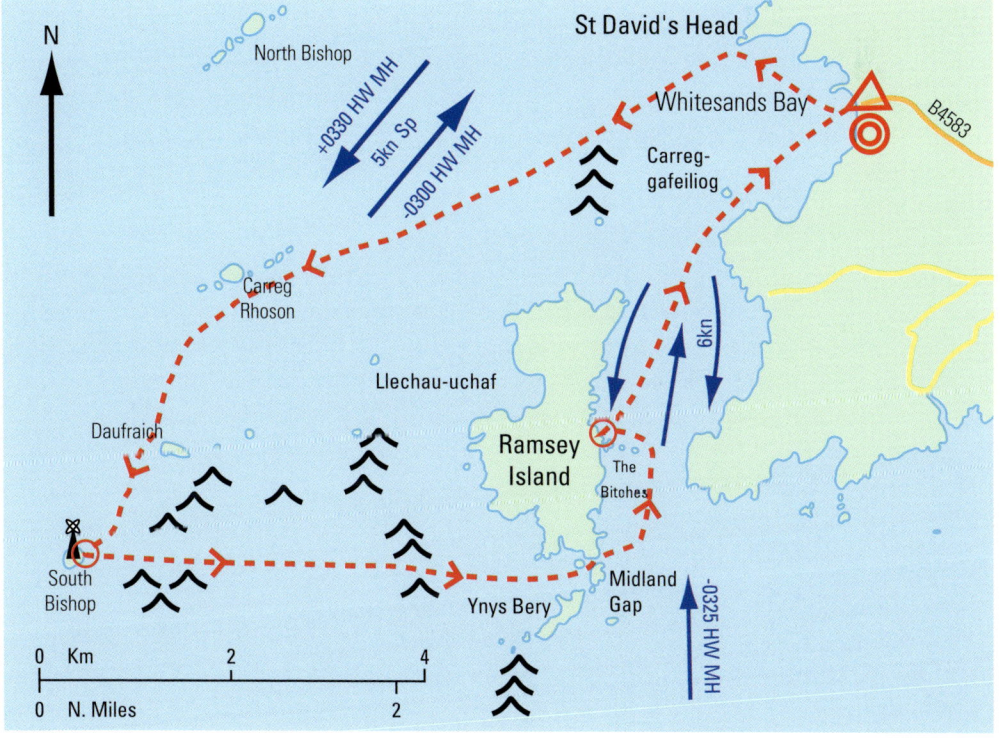

Landing on South Bishop | Mark Rainsley

see you through to the eastern side of Ramsey Island. As you turn north be aware that you are being drawn into The Bitches. To avoid this aim over towards the mainland and then break out behind the end of The Bitches to land near the jetty on the island, or use the natural arch at the western end of the rocks. Notice that there may be a south-flowing stream close into the island, which will make for some confused water near where you land. Take a well-earned break here and then head down Ramsey Sound with a northerly-flowing stream behind you. Look out for Horse Rock, which is normally submerged but can cause eddies and whirlpools that can be dangerous. Once past Horse Rock you can head over to St Justinian, which is named after the 6th Century saint that lived on Ramsey. He was later murdered and tradition has it that he picked up his head and walked over to the mainland before dying.

During October 1910 the lifeboat was launched from here and rescued three people from the ketch Democrat, but then the lifeboat itself was wrecked, drowning the coxswain and two other members of the crew. The rest were rescued from The Bitches by 18 year old Sydney Mortimer, who was awarded a Silver Medal for his bravery and appointed as the new coxswain. In 1910 a motor powered boat was obtained and the existing lifeboat house was built in 1911 to house it. From here the return to Whitesands will seem an easy stretch when compared to the challenges you will have faced during the day.

Tide and weather

The area between South Bishops and Ramsey has numerous overfalls and it can become rough even in light wind conditions. At the south end of Ramsey a north-east current flows through Midland Gap into Bay Dillyn. This can run quite fast and may last for 9 hours, making progress from the west difficult.

Grassholm | Mark Rainsley

Grassholm

No. 35 | Grade C | 28km | OS Sheet 157 | Tidal Port Milford Haven

Start	△ Whitesands Bay SM 734 271 / SA62 6PS
Finish	◯ Whitesands Bay SM 734 271 / SA62 6PS
HW / LW	in Ramsey Sound is 30 minutes after Milford Haven.
Tidal times	For tidal times around Ramsey Island and The Bishops and Clerks, see Routes 33 and 34. The south-flowing stream around Grassholm starts 4 hours 40 minutes after HW Milford Haven. The north-flowing stream around Grassholm starts 1 hour 35 minutes before HW Milford Haven.
Tidal rates	In Ramsey Sound the tide can flow at 6 knots at springs. On the west side of Ramsey and around Grassholm, the tides reach 5 knots at springs.
Coastguard	Milford Haven, Tel. 01646 690909, VHF 0150 UT repeated every 3 hours

Introduction

Grassholm (Ynys Gwales) is an uninhabited island located far offshore of the Welsh mainland and guarded by ferocious tidal flows and rapids. Visiting the westernmost point of Wales is an exceptional but very worthwhile paddling and planning challenge, rewarded by experiencing the sight, sounds and smell of the 39,000 pairs of northern gannets crammed onto this 400m-wide lump of volcanic rock.

Grassholm gannet | Mark Rainsley

Description

Grassholm (SM 598 093) is about 16km west of the Marloes Peninsula. However, the easiest approach is via the longer route from Whitesands Bay, hitching a lift on the tide stream. Time your launch to arrive at Grassholm around slack water, likely taking under three hours. Ferry glide from Whitesands Bay north of Ramsey Island and then ride the tide past The Bishops and Clerks to South Bishop Lighthouse. Paddlers are recommended to already be familiar with these wonderful but challenging locations; the lighthouse (Route 34's ultimate destination) is reached and ticked off within the first hour! Passing South Bishop, expect to encounter lively tidal rapids.

It's not hard to identify your target; Grassholm's 45m-high summit and north-western half is covered by a gleaming white cap of gannet poo. Set a bearing for the isle and enjoy 14km of deep calmer waters. Porpoises and bottlenose dolphins are a common sight. The distance passes quickly as Grassholm grows in size; keep checking your position relative to your intended course and adjust as necessary.

The skies fill out with wheeling gannets and you need to be careful not to let this awe-inspiring assault on your senses distract you from a safe approach: if you are a bit early for slack water, you'll encounter tide races flowing around Grassholm (in a NE-SW direction across your path) which will need to be crossed. The author has been here at the height of the tidal flow, the races were notable.

You can't land! The RSPB, who have owned Grassholm since 1948, only permit this in the company of a licensed ornithologist. However, limited shelter can be found in two tiny inlets, the North Gut and South Gut. The latter, on the far side of the isle from your approach, is more spacious and further from the nesting birds; avoiding unnecessary disturbance should be your priority. Paddling around Grassholm whilst waiting for the tide to turn is a wildlife bonanza. The gannets dominate, packed onto the cliffs and filling the skies. These massive birds (two-metre wingspans!) have been here since at least 1872, when a dozen pairs arrived from Lundy in Devon. Grassholm's colony is now a tenth of the world's population, only surpassed in size by St Kilda and Bass Rock in Scotland. One depressing aspect is the jarringly colourful nature of their nests, about 80% of which utilise marine plastic. Other nesting birds include guillemots and razorbills. At the water's edge, around 120 grey seals bask, although they pup elsewhere. It is hard to discern much of the island's interior due to the gannet colony, but you may spot traces of ruined stone shelters believed to be early Christian or Viking in origin; settlement of the island dates back into prehistory. The landscape is pock-marked by craters from USAF target practice during WW2.

The trickiest bit is still to come: your return. You will be passing Ramsey Island at the height of the tidal flow (yes, completing a 48km no-landing paddle with a run past The Bitches and Horse Rock) and this needs consideration. Furthermore, your passage is severely complicated by the tide flowing out of the northern end of St Brides Bay. This powerfully pushes west and north-west (i.e. offshore) across your path as you approach Ramsey Island and The Bishops and Clerks. The author has tackled this by aiming nearly east-north-east from Grassholm; this still involved a tough wrestle against the current to squeeze into Ramsey Sound. On a later occasion, we adopted a more laid-back approach, aiming for the southern tip of Ramsey Island with the intention of passing along Ramsey's west coast. The actual outcome was being dragged west of South Bishop(!) and having to fight and ferry-glide our way from eddy to eddy along The Bishops and Clerks, through enormous tidal rapids which made The Bitches seem rather underwhelming. You don't want to do this.

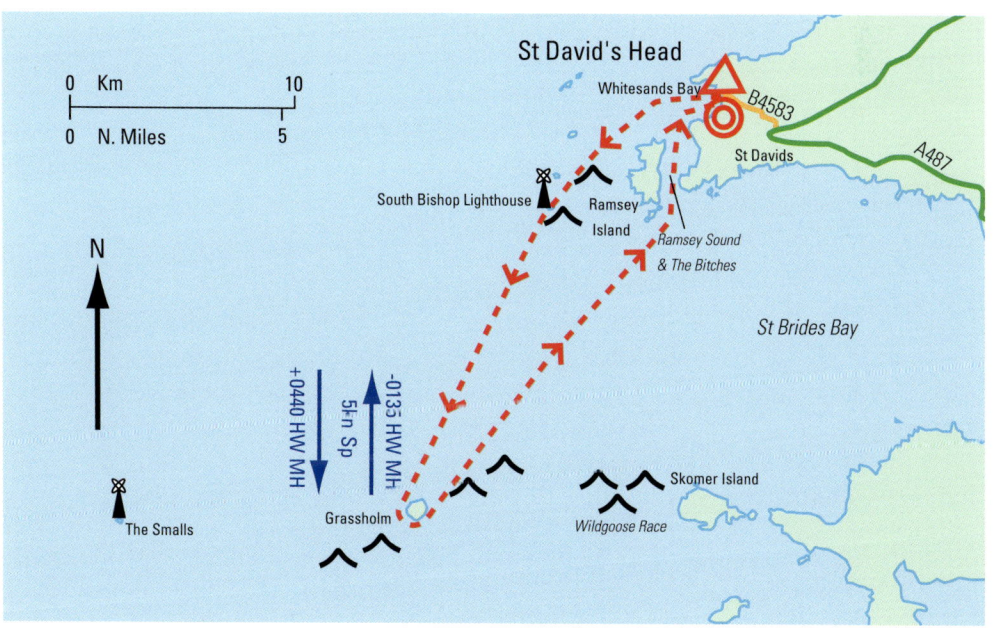

The Smalls

Grassholm is the westernmost point of Wales. Or is it? The Smalls rocks (SM 466 088) are 13km further west, with four reefs spread over several hundred metres. The 41m-high white lighthouse on North West Rock, lit in 1861, is Trinity House's most isolated. It is infamous for the tragedy of 1801, described in Route 34.

Only a handful of sea kayak groups have made it out here and landing is not officially allowed.

'At 21 miles offshore and maybe only 50 square metres visible at high water, it was a small target to find. Getting there involved navigating the infamous Bishops and Clerks as well as five knot tides around The Smalls themselves.

As we launched, The Bishops and Clerks were rising mysteriously from the misty waters on the horizon and the light from South Bishop cast its eye towards us every five seconds.

In the last hour, we were able to see how small the reef really is. It was covered with seals and gulls, none of whom seemed bothered by our arrival. We didn't want to land as this is their home and we are but guests.

We have since heard that the first successful kayak trip was in 1984, led by Nigel Foster. As far as he knew, we were the second group to reach The Smalls.' - Mike Mayberry.

The south-flowing stream around The Smalls starts 5 hours 15 minutes after HW Milford Haven. The north-flowing stream around The Smalls starts 45 minutes before HW Milford Haven. Between Grassholm and The Smalls, the tides flow up to 5 knots on springs.

Tide and weather

This trip favours perfect weather and visibility coupled with settled seas. If after launching you decide that conditions are not favourable, an early decision to abort (into St Brides Bay?) must be made. Once past Ramsey Island, you are probably committed for the duration.

As noted above, familiarity with Routes 33 and 34 is advisable; even so, note that you'll be experiencing the races west of Ramsey at the height of the tide, rather than at the slackish flows normally used to visit them.

Additional Information

A number of tour boat companies visit Grassholm on wildlife-watching tours. It may be worth checking their schedules to find out if you will have company out there.

Variations

Grassholm can be reached from Martin's Haven (Route 39); the author (Mark Rainsley) has not attempted this. This shorter option (c33km) involves crossing a complex series of overfalls, including Jack Sound to the east, and the Wildgoose race to the west, of Skomer Island. Make sure that your planning is spot-on!

Cliff line east of Solva

Green Scar

No. 36 | Grade B | 12km | OS Sheet 157 | Tidal Port Milford Haven

Start	△ Porth Clais SM 740 242 / SA62 6RR
Finish	◯ Newgale SM 847 223 / SA62 6AS
HW / LW	along this coastline is approximately 15 minutes after Milford Haven.
Tidal rates	There is little tidal assistance here, however at the height of the main southerly flow, a small tidal stream flows east along the coast, and an equally small westerly flow occurs when the main stream is running north.
Coastguard	Milford Haven, Tel. 01646 690909, VHF 0150 UT repeated every 3 hours

Introduction

While many will head to the playgrounds and tidal races of the offshore islands, they can easily miss this stretch of sheltered coast, which offers the kayaker the opportunity to explore a variety of history, culture and natural features. It would be easy to complete a return trip to Porth Clais by stopping for lunch at Solva as there is little tidal flow in this area and the trip could be completed at any time.

Solva at low water

Description

At Porth Clais there is a good-sized car park, toilets and a small café. This is a narrow harbour that dries out as far as the outer quay wall, which makes for a long carry or drag through the shallow stream that flows here, if departing near low water. It was created by glacier melt water at the end of the ice age and had been a busy port, which is shown by the restored limekilns on the quay wall. Soon after leaving, you'll pass St Non's Bay, which is reputedly St David's birthplace and named after his mother. The spring is said to have started to flow when he was born and to have special healing powers. The area is used by educational groups, so look out for their presence.

Crossing Caerfai Bay you'll see the rock outcrop of Penpleidiau and a promontory fort on the end of the headland. Rounding the corner will bring you into Caer Bwdy Bay, where there is a quarry which provided the stone for St David's Cathedral. Spend some time exploring the caves around the bay, before heading out to sea and around the Black and Green Scar rocks.

Look north and you'll see the entrance to Solva marked by Black Rock. The harbour frustratingly dries out at low water. However there is a stream so you can float your boat down to the water's edge if launching from here. It was created by the meeting of two ice age melt streams. In the past it was an active port, with a vibrant industry based around processing lime. The materials for the Smalls lighthouse were shipped from here. It is now a picturesque village, which makes its money from tea shops and galleries. Hence the car park can soon fill up, so arrive early. There is a woollen mill 2km north of Solva, which was built in 1907 and was originally powered by a waterwheel. It makes for an interesting visit if it is too rough to go out paddling.

Arriving at Solva near high water

Between here and Newgale there are two prominent headlands, Dinas Fawr and Dinas Fach, where you'll find plenty of caves to explore so allow time at the end of the trip. Pass these and start looking out for the size of the surf. Newgale is a popular venue for a wide variety of outdoor activities, hence be careful when landing. It is best to avoid high water because of the steep stony bank which is at the back of the beach. The beach is a 3km long expanse of sand with a pebble bank. At the north end the remains of an ancient forest can be seen at very low tides. Brandy Brook enters the sea here, which marks the western end of the Norman "Landsker" defensive

36

Green Scar

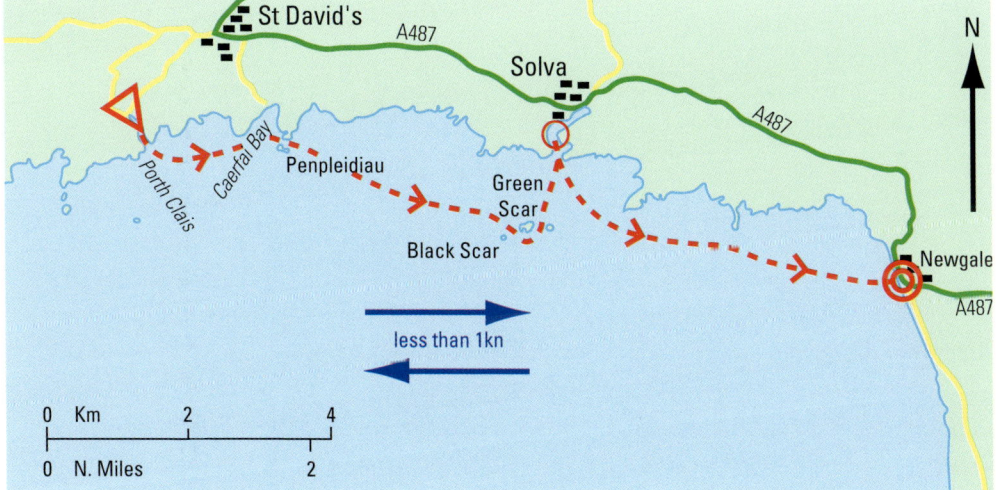

193

Watching climbers near Caerfai Bay

line and identifies the imaginary cultural boundary where the Welsh speaking north is separated from the English speaking south. Inland you will find the remains of Roch Castle, which formed part of this line that ran to Laugharne in the south. Landsker is derived from the Norse word for 'divide'.

There is a campsite, popular with surfers, on the other side of the road and next to the pub. This site could be used as an overnight stop for those wanting to continue along the coast. There are toilets and a number of other facilities within easy walking of the beach.

Tide and weather

With little tidal flow and protected from northerly winds this stretch of coastline is ideal for a group who want a more relaxing day's exploration without the constraints that strong tides can bring.

Additional information

There are two campsites at Caerfai which are within a short distance of this sandy beach and could be used for overnight stops, although you'll have to carry everything up some steep steps to reach either site. The sand is covered at high water. Caerfai Farm Campsite is the nearest and is a tent only site, Tel. 01437 720548 www.caerfaifarm.co.uk

If you want to stay in the area Brandy Brook Caravan & Camping Site (SA62 5PS) Tel. 01437 711020 is in a sheltered, quiet spot inland from Roch and is kayak friendly. You are warned not to arrive from the west using the ford, which usually is too deep for normal cars.

Arch between Nolton Haven and Broad Haven | Eurion Brown

St Brides Bay

No. 37 | Grade A | 9km | OS Sheet 157 | Tidal Port Milford Haven

Start	△ Newgale SM 847 223 / SA62 6AS
Finish	◯ Little Haven SM 856 128 / SA62 3UN
HW	along this coastline is approximately 15 minutes after Milford Haven.
Tidal times	There is little tidal assistance here, however at the height of the main northerly flow, a small tide stream flows south along the coast.
Coastguard	Milford Haven, Tel. 01646 690909, VHF 0150 UT repeated every 3 hours

Introduction

If the surf is up you may find that spending a day playing at Newgale is all you want. This is Pembrokeshire's most impressive beach and is a popular destination. You'll find a mixture of different water users, from sunbathers to anglers and surfers. Be here on a day when there is a strong westerly blowing and you'll have a totally different experience. The Duke of Edinburgh Inn that shelters behind the stone bank has already been rebuilt once when in 1890s it was engulfed in a particularly bad storm. Before you leave, climb the path at the north end of the beach and

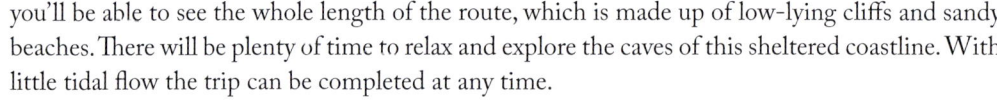
Exploring the cliffs north of Nolton Haven

you'll be able to see the whole length of the route, which is made up of low-lying cliffs and sandy beaches. There will be plenty of time to relax and explore the caves of this sheltered coastline. With little tidal flow the trip can be completed at any time.

Description

There is plenty of parking near the beach, as well as toilets and a café, and surfboard hire is available should you want to develop your skills. Leaving from the beach you may need to carry the boat some distance and then punch out through the surf. At high water launching can be difficult because of the steep stony bank at the rear of the beach. Turning south you'll soon see Rickets Head and the remnants of the once busy Pembrokeshire coal mining industry, which was active here until 1905. Many of the galleries ran out under the sea and required constant pumping. Once extracted, the coal was hauled by traction engine south to Nolton Haven, where it was transported on by boat. Here there is a pleasant sandy beach to land on. However it is stony at high water, but has a slipway, toilets, car park and the Mariners Inn, Tel.01437 710469, which also does B&B for those looking for an overnight stopping point with comfort. At low water the tide does run past the entrance to the beach, which can be dangerous for swimmers.

At Druidston Haven you'll find another expanse of golden sands, named after a knight who settled here in the 12th century. Leaving Druidston Haven you see more evidence of coastal erosion, many examples of cliff collapse and it cannot be long before the coastal path that hangs onto the edge here has to be moved back. At Black Point there is another Iron Age fort and further

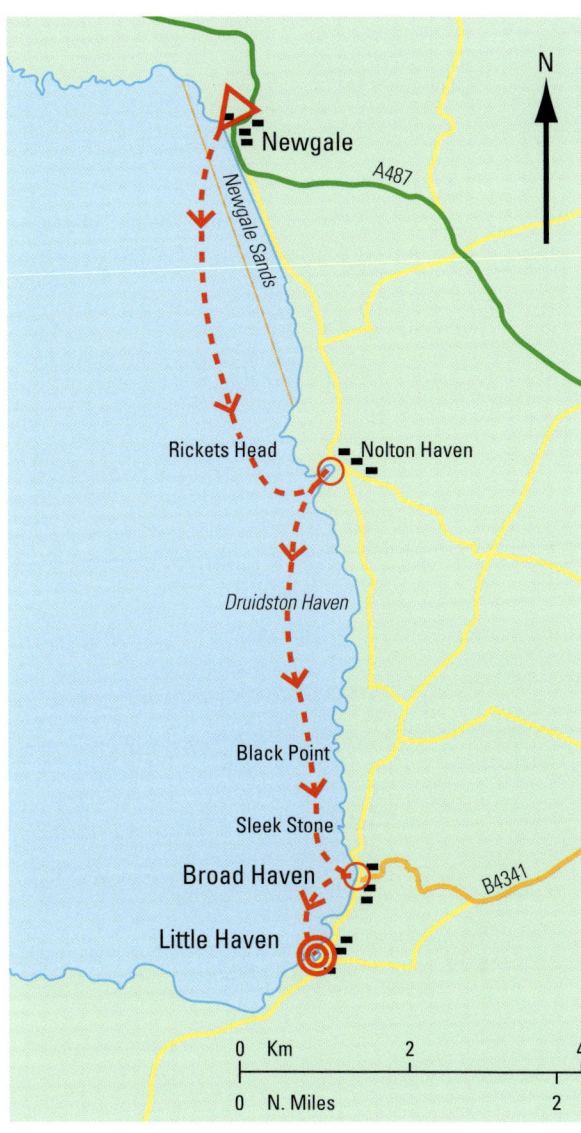

south there are some interesting rock formations, Den's Door and Sleek Stone.

Arriving at Broad Haven you'll find a wide, open and popular beach. There is a good-sized car park, toilets and information centre, and surf shop Haven Sports, Tel. 01437 781 354, which does sell some kayaking equipment just up from the beach. The Youth Hostel, Tel. 0870 770 5728, is here as well and could be used for another night stop. There is a smaller car park at the south end, which is nearer the beach but this soon fills up. You can carry on for another kilometre to Little Haven. During the summer the narrow roads here can become congested and parking is more difficult. However after a peaceful day you can sit at the top of the beach with an ice cream in hand, looking back across St Brides Bay towards Ramsey Sound, thinking about the size of the waves as the tide is rushing around The Bitches rocks. The coastal bus service calls here and can provide you with a ride back to Newgale.

Tide and weather

Generally this section of the coast is well protected except from westerly winds. There is little tidal movement that would affect a sea kayaker.

Additional information

If you want to develop your surfing skill or check the height of the waves then contact Newsurf www.newsurf.co.uk, Tel. 01437 721398 or 01437 720698.

Broad Haven

Stack Rocks

No. 38	**Grade A** **13km** **OS Sheet 157** **Tidal Port Milford Haven**
Start	△ Little Haven SM 856 128 / SA62 3UN
Finish	◯ Martin's Haven SM 760 091 / SA62 3BJ
HW / LW	at Little Haven is 10 minutes after Milford Haven.
Tidal times	There is a westerly flow from Goultrop Roads towards St Brides that starts 2 hours 30 minutes before HW Milford Haven and lasts for 9 hours. This is caused by an eddy as the tide floods into St Brides Bay.
Tidal rates	The above mentioned eddy flows up to 1 knot.
Coastguard	Milford Haven, Tel. 01646 690909, VHF 0150 UT repeated every 3 hours

Introduction

This stretch of coastline will provide an interesting trip, as you turn a series of small headlands, slowly feeling the pull of the tide as Skomer Island comes into view. There are offshore rocks, sheltered bays and sandy beaches for you to explore. The low cliffs are made up of different rock layers, which can be clearly seen from the sea. Well protected from southerly winds and with a reliable westerly tidal flow, this trip can be completed at most times of the day. There are plenty of opportunities to stop off in secluded bays, where your only company may be some seals.

St Brides Haven

Description

You can depart from Broad or Little Haven, which has the feeling of a Cornish village, at most states of the tide. However leaving around HW Milford Haven will give you tidal assistance all the way along to Martin's Haven. Head across Goultrop Roads for Borough Head looking out for the old lifeboat station that was abandoned in 1922. From here follow the coastline to Howney Stone and then head out to Stack Rocks. You should be able to find some seals that have pulled themselves out of the water. By now Skomer Island will have come into view but don't rush things, head ashore and take a break at St Brides Haven. Here you'll find a medieval church, built after the original had been washed away due to erosion. You can find the ends of stone-lined coffins from the original graveyard near the old limekiln. The large house behind was once owned by the Edwards family from Kensington; you'll also find a restored pump house that would have supplied the house with fresh water.

St Brides may have been named after Saint Brigid of Ireland (AD 451-525) who was born in County Lough. Many houses in Ireland have a Brigid's Cross, as it is believed that a Brigid's Cross protects the house from fire. A new cross is made each St Brigid's Day, February 1, and the old one burned to keep the house safe. There are toilets and a car park at St Brides but this can become busy and is popular with divers.

Leaving St Brides head west and look up at The Nab Head, which is the former site for Mesolithic flint production. Its name comes from the old word 'knap' meaning the process of striking flint. Tower Point was the ideal location for an Iron Age fort, from which gave outstanding views of the whole of St Brides Bay. Further along the coast are the golden sands of Musselwick;

Martin's Haven

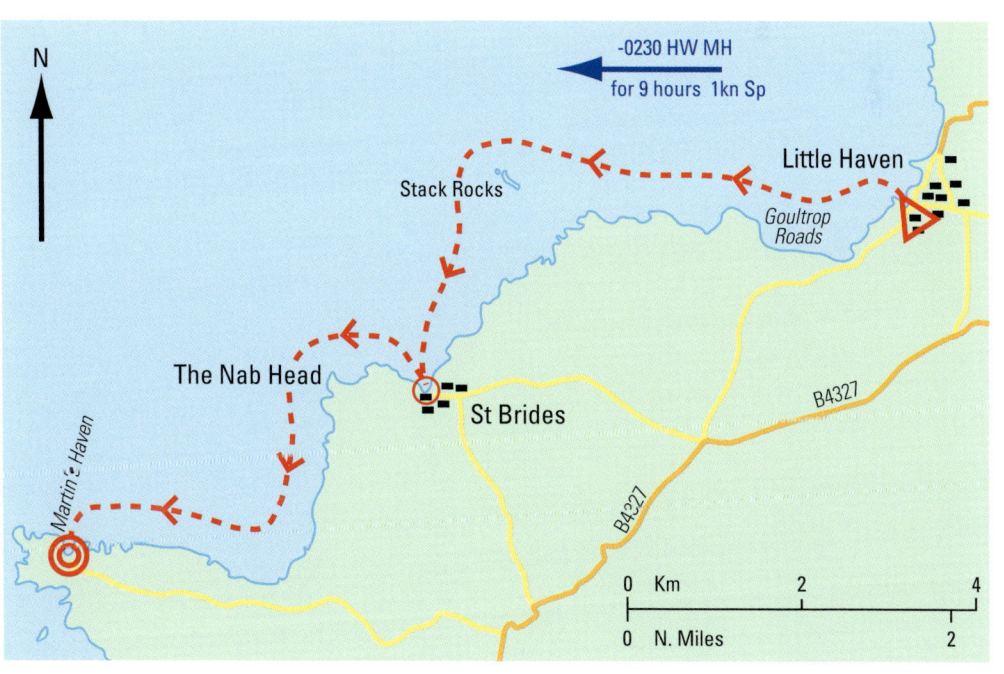

38 Stack Rocks

Looking towards The Nab Head

these are backed by a steep embankment, made up of folding layers of different coloured rocks. These mark the change from the hard volcanic rock that makes up Skomer to the soft sedimentary rocks of the eroding coastline.

As you approach Martin's Haven, your peace will be broken as commercial boats ply their trade, taking bird watchers and divers out to Skomer; it can become a busy place. Try to keep clear of the jetty and also be prepared to encounter shore-based divers – look out for their marker buoys. There are toilets and an information point in some restored cottages near the beach but no café and the car park is 200m away up a steep road. As you carry your boats up, take a rest and look for an inscribed Celtic cross in the wall near the cottages. This trip will have broadened your understanding of local history and brought you to within striking distance of one the most important nature reserves in UK waters. There is a campsite at West Hook Farm, Tel. 01646 636424, 500m further along the road, which could be used for an overnight stay if you were prepared for the carry. A shared set of wheels would ease the load.

Tide and weather

This stretch of coastline is quite sheltered, with favourable tides and plenty to explore, making it a relaxing trip for those new to sea kayaking.

Additional information

For those not wanting to paddle back, the coastal bus service calls at both St Brides and Martin's Haven, enabling you to make an easy return to Little Haven for your car.

Skokholm | Eurion Brown

Skomer and Skokholm

No. 39 | Grade C | 19km | OS Sheet 157 | Tidal Port Milford Haven

Start	△ Martin's Haven SM 760 091 / SA62 3BJ
Finish	◯ Martin's Haven SM 760 091 / SA62 3BJ
HW	at Martin's Haven is 10 minutes after Milford Haven.
Tidal times	The tides are complex and can be strong. There are serious overfalls in Jack Sound, near Garland Stone and on the west end of Skomer.
	A southerly-flowing stream in Jack Sound starts 2 hours after HW Milford Haven; this creates a strong eddy around the south side of Midland Isle.
	The north-flowing stream starts 4 hours 25 minutes before HW Milford Haven. The period of slack water in Jack Sound is very short and during spring tides can be non-existent.
	At the west end of Skomer the southerly flow starts 4 hours after HW Milford Haven. The northerly flow starts 2 hours 30 minutes before HW Milford Haven.
	Further west is the Wildgoose tide race where, once the main flow has started, the water can become very rough, especially during spring tides.
	In Broad Sound a SE stream starts 4 hours 30 minutes after HW Milford Haven and the NW stream starts 2 hours before HW Milford Haven. Once the main flow has started in Broad Sound an eddy flowing in the opposite direction can start close into the shore, south of Gateholm Island.
Tidal rates	The tide can reach 6 knots in Jack Sound and 4 knots at the west end of Skomer.
Coastguard	Milford Haven, Tel. 01646 690909, VHF 0150 UT repeated every 3 hours

© Skomer Island | Mark Rainsley

Introduction

A trip by kayak around the islands of Skomer and Skokholm must be near the top of anyone's list of 'must go' destinations. Tidal streams of up to 6 knots and overfalls all set against a backdrop of an abundance of wildlife and wonderful views will make this a day to remember. The area is littered with shipwrecks that have been swept onto rocks by the strong tidal streams, one of the most visited being the wreck of 'The Lucy'. She sank on Valentine's Day in 1967 after hitting a rock on the south end of Jack Sound and now lies in 36m of water in North Haven.

Description

Martin's Haven can become busy as tourists catching boats over to Skomer, divers and kayakers all jostle for space. It is easiest to arrive early, park at the top of the hill and carry your boat down to the water, before you get caught up in a traffic jam of trailers from dive boats. There are toilets and an information point in some restored cottages near the beach but no café, so remember to pack your sandwiches. Try to keep clear of the jetty and also be prepared to encounter shore-based divers, look out for their marker buoys. Expect to spend much of the day in your boat due to landing restrictions on both islands. There are numerous places around the islands to explore. However be aware of seals who may have pups, especially around 'The Neck' during the breeding season, which runs from September through to March, when you should keep well away from the shoreline in these areas.

Due to the complex nature of the tidal flow around the islands it's difficult to obtain a free ride for the whole trip, times will vary between springs and neaps. However to make best use of the tides leave Martin's Haven 4 hours before HW Milford Haven and use the last of the south-flowing stream to take you around the west end of Skomer and down to Skokholm, trying to arrive here around slack water. During a fast-flowing southerly stream the water can become quite rough to the NW of the Garland Stone. However you should be able to avoid the worst of this by going inside of the rock and keeping close to the cliffs. The north-flowing stream starts 2 hours before HW Milford Haven; use this to take you back across Broad Sound, either to land on Albion Sands on the mainland or go straight through Jack Sound and land at North Haven. By the time of your return to Martin's Haven the north-flowing stream will be a full force; either ferry glide across the sound, judging your progress against Tusker Rock or stop and practise your boat handling.

Tide and weather

Jack Sound can become very rough, especially in any wind against tide conditions. Although it can be a good place to practise your boat handling, be prepared to realise when things are getting out of hand and retreat to the safety of Martin's Haven. With careful reading and use of eddies it is possible to make your way through the sound against the main flow. In this way you can retrace your steps and continue to build your confidence in moving water.

Additional information

Skomer is of international importance for its seabird population, especially Manx shearwaters, as over 40% of the world's population breed here. It is also a good place to see puffins and Atlantic

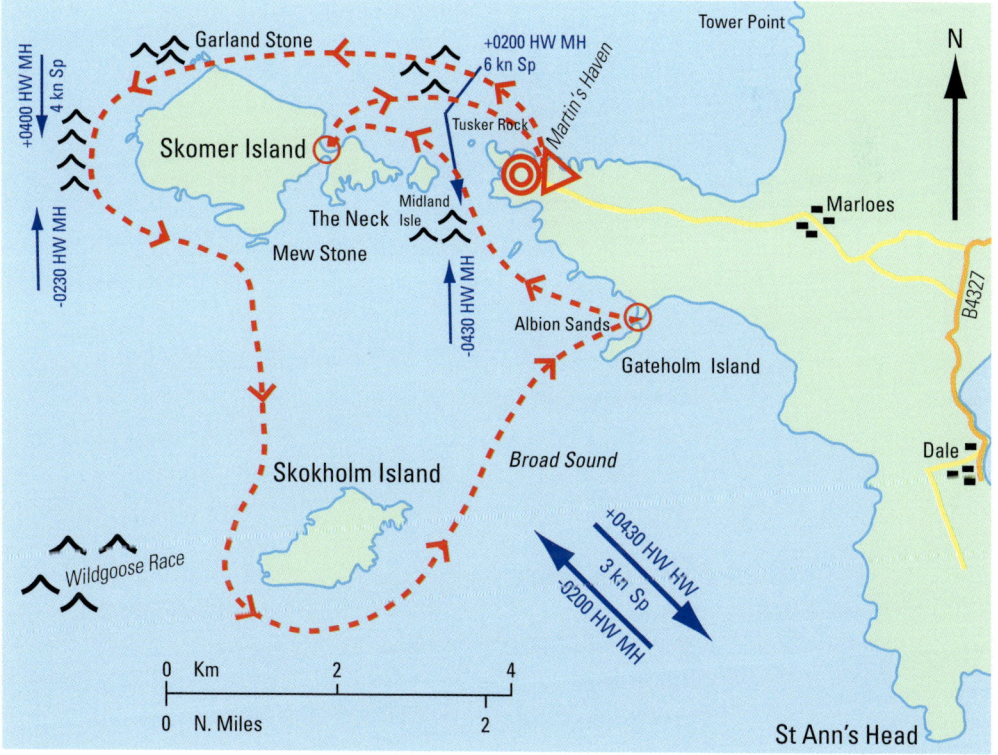

Puffin, a Skomer local | Mark Rainsley

grey seals. All the puffins leave at the start of August, so if you're keen to see them, come earlier in the year. The island has a large rabbit population and a unique type of vole but there are no predatory mammals such as rats, so the ground-breeding birds flourish. There is much evidence of early human habitation in the form of a small fort and remains of four settlements with field boundaries. The area around both islands is a National Nature Reserve and a Code of Conduct is in operation; this is displayed at Martin's Haven. Landing on Skomer is only permitted at North Haven. It is best to discuss your plans with the car park warden at Martin's Haven, who will phone over to the island and advise you of any further restrictions. Certain points around the island such as The Wick and Bull Hole have large numbers of cliff-nesting birds and you are asked to stay well clear of these places at all times.

Skokholm was privately owned until 2006 but was then bought by the Wildlife Trust who manage the island, and landing should only be with prior arrangement with the Wildlife Trust

The Manx shearwater

The Manx shearwater likes to nest on grassy slopes of the edges of cliffs, and because of this they are vulnerable to ground rodents such as rats. They breed on a few islands on the west coast of Britain including Skomer and Rhum in Scotland. It is quite a small bird, black from above, with white underneath. It tends to fly with a series of short flaps and then glides. By July they head off to their winter feeding grounds in South America.

◎ *Dinner is served!*

Puffins

This cheeky little bird has a special place in everyone's heart and when spotted will lead to a delightful yell from all around. Its unique appearance of white underbelly and black back, with its colourful beak make it easy to identify and it carries the crown as the clown of the bird population. Puffins moult their colourful bill every autumn, and regrow it the following spring. They are part of the auk family and live in a burrow rather than a nest which differentiates them from most other birds. They are also remarkably friendly and it is surprising how closely you can approach them. They tend to collect in groups and can regularly be seen bobbing around near cliffs. Even if you are not close they are easy to recognise by their fast wing movements. They are also good swimmers and their staple diet is the sand eel. The record number of fish carried in a single puffin's beak is 62.

Puffins spend much of the year afloat and only arrive on land in April to breed, leaving again during August. Some colonies, such as the one on Cardigan Island, have been devastated by rats that eat the eggs incubating in the burrow. As they only produce one egg per year, any loss can have considerable effect on the population. The incubation period is between 36–45 days and they will live for over 20 years. Efforts have been made to clear such places of rat populations and strategies are being employed to encourage the birds to return. There are colonies on many islands as well as the mainland along the British coastline. Skomer and South Stack both have established colonies where you should be able to see them during a springtime paddle. Other good locations are Bempton Cliffs and the Farne Islands, both of which are good sea kayaking venues.

Skokholm Island | Mark Rainsley

of South and West Wales, Tel. 01239 621600, www.welshwildlife.org/, who also manage Skomer. In 1927 Ronald Lockley took over the tenancy of the island and his research led to the establishment of Britain's first bird observatory there in 1933. He wrote about his experiences of living on the island to his fiancée, and their letters are reproduced in his book 'Dear Islandman'. The lighthouse on the SW tip of the island was established in 1776 and the construction materials were transported from the jetty over the island on a small railway, the trucks being pulled by a pony.

St Ann's Head

No. 40 | **Grade B** | **16km** | **OS Sheet 157** | **Tidal Port Milford Haven**

Start	△ Martin's Haven SM 760 091 / SA62 3BJ
Finish	○ Dale SM 811 058 / SA62 3RB
HW / LW	at Martin's Haven is 10 minutes after Milford Haven.
Tidal times	A southerly-flowing stream in Jack Sound starts 2 hours after HW Milford Haven. Further south towards St Ann's Head the flow starts an hour or more later. The ingoing stream in the entrance to Milford Haven starts around LW Milford Haven. The outgoing stream starts around 30 minutes after HW Milford Haven. Once the main flow has started in Broad Sound an eddy flowing in the opposite direction can start close into the shore, south of Gateholm Island.
Tidal rates	Through Jack Sound the tidal flow can reach 6 knots, further south towards St Ann's Head it will drop to 3 knots.
Coastguard	Milford Haven, Tel. 01646 690909, VHF 0150 UT repeated every 3 hours

Introduction

This is a wonderful trip that will take you through a serious tidal race, past glorious sandy beaches and round a major headland to finish in one of the world's largest natural deep-water harbours. You will also have an opportunity to see the site of a tragic shipwreck and evidence of 130 hut circles that made up an Iron Age community.

Lunch stop at Westdale Bay | Eurion Brown

St Ann's Head

Description

Try to leave Martin's Haven soon after the tide starts to flow south through Jack Sound, 2 hours after HW at Milford Haven, and aim to arrive at St Ann's Head at or soon after LW Milford Haven, then the start of the flood will take you round to Dale. This will give you time to explore the coastline and have a break. You can leave later than this but you may encounter a north-flowing eddy south of Gateholm Island.

Once through Jack Sound and heading SE you'll see Gateholm Island and Albion Sands before you. These are named after the SS Albion that was wrecked here in 1837. Local tradition says that the ship's cargo of pigs swam ashore, only to find themselves served on the dinner tables of the inhabitants of Marloes. Remnants of the Albion's paddle can be found on the beach at low tide.

There may still be enough water to pass inside of Gateholm Island. This was an Iron Age fort and had later been used by the Romans. Next is Marloes Sands; here you'll find three natural chimney-shaped columns which are formed from alternating coloured layers of mudstone and sandstone. Just inland is Marloes Youth Hostel, Tel. 01646 636667. This is housed in some refurbished farm buildings and is a great place to stay but at nearly 1km from the beach, a long carry. At Westdale Bay the land drops to nearly sea level and it is just over 1km to Dale along the road. This also marks the western end of the Ritec Fault that extends as far as Tenby and is a flooded river valley that now makes up Milford Haven. All this happened during the last ice age, when sea levels were much lower. Water from the melting ice gouged out the river bed and as sea level rose Milford Haven was created. This is called a "ria" or drowned river. Westdale Bay also provides an emergency egress if the weather changes, for anyone not wanting to round the headland.

On Great Castle Head there is another Iron Age promontory fort and if you continued heading south from here your landfall would be the north Cornwall coast. However keep close into the cliffs and look up for the swirling rock formations that make up the Cobbler's Hole. Within 300m the cliffs will run out and you'll be able to look east over to the surf beach of Freshwater West. You are now at St Ann's Head; the lighthouse was established in 1714. Originally it had two separate towers, which distinguished it from the light at Mumbles, which had one light above another. In 1841 the current light was rebuilt further back from the cliff edge due to erosion. The rock formations here are particularly impressive and just before the headland you will see the Cobbler's Hole which is formed by a series of folds in the different layers of rock. It is worth walking out to see this afterwards from above. There is a signed path just before the lighthouse.

On 15 April 1996 the Sea Empress spilled 72,000 tonnes of crude oil and it struck the Milford Channel Rock on the way into Milford Haven harbour. The ship had attempted to steer west of the rock, which lay in the middle of the harbour. However a strong east-flowing tidal stream pulled the ship down onto the rock. It remained stuck there for the next eight days, before it finally limped into Milford Haven. If you've got your timing right, the start of the flood tide will now take you around the headland and into Milford Haven. You'll soon pass Mill Bay, where in 1485 Henry Tudor landed with his army aboard 55 ships. He then marched through Wales and two weeks later won the Battle of Bosworth, along with the English crown.

As you round the final headland, Dale Point, you'll be facing back towards Martin's Haven, from where you started. Above you is Dale Fort that was built as part the defences constructed during the 1850s. It is now run by the Field Studies Council as a study centre. The last kilometre will be in sheltered water and you'll be able to relax as you quietly glide into Dale. This is a popular

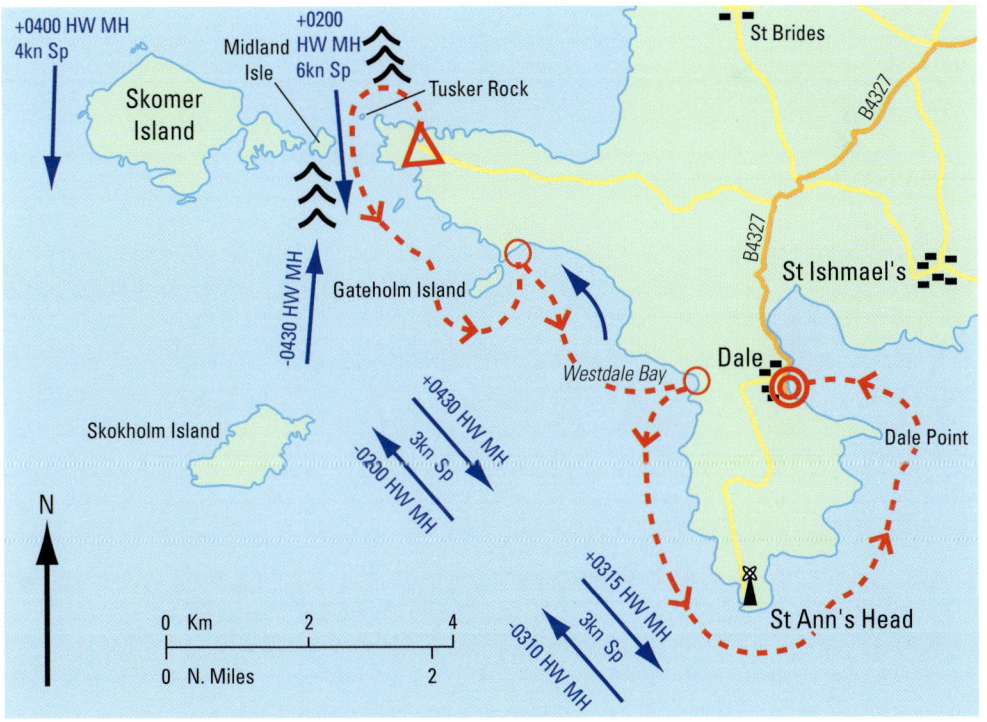

© Watwich Point Beacon, Castlebeach Bay | Eurion Brown

St Ann's Head

centre for a wide range of water sports and on windy days look out for windsurfers who relish the protected waters of Dale Roads. There is a good-sized car park here, toilets and a café. It is also possible to hire a windsurfer if you fancy a try, from West Wales Wind Surf and Sailing, Tel. 01646 636 642. http://www.surfdale.co.uk/index.htm

It will have been a day of continually changing views, as you turn one corner after another, but one of great historical interest, going back to early Iron Age forts and right up to the modern consequences of our current dependency on oil.

Tide and weather

The tides do tend to eddy round several of the headlands, especially south of Gateholm Island. Try not to arrive at St Ann's Head too early. At 4 hours after HW Milford Haven, on a strong south-flowing stream, you will encounter confused water caused by the outgoing stream from Milford Haven and a rock shelf that extends south from St Ann's Head by 1km. Try to arrive here soon after low water and the tidal stream will take you round the headland and into Milford Haven.

Additional information

The coastal bus service connects both ends of this trip and in less than 20 minutes will get you back to Martin's Haven, saving the problems of moving cars around at the beginning of the day. There is a pleasant pub and café here for you to wait, and showers are available.

West Angle Bay with St Ann's Head in the distance

Milford Haven

| No. 41 | Grade A | 20km | OS Sheet 157 | Tidal Port Milford Haven |

Start	△ Dale SM 811 058 / SA62 3RB
Finish	○ Dale SM 811 058 / SA62 3RB
HW / LW	Milford Haven
Tidal times	The ingoing stream starts at LW Milford Haven. The outgoing streams start around 30 minutes after HW Milford Haven.
Tidal rates	The ebb flow out of Milford Haven can reach 2 knots at springs.
Coastguard	Milford Haven, Tel. 01646 690909, VHF 0150 UT repeated every 3 hours

Introduction

Milford Haven is one of the largest natural harbours in the world. It was also the scene of an environmental disaster, when in 1995 the Sea Empress oil container spilled 72,000 tonnes of crude oil when it struck the Milford Channel Rock on the way into the harbour. Since then the visible evidence has been removed but longer term consequences are yet to be uncovered. Further upstream the area can provide an ideal location for a sheltered day's paddling and an opportunity to explore the number of tidal creeks that flow into the Haven. It also gives you a chance to look for the wide range of wildlife that live in the area.

213

At the Ship Inn Lawrenny

Sir William Hamilton established the port of Milford Haven during the 1790s and its rapid growth was further accelerated by the arrival of the Naval dockyard. Early commercial users were Quaker whalers but later these were joined by local fishermen. During the 1800s the area was heavily fortified and these installations can still be seen on Stack Rock and Thorn Island. By the 1950s the fishing industry had started to decline but the Suez crisis of the 1950s led to the development of the port as a major oil terminal, and in 1960 Esso opened an oil terminal. However this has now closed, and after the Sea Empress disaster questions are now being asked if having such a port in an area of outstanding natural beauty is a good idea.

Description

Dale is a popular centre for a wide range of water sports and on windy days look out for windsurfers, who relish the protected waters of Dale Roads. There is a good-sized car park here, toilets, a post office and café, as well as a chandlery. There is another car park by the beach just north of the village. However this does involve a long carry at low water. It is also possible to hire a windsurfer, sailing dinghy and kayaks from West Wales Wind Surf and Sailing, Tel. 01646 636 642, http://www.surfdale.co.uk/index.htm. There is a one-way system to take you round the village but even then it can get busy, especially at weekends when dingy sailors and windsurfers are unloading their boats.

The beach is sheltered and makes a good practice area. However once you pass Dale Point you are into Milford Haven. This is a large piece of water and, although the quantity of shipping using it has fallen in recent years, it is still very busy with commercial boats. These are not manoeuvrable, hence you need to keep a very clear outlook and try to predict their course of action. Always try to cross the shipping channels at 90°, so keeping the time you are at risk to a minimum. It is worth looking at the Imray chart C60, *The Gower to Cardigan* or the *Lundy and Irish Sea Pilot* to gain an understanding of where the main shipping channels are.

Aim to leave from Dale around 2 hours after low water and use the rising water level to help you explore some areas such as Angle Bay and Sandyhaven Pill. However it is possible to paddle in Milford Haven at any state of the tide. Head towards Dale Point and the Dakotian buoy, from here you'll get a clear view of any ship movements. Continue to head east, parallel with the shipping channel until Thorn Island is directly south; look out for any buoys that are marking the channel and ferry glide over to Thorn Island. This is now a very exclusive hotel and out of the budget range of any sea kayaker I know. However the island is the scene of a Welsh Whisky Galore; when bound for Adelaide, the 'Loch Shiel' broke up in heavy seas on 30 January 1894 and lost its cargo of 7,500 cases of whisky. These were soon gathered up by local people and are still being found as recently as 1999, when some divers found six bottles on the seabed near Thorn Island.

You can continue onto Angle but only try and land during the top half of the tide, as there are large expanses of exposed mud at low water. There is a small jetty and pub just south of Angle Point making an ideal stopping-off point. Leaving Angle you will face the oil terminal and jetties. Head to the west of these and onto Stack Rock, which protects the entrance to the Haven. If you are on a rising tide you can cross the coastal path and explore Sandyhaven Pill. The path actually uses some stepping stones to cross the water at low tide. There is a small car park here and could provide another place to launch as well as official campsite.

Heading around Great Castle Head and its promontory fort you will see Dale in front of you. This will have a been a relaxing day, although you will have kept your eyes open, not just for passing ships but also for the wildlife and history that once made this a major naval port.

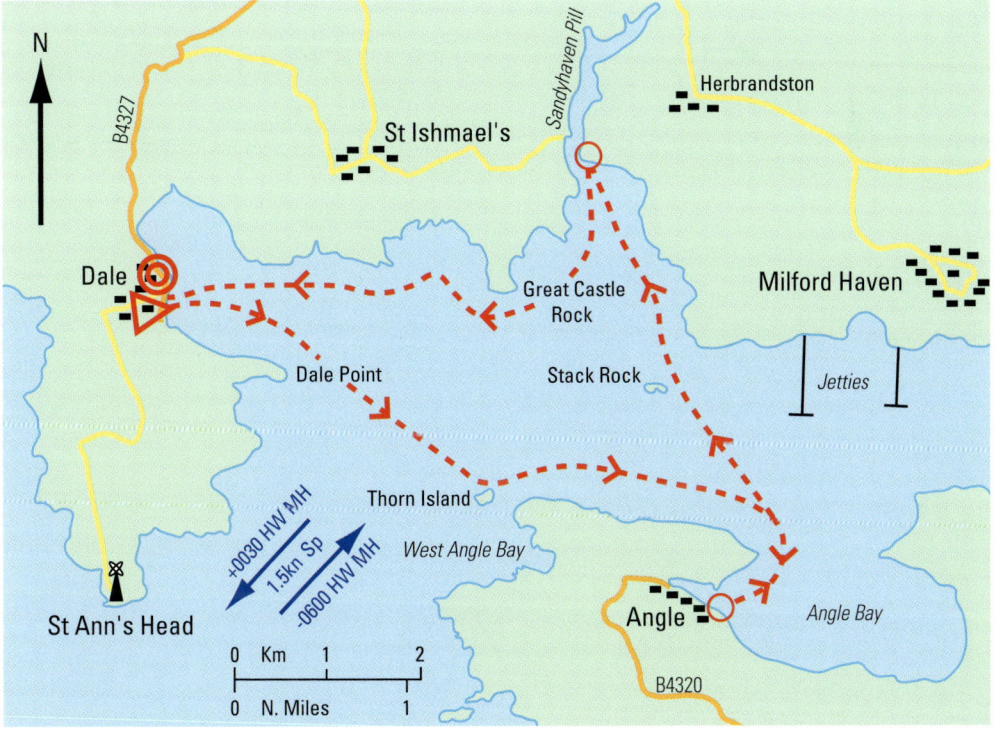

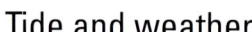
Dale at low water

Tide and weather

The entrance area of Dale Roads can become quite rough in strong SW winds, especially during an outgoing tide. However further upstream and towards Neyland and Pembroke Dock it is well sheltered and gives the option, like the Menai Strait in North Wales, to paddle whatever the weather. To make the most of the area try to set off on a rising tide.

Additional information

If the weather gets really rough or you want a change then consider exploring the Inner Haven and Daugleddau Estuary. There is an abundance of wildlife, including otters. The area also has important bird-feeding sites, which are protected by a special Act of Parliament. Get your timing right on a good spring tide and you can have lunch in Haverfordwest. HW here is about 30 minutes after Milford Haven, or visit the popular pub at Landshipping.

Due to the wide expanses of mud in the estuary, it is best to use one of the several slipways that can be found along its course. The most accessible of these is at Neyland (SM 963 047 / SA73 1QB) where there is a large car park and toilets. It is also near the marina, a chandlery and café, Tel. 01646 601601. Hobbs Point (SM 967 042 / SA72 6TR) is on the opposite, south side of the estuary, where there is the Pembroke Haven Yacht Club, a slipway, toilets and Lelpie Boats, Tel. 01646 683661. Signposted just south of the Neyland Bridge is Cleddau Reach and a watersports centre. It is possible to use the slipway here but it can become busy. Further upstream try Black Tar Point (SM 998 095 / SA62 4HL) where there is a pleasant grassed area and would give the option of using a south-flowing ebb to take you down to Neyland. All these slipways give good access at most states of the tide. Although it is not possible to launch at Lawrenny, it does make a good destination, where there is the Ship Inn, a pleasant café and a marina.

St Govan's Head | Eurion Brown

St Govan's Head

No. 42 Grade B 28km OS Sheet 158 Tidal Port Milford Haven	
Start	△ West Angle Bay SM 853 032 / SA71 5AW
Finish	◯ Freshwater East SS 017 977 / SA71 5LN
HW / LW	at West Angle Bay is 5 minutes before Milford Haven.
Tidal times	As the flood tide enters Milford Haven it sets up a SE eddy in Freshwater West, which then flows around Linney Head. During the ebb tide this eddy continues to flow in the same SE direction, so when it meets the main NW flow at Linney Head it can cause confused water. Off St Govan's Head the NE flood starts 4 hours 30 minutes after HW Milford Haven and the SW ebb starts 2 hours before HW Milford Haven.
Tidal rates	Off St Govan's Head the tide can reach 4 knots.
Coastguard	Milford Haven, Tel. 01646 690909, VHF 0150 UT repeated every 3 hours

Introduction

This has to be one of the most impressive and varied trips along the Welsh coastline. There is a continual line of cliffs with few places to get out until you reach the safety of Broad Haven. You will also pass the spectacular Green Bridge of Wales (925944), near Elegug Stacks, which are marked on the OS map. Add to this tidal overfalls, surf beaches, caves to explore and a military firing range, making this a challenging trip that requires some careful planning.

217

Barafundle | Eurion Brown

Description

At West Angle Bay there is ample car parking and toilets, it is a sheltered beach and launching should be quite straightforward when the surf is quite big around Freshwater West. The west flowing tidal stream starts 4 hours after HW Milford Haven, so it is best to try and leave around then, this will give you 6 hours to reach your destination. Follow the coast round past Rat Island and Sheep Island to enter Freshwater West. Large ships do wait here before entering Milford Haven and one foggy day I remember coming across one quite by chance; although it was anchored we considered there may be another manoeuvring, so from then on we kept close into the coastline. There are several submerged rocks around Linney Head and you may encounter some rougher water. Look further down the coast and you will see an impressive stack. There are some small coves where it is possible to land, but they don't provide any form of escape route and are strictly prohibited as they fall within the firing range. Look out for seals in this area, as well as the firing range control boats. The land here is a flat plateau made up of limestone, which was formed around 350 million years ago.

Further along you'll come to the Green Bridge of Wales, which can be paddled through 3 hours either side of HW. Elegug Stacks that follow had been similar arches but have now collapsed. They now provide safe nesting sites for an abundance of seabirds, such as guillemots or 'elegug' in Welsh. This area is a maze of impressive rocks and caves. All along this coast you'll share the views with rock climbers, this is Pembrokeshire's prime climbing area.

Further along the coast are a series of narrow gaps leading to stony beaches including Huntsman's Leap, where tradition has it that a horseman jumped the gap, only to look back and die of shock from what he saw. Next to here is St Govan's Chapel, which was built in the 13th century. It has now been restored by the National Trust and the water from its well is supposed to have special healing powers for your skin and eyes, although now it is dry for much of the year. It was probably named after the Irish abbot Gobhan but stories also link it with Sir Gawain and King Arthur. It is difficult to land here due to the rocky foreshore.

As you leave here and round St Govan's Head you will be at the most southerly point of your journey along the Pembrokeshire coast. Broad Haven is popular with families during summer months. There is a car park and toilets and it provides an ideal finishing point for those wanting a shorter trip. The coastal bus service calls here, which will take you back to Angle or Freshwater West.

At Stackpole Head there are a number of spectacular blowholes and caves to explore, as well as many nesting birds. Further round you'll come into the beautiful Barafundle Bay, which tends to be quite quiet, as there is no road access. Around the next headland is Stackpole Quay, which was built for the export of limestone from the nearby quarry. It was also used to bring luxury goods into Stackpole Court, which was built in 1735 by the Campbell family of Cawdor. However it was later demolished in 1963 when the family moved back to Scotland. The estate was then passed onto the National Trust in 1970. There is a car park, toilets and a delightful tea room.

By the time you round Trewent Point your arms will be aching and legs feeling numb, but it will have been all worth it. As you slide the boat up the sandy beach of Freshwater East your face will be filled with a smile and the sunbathers and swimmers may ask you where you have come from. "Freshwater West and through the firing range" will be your answer. They may not appreciate how far that is but your sense of satisfaction will be there for all to see.

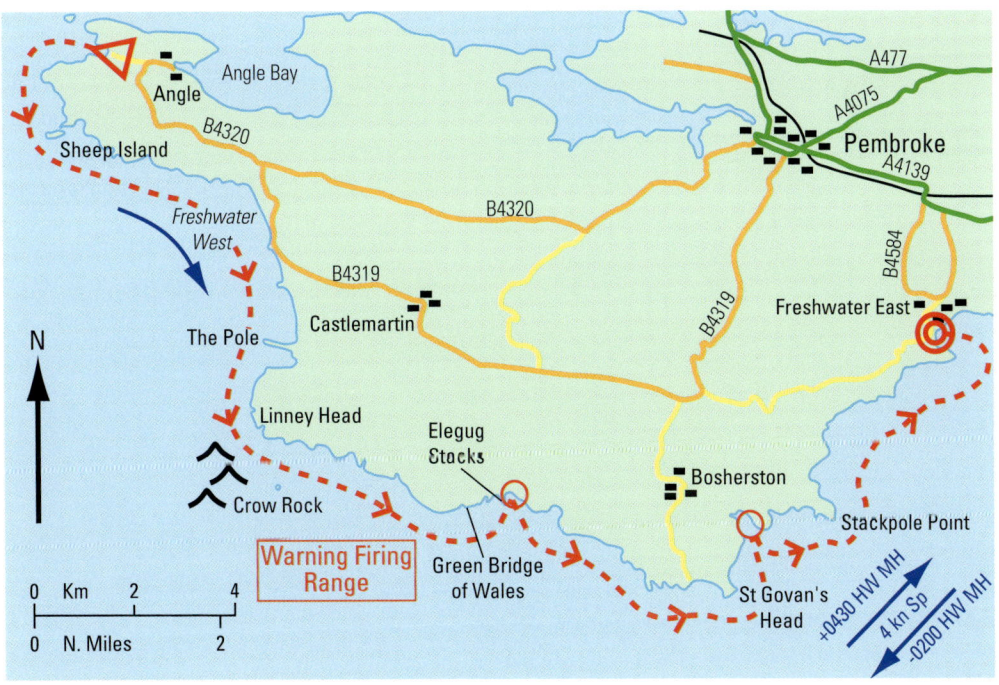

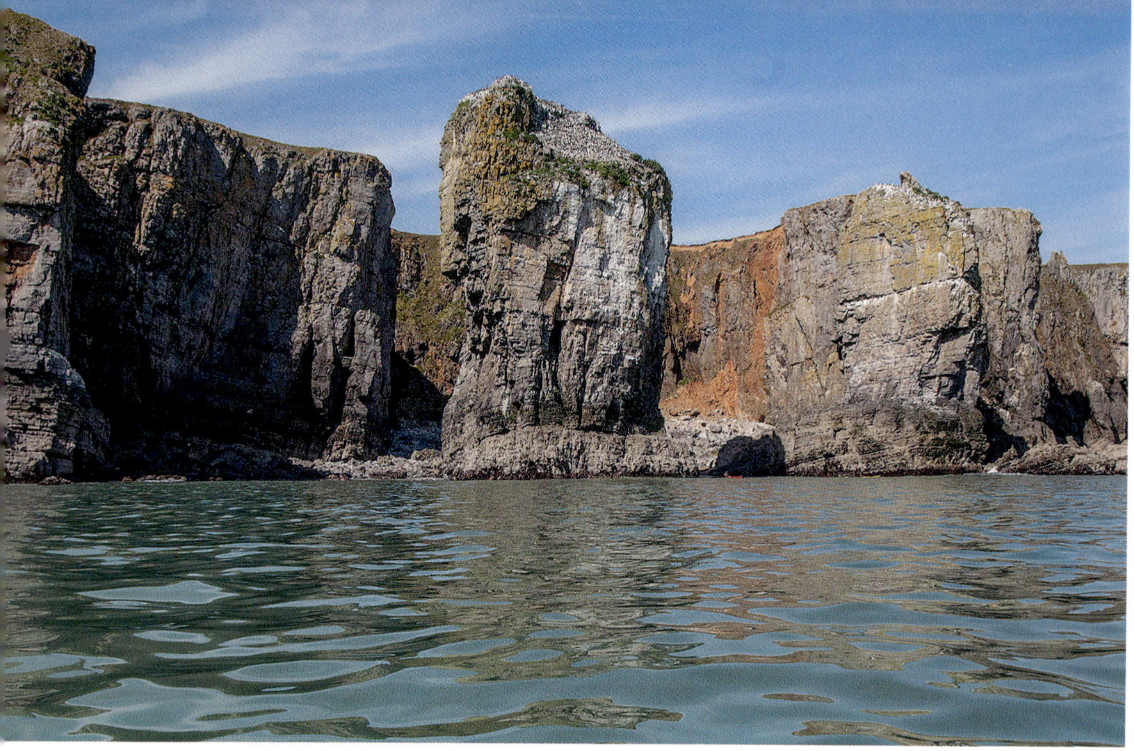

Elegug Stacks | Eurion Brown

Tide and weather

This is an exposed section of coastline and the tides can reach 4 knots. If the wind is against the tide you can expect a rough ride especially off the headlands. Also there are few places to escape, so don't set out unless you have a settled forecast.

Additional information

It is worth finding out if the range is closed in advance. Phone the Range Office, Tel. 01646 662496, (or 01646 662367 to hear a 24hr. answer phone message detailing the firing programme for the following days).

Warren Tower, Tel. 01646 662336

Guard Room, Tel. 01646 662280

Milford Haven Coastguard, Tel. 01646 690909

They also state that "unscheduled firing may take place without prior warning, and firing may be cancelled without notice". Therefore it is worth listening out on CH16 and looking out for the range boats displaying a red flag. The range extends up to 12 miles offshore, so it is a long detour to keep out of the way. There is normally no firing at weekends or bank holidays. The schedule is also displayed in the PO at Bosherston and in the local press. If you do land anywhere along this coast treat any metal objects with suitable caution.

Caldey Point | Mark Rainsley

Caldey Island

No. 43	**Grade B** **19km** **OS Sheet 158** **Tidal Port Milford Haven**
Start	△ Freshwater East SS 017 977 / SA71 5LN
Finish	○ Tenby, South Beach car park SN 131 001 / SA70 7EG
HW / LW	at Tenby is 15 minutes before Milford Haven.
Tidal times	The east-flowing stream in Caldey Sound starts 5 hours after HW Milford Haven and the west-flowing stream starts 1 hour before HW Milford Haven. SE of Caldey Island the flow turns about an hour later.
Tidal rates	Through Caldey Sound the flow can reach 2.5 knots at springs.
Coastguard	Milford Haven, Tel. 01646 690909, VHF 0150 UT repeated every 3 hours

Introduction

This is another beautiful stretch of the Pembrokeshire coastline and with an island to circumnavigate makes for an interesting and varied day out. During the trip you can experience some strong tidal streams, and with two firing ranges good planning is required.

Secluded beach on south side of Caldey Island | Eurion Brown

Description

There is a large car park at Freshwater East, the toilets are on the beach but the campsite is 500m up the hill, which makes it a hard carry if you want to stop overnight. The water also goes out a long way at low tide, unfortunately the best time to launch if you want to make use of the tidal flow along the coast, which is no earlier than 4 hours after HW at Milford Haven. So you may be faced with a long carry anyway.

Leaving the beach you will pass Swanlake Bay and see Manorbier in front of you, with its castle. Here the beach is sandy with only shingle being exposed at high water; there is a good-sized car park next to the castle and toilets. It also is a great surf beach and there are consistent quality waves, so look carefully before landing. As you leave the bay look up at Priest's Nose, where there is a Neolithic burial chamber, and several deep faults in the cliffs caused by the collapse of soft shale, which is surrounded by harder sandstone. The MOD still has a presence here and the camp now covers the site of a promontory fort, on Old Castle Head. The base is used as an air defence testing station. Further along the coast is the Penally small arms range, look out for red flags and check before you depart if firing is planned for that day. If you have time land in Skrinkle Haven where you will find the Church Doors, which is a natural limestone arch.

There are several caves to look in as you round Lydstep Point to find yourself in the sheltered bay of Lydstep Haven. This would look like an ideal place to use as a landing or departure point. However the foreshore road is owned by the caravan park and the public car park is 500m up the hill. It is best to carry on and cross over to Caldey Island. Be aware of the tide taking you down into the Sound. If it is approaching high water you could come into the north side of St Margaret's Island and use the south-flowing eddy to take you through Little Sound and into Sandtop Bay. St Margaret's Island has been quarried in the past and there are remains of cottages and a walled garden, but it is now a nature reserve.

In an east-flowing tide there is normally some rough water off West Beacon Point. The lighthouse was constructed in 1829 and can be seen on Chapel Point as you round the point. It was the last lighthouse to be powered by acetylene gas, until its conversion to electricity in 1997. Continue to follow the coast round, looking out for seals in the bays on the east side of the island near Caldey Point. Land in Priory Bay trying to avoid the day trippers who come across by boat from Tenby.

Monks arrived on the island during the 6th century and Pyro was the first abbot; he is remembered in the island's Welsh name, Ynys Byr. He was followed by St Samson, from the Celtic monastery at Llantwit Major. In the 12th century Benedictine monks from St Dogmaels arrived and stayed until the Dissolution in 1536. Much of their medieval priory is still standing. In 1906 a group of Anglican Benedictines purchased Caldey and built the present abbey but financial difficulties forced them to sell the island in 1925. The present monks of Caldey Abbey are Cistercians, a strict offshoot of the Benedictine Order. Their income comes from farming and tourism. There is a café, perfumery and post office, which can add a unique touch to your postcards home. Visitors are requested to keep to the marked trails.

Leave the shelter of Priory Bay and paddle across Caldey Roads to land on South Beach near St Catherine's Island. Here you'll find all the facilities of a seaside resort, including a good-sized car park with toilets. Today will have given you a variety of experiences, and sitting on the fine sands of the beach eating an ice cream will allow you to savour these for a little longer. It is possible to land or depart from Penally, but it is a long carry through the sand dunes that make up the Burrows.

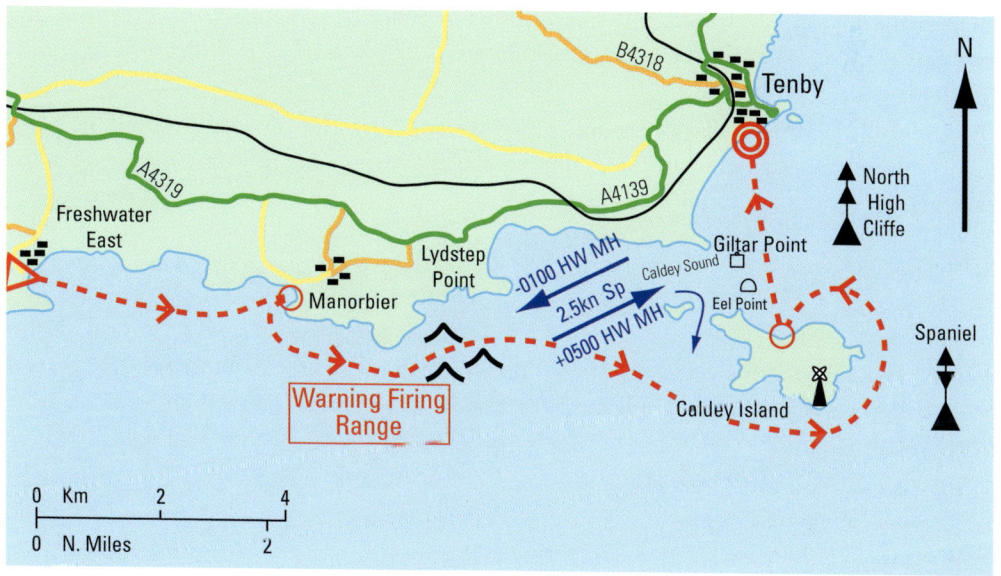

Manorbier Castle | Eurion Brown

Caldey Island

Tide and weather

With a westerly wind and ebb tide the water can become quite rough through Caldey Sound, especially over Eel Spit that runs across the Sound. A strong flowing easterly stream will cause a southerly-flowing stream in Little Sound between St Margaret's Island and Caldey Island. Overfalls can also build up around Old Castle Head.

Additional information

Unlike elsewhere in the country, the foreshore of Caldey is owned by the island community and therefore any landing should be at Priory Bay where a fee is payable. There should be no landings on Sunday.

Caldey Island, Tel. 01834 844453, www.caldeyislandwales.com

There are two firing ranges along this piece of coast and it is advised to check before departure whether they are operational by telephoning the Range or Tenby Tourist Office. Times are also displayed at the Harbour Master's Office that overlooks the harbour and North Beach. While here walk along and look at the impressive new lifeboat station and its interactive display.

Penally Range, Tel. 01834 845950

Manobier Range, Tel. 01834 871282, recorded message Tel. 01834 870098

Tenby Tourist Office, Tel. 01437 775603

Llangennith Beach and Burry Holms

Carmarthen Bay

No. 44 | Grade B | 40km | OS Sheet 158 &159 | Tidal Port Milford Haven

Start	△ Tenby South Beach car park SN 131 001 / SA70 7EG
Finish	○ Llangennith car park SS 410 911 / SA3 1JH
HW / LW	at Tenby is 15 minutes before Milford Haven.
Tidal times	The NE stream starts 5 hours after HW Milford Haven.
Tidal rates	are greatest during the NE flood stream and may reach 1.5 knots.
Coastguard	Milford Haven, Tel.01646 690909, VHF 0150 UT repeated every 3 hours

Introduction

This trip will take you from the popular holiday resorts of Tenby and Saundersfoot across Camarthen Bay to the surf beach of Llangennith and the dramatic cliffs of Worms Head. It is a long way and will link these two parts of the South Wales coastline. The tidal stream is not strong but the route does cross the firing ranges of Pendine and Pembrey Sands. Most yachts miss out this area and cross directly in a straight line, passing to the south of the firing area. However this is a long way out for a kayaker. Unless you have a settled forecast and are prepared to be in your boat

© Pembrey Sands

all day, it is best to keep closer to the shore. You will pass where world land speed records were set and see the practice sites for the D-Day landings.

It is best to leave Tenby soon after the NE flood stream starts, as this runs around the bay in a clockwise direction and means you will arrive at Llangennith near high water, which will save you a long carry after a tiring day afloat.

Description

The walled town of Tenby can become very busy during summer months; parking can become a problem, but the south beach provides a good starting point and you can normally drop your boat off there. The area around North Beach gets very congested and it's very difficult to drop your boats off. The town's walls date back to the 13th century and during the 15th century it developed as an important port. Fearing an invasion of Milford Haven a fort was built in 1869 on St Catherine's Island; this can still be clearly seen. However it was the arrival of the railway during the 19th century that turned the town into a popular holiday destination, which it still remains.

Leaving South Beach you will round St Catherine's Island to see the full extent of Camarthen Bay in front of you. Further along the coast you will round Monkstone Point and enter Saudersfoot Bay. This makes an ideal stopping point for those wanting a shorter trip. You could arrange to arrive here around 2 hours before HW Milford Haven, have a rest and then return using the SW stream that starts around 1 hour before HW Milford Haven. Although there are two car parks here, like Tenby's North Beach it gets very busy and therefore is not ideal for launching or recovery. It is better to continue a further 1km along the coast to Coppit Point, where there is a large car park. Saundersfoot harbour was built in 1829 for the exporting of locally mined anthracite. This was carried down to the shore on a narrow-gauge railway that ran parallel to the coast through a series of tunnels, which are now used by the coastal footpath. A further 2km will see you reach Wiseman's Bridge, which in August 1943 saw the rehearsals for the D-Day landings and were watched over by both Churchill and Eisenhower.

From here the coastline sweeps round in a gentle curve, past Amroth, which marks one end of the Pembrokeshire Coastal Path and where you can find evidence of an ancient wood that was drowned by the rising sea levels of the last ice age. There is some parking here and a reasonable carry at low water. The castle here forms part of the Lansker line that runs up to Newgale. This marks the boundary between English and Welsh speaking communities. Landsker is derived from the Norse word for 'divide'.

Pendine marks the last place to easily land until you reach Llangennith and the Gower Peninsular. Pendine Sands was the scene for many of the early attempts of the land-speed record. The first person to use Pendine Sands for a world land-speed record attempt was Malcolm Campbell and on 25 September 1924 he set a record of 146.16mph in Bluebird. Over the next two years Campbell and Parry Thomas traded places as the fastest man on earth. In March 1927 Parry Thomas attempted to beat Campbell's record. Using his car, Babs, Thomas was killed when he lost control and crashed at over 180mph. The car was then buried in the sand until 1969, when a local college lecturer Owen Wen-Owen obtained permission to excavate the wreckage and restore it to its former state. It can now be seen at the Museum of Speed in Pendine village.

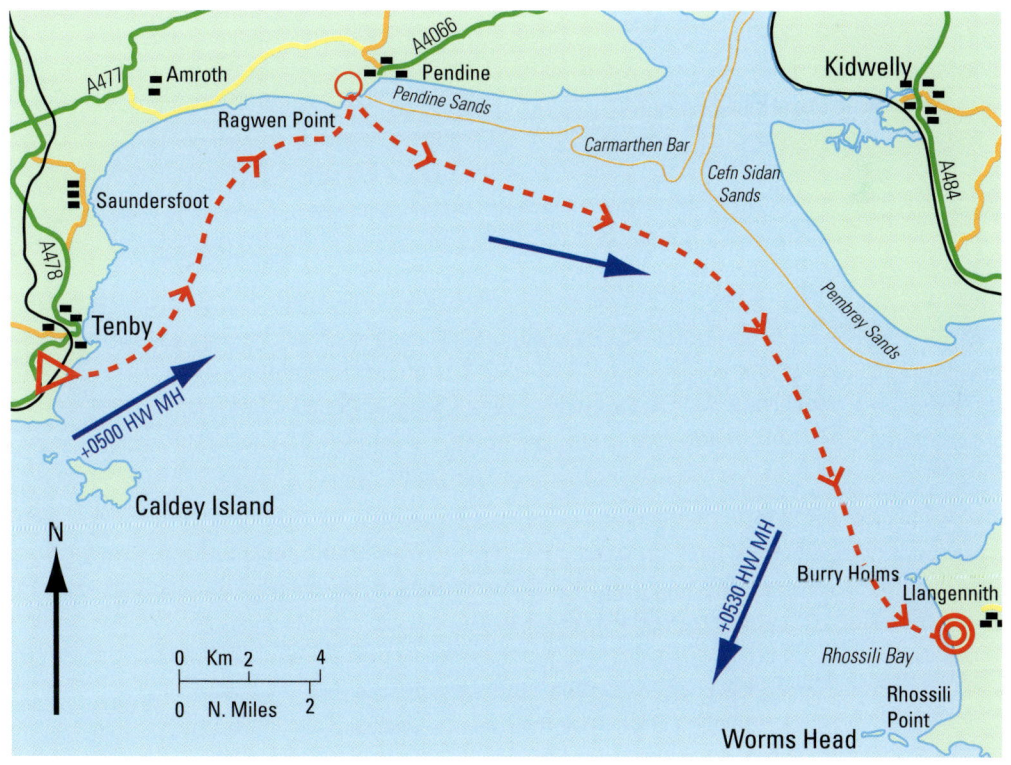

Worm's Head, seen from Saundersfoot | Mark Rainsley

It is still a long way to go and you may wish at times that you could travel at 1/10th of the speed of Campbell or Thomas. But slowly the Gower peninsular will come into view. Be aware of the flood tide that will try to take you north and onto the Carmarthen Bar, which extends well out to sea. Look for Worms Head and Burry Holms, which is a prominent outcrop of rock that forms the north end of Llangennith beach. The beach is popular with surfers so look out for them as you land. This will have been a long day and you'll need a good pair of binoculars to see where you have come from. The full satisfaction of your endeavours will slowly emerge as you lay back in the warm sand and gaze across the empty horizon.

Tide and weather

At low water large sandbanks are exposed and when the wind comes in from the SW you can find breaking waves a long way from the shore in the shallow water. It is then best to keep away from the shore especially near the estuary mouth formed by the confluence of the rivers Taf and Towy.

Additional information

The operating hours of Pendine Range are from 0800 hrs to 1615 hrs, Monday to Friday throughout the year. However, these hours may be extended either side of those times with very little notice. The area is patrolled by a safety boat.

Further information https://www.qinetiq.com/en/pendine

Listen on VHF ch 16.

Gower and Bristol Channel

An Introduction

The Gower peninsular is more like an island, leaving the City of Swansea behind; you are transported to a paradise for those interested in outdoor activities. Like its neighbour, Pembroke, the Gower also boasts sea cliffs, big tidal flows and also some of the best surf beaches in the country. In 1956 the Gower was designated as the UK's first Area of Outstanding Natural Beauty. There are good introductory rock climbs at Three Cliffs Bay and the quiet lanes lend themselves to cycling.

Abertawe is Swansea's Welsh name and comes from the River Tawe, which flows through the city. Upstream of the city the river can provide some challenging white-water paddling. The north coast of the peninsular and River Loughor provides sheltered paddling during rough weather, while kayakers wanting more adventure can head out to Worms Head and the surf beach of Llangennith or practise their boat handling in the tide race off Mumbles Head. There are three good locations to camp where there is easy access to the water, Hillend (Llangennith), Port Eynon or Penmaen, near Three Cliffs Bay. For a specialist kayak shop you will have to travel into Cardiff to 'Up & Under', Tel. 02920 578579. However there is a chandlers 'Force 4 Chandlery', Tel. 01792 4655704 in Swansea Marina.

The Bristol Channel has the second highest tidal range in the world. As you travel up its length you will see how the clear waters around the Gower are transformed by the silt which is swept down from the upper reaches of the River Severn. This waterway is still a major shipping channel and the development of ports such as Barry and Avonmouth were central to the industrial growth of South Wales during the last 150 years. It is a venue that will challenge the experienced paddler but can also provide quieter locations for those new to the sport.

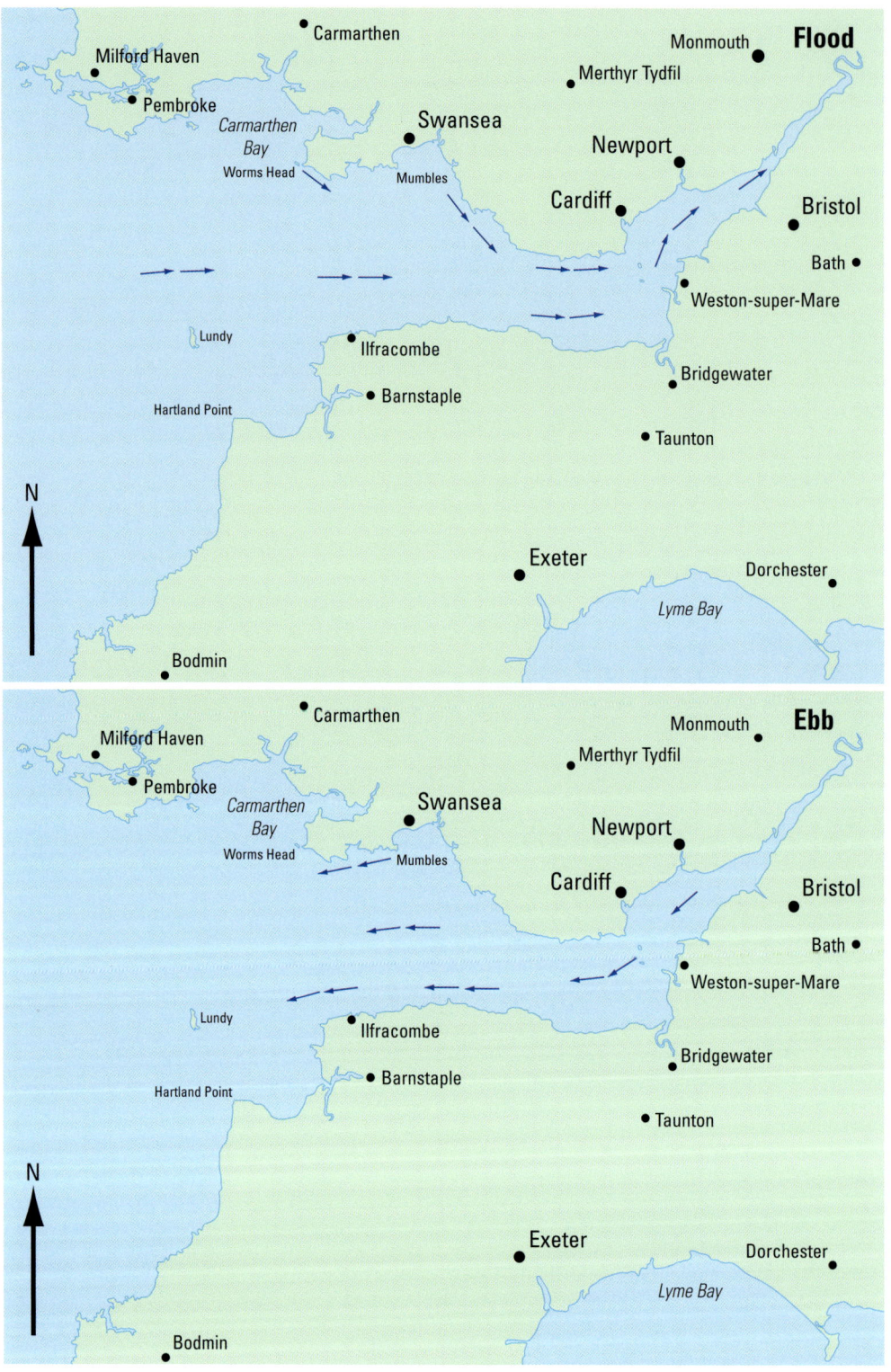

The above charts are intended to give a general overview. Consult the relevant chapters and other sources for more precise information.

Burry Holms

No. 45	**Grade A**	**20km**	**OS Sheet 159**	**Tidal Port Milford Haven**
Start	△ Pen-clawdd SS 544 959 / SA4 3YF
Finish	○ Broughton Bay SS 418 929 / SA3 1JP
HW / LW	at Pen-clawdd is 15 minutes after Milford Haven.
Tidal times	The ebb tide starts soon after local high water and drops quickly, especially around Whiteford Burrows.
Tidal rates	The ebb tide can run at 3 knots past Whiteford lighthouse.
Coastguard	Milford Haven, Tel. 01646 690909, VHF 0150 UT repeated every 3 hours

Introduction

Whether it is the surf on Llangennith beach or the wildlife on Whiteford Burrows, the often forgotten, north-west coastline of the Gower peninsular can provide a variety of experiences for both the beginner and more competent paddler alike. With the aid of a tide table, the River Loughor can provide a sheltered venue for a variety of trips. It is possible to launch upstream of the

231

© Pen-clawdd

road and railway bridge at Loughor, near the Loughor Boating Club and inshore lifeboat station, then take the flood tide as far as Hendy. However the water soon disappears and those slow on the return trip need to be careful not to be left high and dry on a mud bank. It is also possible to leave from Burry Port, which is more accessible at all states of the tide, and complete a round trip taking in Llanelli, as well as the western beaches of Whiteford and Rhossili. As the tide falls these beaches can become large which means a long carry of your boat at the end of the day and are not recommended as launch sites.

Description

This trip starts at Pen-clawdd, where there is ample car parking, as well as other facilities such as shops and a pub. It is best to aim to leave at or near high water and take the start of the ebb out towards Whiteford Point, looking for the disused Whiteford lighthouse as a point of reference. This is made of cast iron and stands like a skeleton exposed to the weather. It was built in 1865 but has not been in use since 1926. At low tide it is possible to walk along Whiteford Sands to this structure, but as you near here on the water your rate of approach will increase as the mass of water sweeps out to sea, and the lighthouse structure forms a large eddy. All around this area there are many breeds of wading birds, especially oystercatchers which can be seen in the salt marshes of Whiteford Burrows. During WW2 the estuary was used as a firing range and unexploded bombs are still found. On the opposite bank are Burry Port and Llanelli. Both towns have been redeveloped recently but only the former gives easy access to the water at all states of the tide.

However both provide destinations if you are trapped in the estuary by bad weather. Llanelli was formerly described as a small and insignificant place but because of its access to water soon saw growth as a port for the local coal mining and tinplate industry that developed during the 19th century. However with the decline of heavy industry and the silting up of the River Loughor led to the final closure of the docks in 1951.

From Whiteford Point you continue parallel to the coast, which changes from sandy beach to rock cliffs with a cave at Minor Point which is possible to paddle through during the top half of the tide. Burry Holms is a prominent outcrop of rock which forms the north end of Llangennith beach and during 2 hours either side of HW becomes an island and therefore possible to make a complete circumnavigation. If you land and walk up to the rocks you will find several remains of an old fort and church.

You can finish the trip with some surf practice here, before returning to Broughton Bay where it is easier to carry the boats through the caravan park and up to the car park (SS 416 925). In strong SW winds this is an excellent location for surfing. There are no facilities here other than lots of space.

Tide and weather

In strong W to S winds it can become quite rough near Whiteford lighthouse and Hooper Sands on an ebb tide.

Additional information

There is a shellfish industry in Crofty and you will also see the wild marsh ponies as you head out towards Whiteford Point. Be aware that large areas dry out and you can find yourself stuck in mud some distance from a firm shoreline. For those who want to find out more about local wildlife visit the National Wetlands Centre in Llanelli. www.wwt.org.uk, Tel. 01554 741087.

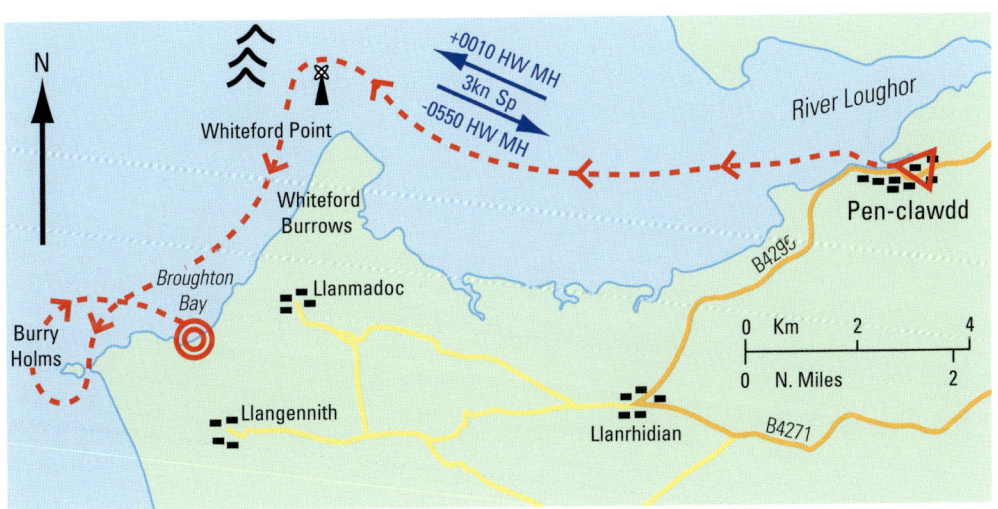

Broughton Bay

Worms Head cut off by a high tide

Worms Head

No. 46 | Grade B | 16km | OS Sheet 159 | Tidal Port Milford Haven

Start	△ Car park, near Llangennith SS 413309 / SA3 1JH
Finish	○ Port Eynon SS 468850 / SA3 1NN
HW / LW	times are similar to Swansea, which is approximately 5 minutes after Milford Haven.
Tidal times	The tide flows in a clockwise direction around Carmarthen Bay and runs SE past Worms Head until approximately 10 minutes after HW Milford Haven.
Tidal rates	can reach 3 knots along the coast and past the East Helwick Buoy.
Coastguard	Milford Haven, Tel. 01646 690909, VHF 0150 UT repeated every 3 hours

Introduction

The dramatic cliffs of Worms Head form a 3km long headland that hangs off the SW corner of the Gower peninsular like a foot. Viewed from Llangennith beach it looks like a monster swimming out to sea. Exposed to both wind and tide its location can provide a challenging trip. If the weather is unfavourable, a walk out to the end of the headland can be as exhilarating as a trip

Port-Eynon Bay | Mark Rainsley

in a kayak. The view down to the sea below will concentrate the mind, while the local bird life soars above, gliding on the up drafts caused by the steep cliff face. There are seabird colonies on the outer headland, as well as seals. The causeway is made up of numerous rock pools where an abundance of sea life is found and can be crossed on foot, 2 hours either side of low water. You can park at the NT visitor centre in the village of Rhossili, where there is a National Trust Centre.

This trip departs from Llangennith; in the village there is a 12th century church, which is dedicated to St Cennydd, who in the 6th century founded a priory on the site. The car park is reached through the campsite at Hillend. However there are no other facilities and you'll probably be faced with a long carry through the dunes and across the beach. The beach here has seen many shipwrecks and the remains of the barque Helvetia can still be seen at low tide. This ship was blown ashore in a storm during November 1887. Later its shipment of timber was taken off and sold on to merchants before the wreck was sold locally. There is a rumour that the deck timbers found their way onto a local man's kitchen floor.

It is best to start once the tide has started to flow SE as this will take you around the headland and along the coast to Port Eynon. For those not wanting to go all the way around it is possible to cross the causeway 3 hours either side of HW. However when the water is shallow, waves can sweep around the back of the headland making it a short but challenging passage. As well as being one of the country's prime surfing spots, it also provides one of the most beautiful sunsets you'll ever see.

Description

Llangennith is one of Britain's surf beaches, so bring a short boat as well, for if it is too rough to go further out to sea, your trip will not have been wasted, as you can have great fun playing in the surf. Leave the beach and aim for the inner head, normally this is quite sheltered but beware of down drafts coming from the cliffs. Look out for the natural arch and blowhole at the north side of the outer head. The water can become confused, with large waves at the actual headland but once around with a following flood tide you'll soon be heading along the coast. You can take a break at Mewslade Bay but using this as a finishing point would involve a difficult scramble with the boats up the cliffs to Pilton. Like all the exposed beaches on the south side of the Gower, you may need to land through surf. There are some caves to explore at the back of the beach.

Leaving Mewslade you'll pass Paviland Cave, where in 1822 the "The Red Lady of Paviland" was found. In fact it was the skeleton of an Stone Age man, who had been buried with a number of personal belongings, including a seashell necklace. Now start to look for the East Helwick buoy, this is just off Port Eynon Point and will give a good indication of how far you have to go. The water can become quite rough off Port Eynon Point and it is best to keep well to the east as you round the point, which will bring you into calmer waters and the finish of what will have been an exhilarating trip. Arriving near HW will keep your carry at the end of the day to the minimum. At the end of the headland you'll find the remains of a salt house and the strange structure of Culver Hole, that was reputedly used by smugglers. This is made by a masonry wall with three windows that bridges the gap between the sides of a gap in the cliff face.

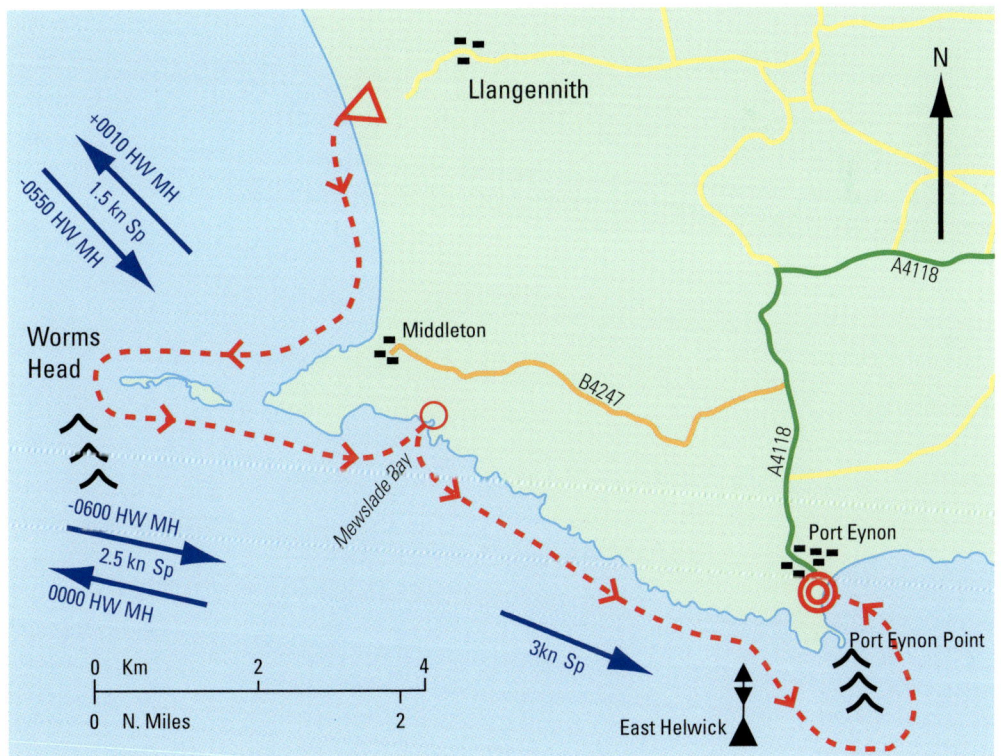

Approaching Worms Head

Tide and weather

Worms Head is not a place to be caught in poor weather, especially if the wind is blowing against the tide. You can contact PJ's Surfshop, Tel. 01792 386669 to give you an idea of the size of the surf at Llangennith. Tides can run at 3 knots along the coast towards Port Eynon.

Additional information

The Welsh Surfing Federation School, Tel. 07702 568398, www.wsf.wales or Gower Surfing, Tel. 07739 536122 can provide lessons if you fancy a change. The NT's Rhossili visitor centre is situated at the start of the path out to Worms Head. From the car park here there are superb views over the length of Rhossili Bay. Skysea Caravan and Camping, 01792 390795 at Port Eynon, Tel. 01792 390795 is 200m from the water and could be used for an overnight stop. A youth hostel is housed in the old Port Eynon lifeboat station, and if you arrived at HW you could paddle right up to the door. Tel. 0345 371 9135.

Mumbles Head

No. 47 | **Grade B** | **18km** | **OS Sheet 159** | **Tidal Port Swansea**

Start	△ Port Eynon SS 468 851 / SA3 1NN
Finish	◯ Mumbles SS 626 876 / SA3 4EN
HW / LW	HW times are similar to Swansea, which is approximately 5 minutes after Milford Haven.
Tidal times	An anticlockwise flow starts to form in Swansea Bay approximately 3 hours before HW Swansea, this lasts for 9 hours.
Tidal rates	Along the coastline the tide rate is 2.5 knots but the south-flowing ebb off Mumbles Head can reach 4 knots.
Coastguard	Milford Haven, Tel. 01646 690909, VHF 0150 UT repeated every 3 hours

Introduction

The south coastline of the Gower peninsula is made up of a number of beautiful sandy beaches divided by rocky outcrops. Each of the bays can provide a sheltered training spot but when exposed to southerly winds they can become great surf beaches, which can provide a lot of fun when conditions are too rough to venture out into open water. The whole of this coast is exposed to

Mumbles Pier

Mumbles Head

the main tidal flow of the Bristol Channel and tide rips can build up, especially south of Oxwich Point, when there is a westerly stream. This tidal stream is swept around Oxwich Bay and is turned SE by the headland to hit the main flow also head on. This bay can provide a good practice area but beware of the tide when it is flowing in this direction. Like all the beaches along this coast, it is popular with families and there is ample car parking, toilets and refreshments. The Oxwich Bay Hotel on the west end of the bay can provide more up-market accommodation and food for those who require it. At the west end of the bay you'll find Three Cliffs Bay where there is some good introductory rock climbs. Behind here you'll find Pennard Burrows, which was a Neolithic chambered tomb.

Description

The gravelly beach at Port Eynon is easy to access; there is a large car park, public toilets and shops. There are several campsites in the area, as well as a youth hostel situated in the old lifeboat station. It is best to aim to leave once the flood tide has started to run and use this to speed your progress; with a following W or SW wind the sea will not be too rough and the trip can be quickly completed. It is easy to break this trip along the way and shorten the trip. Caswell Bay and its sandy beach are especially popular with families, where there is a good car park, toilets and a café. As you come round Pwlldu Head look out for the three blocks of holiday flats that are at the back of Caswell beach. This is an ideal place to stop for a break. It has a lifeguard presence during the summer and the safe area for swimmers is normally marked by two flags. Look out for people in the water and the rocks on the west side of the bay which are exposed at low water. There can be reasonable surf here.

Leaving Caswell, the Mumbles lighthouse will soon come into sight and you will pass Langland Bay, which is an excellent surf spot, but can become congested so it is not ideal as a launch site. Past here and you'll soon be under the watchful eye of the coastguard station in Bracelet Bay. Look south and you will see the Mixon buoy that marks the Mixon Shoal. A trip out there can be a rewarding experience but also a challenging one on an ebb tide and SW wind. The lighthouse is built on the outer of two islands and marks the entry to Swansea Bay. There should be enough water for you to circumnavigate these, before continuing under the pier and lifeboat station before landing at the slipway. A lighthouse was first established in 1794 and used two coal fires, one above the other to distinguish it from St Ann's Head, which had two lights on separate towers and Flat Holm that had just one light. There is a car park, toilets and café here. However it can become busy on summer weekends, as a variety of water users and other visitors scramble for any available space.

The tide flows around the mainland and inner island of Mumbles Head and can provide an excellent playground. Inside Swansea Bay an anticlockwise flow starts 3 hours before HW at Mumbles, with the tide actually flowing for 9 hours, this runs between the islands that form Mumbles Head. The flow between the islands can provide a good venue to practise your boat handling and rescues in moving water. There is a small beach on the mainland overlooking the inner passage, which is ideal to get out for a quick break and stretch of the legs, or drive up to the car park by the coastguard station to look down on the water. It is quite easy to launch at Mumbles and return to the same spot. There is some free roadside parking and a larger car park at Knab Rock with a slipway. The water north of the pier is quite safe and an ideal place to introduce beginners to the sport. As the distances are quite short it is also possible to use general-purpose boats. The tide sweeps around the headland and forms some fast-moving water and large waves further offshore. This offshore tide race outside the lighthouse can become challenging, be warned!

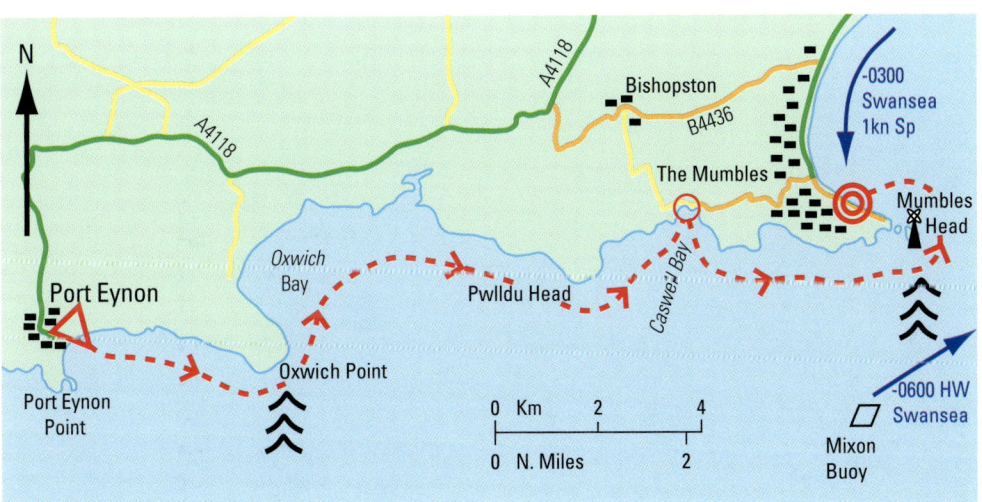

Threecliff Bay | Mark Rainsley

Tide and weather

The tide runs at 2.5 knots along the coast and when this is against the wind the water can be challenging. There can be overfalls south of Oxwich Point. However if you keep close to the shoreline you will be out of most of the flow and will have a smoother ride.

Additional information

Swansea's history goes back to the Vikings; and the Normans built a castle here. However it was the industrial revolution that saw its real growth, which meant it suffered heavy bombing during WW2. Since then it has been rebuilt and now has a number of worthy attractions. The National Waterfront Museum tells the story of the industrial revolution and shows the history of Wales through its contribution of coal mining, slate and steel production to the nation's history. www.nmgw.ac.uk Tel. 01792 459640.

> Swansea was the birthplace of Dylan Thomas and there's an excellent centre dedicated to his work. www.dylanthomasboathouse.com, Tel.01792 463980
>
> Swansea Tourist Information Centre, Tel. 01792 371441
>
> Mumbles Tourist Information Centre, Tel. 01792 361302

Passing Ogmore-by-Sea

Tusker Rock

| No. 48 | Grade B | 19km | OS Sheet 170 | Tidal Port Avonmouth |

Start Porthcawl, Rest Bay SS 809 769 / CF36 3LS
Finish Llantwit Major, Col-huw Point SS 956 674 / CF61 1RF
HW is 50 minutes before Avonmouth.
Tidal times The SE stream starts 5 hours 35 minutes after HW Avonmouth.
The west-going stream starts 35 minutes before HW Avonmouth.
Tidal rates Up to 5 knots.
Coastguard Milford Haven, Tel. 01646 690909, VHF 0150 UT repeated every 3 hours

Introduction

The Severn Estuary has the second largest tides in the world and, as this mass of water moves up the estuary to where it narrows, the tide can cause a phenomenon called the Severn Bore. This takes the form of a wave that moves faster than you can run, which surfers and kayakers aim to ride as far as Gloucester, while a strong ebb tide can mean a succession of whirlpools, eddies and standing waves. This makes the South Wales coastline not a place for the faint-hearted or those looking for a relaxed day.

243

The Tusker Rock Café | Eurion Brown

Description

Porthcawl makes an ideal starting point to this trip. Originally this was a busy commercial port, but with the growth of nearby Barry harbour it is now just used by yachts and other pleasure craft. It was also a popular holiday resort for the nearby mining community, when in the 60s families would create a tented city at Trecco and Sandy Bay. However with the growth of holidays overseas the numbers dropped. There is still a holiday camp there but half the size it was at its peak 40 years ago. During WW2 the area had been used by the Americans as a base before the D-Day landings.

It would be best to use a SE stream to make easy progress along the shore and especially past Nash Point, aiming to arrive at Col-huw Point just before high water.

There is plenty of car parking and several campsites nearby. You can launch from the beach at Rest Bay, where there are toilets. If it is rough here use the car park and beach north of Newton Point (838769). Both locations may require a reasonable length carry. Another option would be to park near Porthcawl Point and use the slipway by the RNLI station. There is another short slip about 500m west from here.

Just south of Porthcawl Point is Fairy Rock and from here Tusker Rock. These rocks are well marked and dry out at low tide. You can land on Tusker Rock and find remnants of a shipwreck, the largest remaining part is the boiler. This is all that remains of the SS Samtampa, which was wrecked in a storm on 23 April 1947 with the tragic loss of all her 39 crew, as well as the 8 crew members from the Mumbles lifeboat that went to her rescue. You can circumnavigate Tusker Rock but look out for breaking waves, especially on the SW side and then head for Black Rocks, SE of Ogmore-by-Sea.

Follow the coastline here, exploring the caves and rock formations created by the continual pounding of the waves. You can land on the sandy beach at Dunraven Bay, although the beach is stony at high water, for an early lunch. There is a good-sized car park, toilets and a café here, however it can become busy on summer weekends. A later departure would make it possible to arrive here at HW slack and then return to Porthcawl at the start of the NW stream, although the tidal streams are not strong along this part of the coast. It is worth a short walk up to the cliff top and look out towards Nash Sands, this will give you a good idea of how rough the water at Nash Point will be.

Continuing along the coast there are opportunities to land on several beaches. Look out for Nash Point lighthouse, which was built in 1832 after the loss of the passenger steamer 'Frolic' in 1830. As you approach Nash Point the water is pushed between the headland and the end of Nash Sands, which is marked by a cardinal buoy. This causes the flow to reach 5 knots and forms overfalls at the end of the sandbank. If there is any wind from the east it can become very rough. The rock formations are quite spectacular along this section of coast, built up by numerous layers, which are now being slowly eroded by the fast-moving waters of the estuary. After Nash Point look out for St Donat's Castle, this was built in 1300 and was once owned by the American millionaire William Randolph Hearst, who bought it for his mistress. It is now a private school but is open to the public on certain days. Tel. 01446 799100 http://www.stdonets.com/.

By the time you reach Col-huw Point you will have experienced a roller-coaster ride. Landing is on an area of shingle, where there is a car park, toilets and a cafe. There are some good cliff-top walks from both here and Dunraven Bay. If you are driving through Llantwit Major it is easy to get lost in the maze of narrow roads. There are some signs to the beach, look out for them.

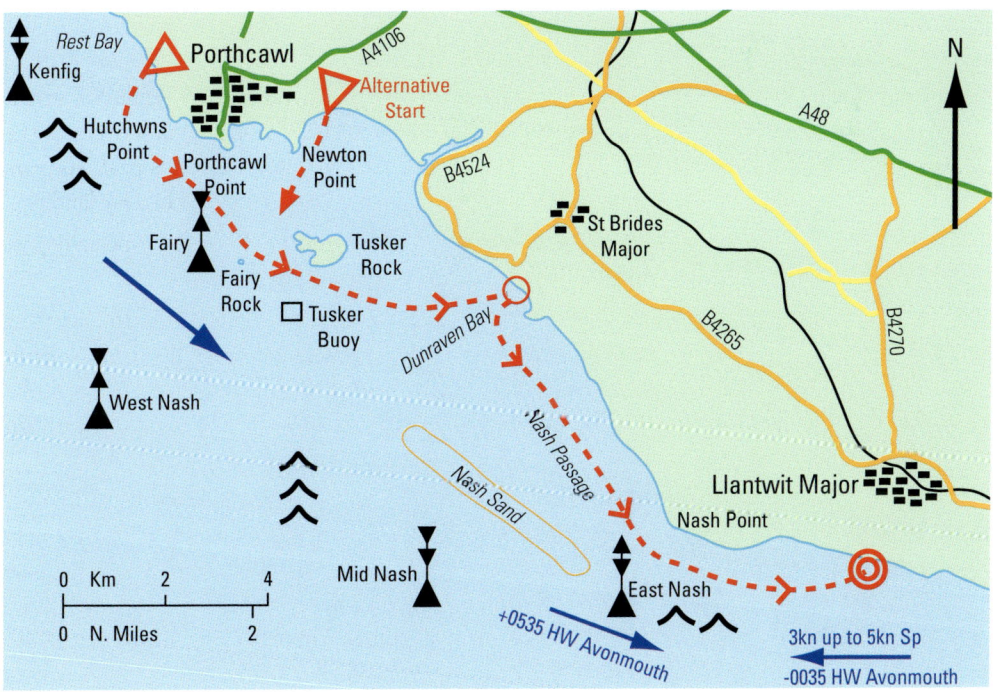

East Nash cardinal buoy, Nash Point in the distance | Eurion Brown

It is easy to run this trip in reverse leaving Col-huw Point once the NW stream starts, landing at Porthcawl near LW. Combined with a trip out to Flat Holm on another day this would make a good weekend's paddling.

Tide and weather

Shallows west of Porthcawl Point can create overfalls and rough water in wind against tide conditions. There can be large overfalls off Nash Point on an east flowing flood tide.

Additional information

For those interested in riding the bore, you will find all the information you need from a number of websites. The first person to surf the bore was Col. Churchill in 1955, while the present record is held by Steve King who covered 7.6 miles in 35 minutes on 30 March 2006.

http://www.severn-bore.co.uk/

Sully Island at high water

The Most Southerly Point

No. 49 | **Grade B** | **28km** | **OS Sheet 170 &171** | **Tidal Port Avonmouth**

Start	△ Llantwit Major, Col-huw Point SS 95629 67485 / CF61 1RF
Finish	○ Penarth ST 189 713 / CF64 3AU
HW / LW	HW at Barry Island is 30 minutes before HW Avonmouth. LW at Barry Island is 1 hour before LW Avonmouth.
Tidal times	The east-going flood stream starts 5 hours 35 minutes after HW Avonmouth. The west-going ebb stream starts 30 minutes before HW Avonmouth.
Tidal rates	4 knots and up to 6 knots at springs through Sully Sound.
Coastguard	Milford Haven, Tel. 01646 690909, VHF 0150 UT repeated every 3 hours

Introduction

This trip is one of contrasts and will take you from the stunning Glamorgan Heritage Coast, past the most southerly point in Wales and on to scenes from our industrial heritage. It can also be a fast trip with tidal streams reaching 4 knots, and you will be swept along on the massive conveyer belt that forms the Severn Estuary flood tide. For those with a GPS it may be worth noting your maximum speed.

© Entrance to Barry Dock

49 Description

The Most Southerly Point

The trip starts from the historical and picturesque community of Llantwit Major, where there is evidence of a Bronze and Iron Age settlements in the area, as well as remains of a Roman villa. St Illtud's Church dates back to the 6th century and is named after St Illud (or Illtyd) who founded a church, monastery and school on the site by Ogney Brook. The current building dates from the 12th century. It is worth a visit as there is a considerable history associated with the church. There is a campsite south of the town, Acorn Caravanning and Camping Site, Tel. 01446 794024, which is 2km from the beach and would make an ideal base for exploring the area.

Travelling through Llantwit Major it is easy to get lost in the maze of narrow roads. There are some signs to the beach, look out for them. Launching is from an area of shingle, where there is a car park, toilets and a café. The beach can be a good venue for surf, so look out for people in the water. There is also an active surf life-saving club in the area and some good cliff top walks from here for those who do not want to paddle. The beach is quite stony in places so be careful when setting off.

Leaving the beach you'll be accompanied by steep, layered cliffs along the coast as far as Summerhouse Point, where a Seawatch Centre is housed in an old coastguard station. In front of you will be the rocky beach that forms Breaksea Point. Here and Rhoose Point, which is a further 4km along the coast, form the most southerly point in Wales and is also the site of Cardiff International Airport. The best place to land is in Limpet Bay, where there is a car park and toilets next to the power station. Watch out for the tower just offshore, south of the power station. Once past Rhoose Point you turn NE and follow the coast round to Barry. The first beach you will reach is The Knap; although stony it makes an ideal place to take a rest, as it is less crowded than the popular sandy beach at Whitmore Bay on Barry Island. There are toilets here and a refreshments van during the summer. During the 1950s The Knap was developed into a pleasant location with a boating lake, gardens and the largest outdoor swimming pool in the country. However there are now plans to develop the area, which includes filling in the pool.

Until the 1880s Barry had been a small village community with a population of less than 100, by 1920 this had rapidly grown to 40,000. This was because of the rapid expansion of the mining industry and the growth of Barry as a port for the export of coal which led to the construction of docks and the building of a causeway to link the island to the mainland. During the 1920s the "Island" also began to develop as a holiday destination, which included an elevated scenic railway constructed of wood that was one mile in length. This was finally demolished after a gale in 1973 and marked the start of the decline of the island's fortunes. A holiday camp was built by Billy Butlin in 1965 and this went through the hands of various owners until it finally closed in 1996, but not before it had been used as the backdrop to several films including an episode of Doctor Who. The island still has the usual facilities of a seaside destination including a steam railway run by volunteers.

With the increase of shipping during the 1920s, this in turn led to several collisions and wrecks. One such incident remains in local folklore, when in August 1926 the Valsesia, loaded with American coal to try to break the miners' strike, ran aground on Friars Point. As the tide fell she broke in half, spilling her cargo onto the beach. Each new tide brought another supply of coal, which was then gathered by local people using any form of wheeled transport they could find. The wreck was finally towed off the rocks in October and out into Whitmore Bay, where she was sunk and so brought to an end the free supply of coal to the Barry community.

Smugglers used the whole coastline in this area during the 1700s. Barry Island was the centre for these activities and the island became the stronghold of Thomas Knight, who built fortifications along the shoreline. He built up a loyal band of supporters from within the local community, which made the customs officials' task even more difficult. However by 1785 the authorities had become tired of his presence and forced him to leave; rumour says he retreated to Lundy. As you

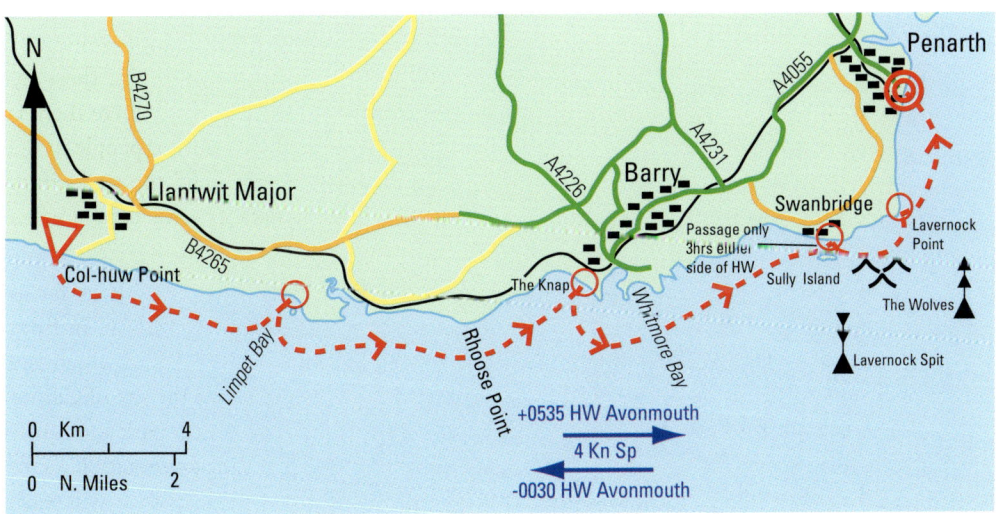

leave Barry Island and pass Nell's Point you'll be able to see the entrance to the docks on your left. Look out for pleasure boats in this area, including the Waverley steamer; Barry Dock lifeboat is also based here. A further 1km along the coast is Bendrick Rocks and then Sully Bay where at low tide you can see footprints left by a dinosaur. Some have been removed and are now on display in the National Museum in Cardiff. However the remaining ones give an indication as to the size of these creatures who roamed the earth millions of years ago.

The tide along this piece of coast flows very fast and can become quite dangerous as it runs through Sully Sound 3 hours either side of HW. Outside these times a natural causeway appears which gives access from the mainland. On the SE corner is the site of a Saxon fort, which is slowly being eroded. There are remains of a shipwreck on the island, which come from the 'Scotia' that was used to explore the Antarctic by William Bruce in 1902-04.

Further along the coast is Lavernock Point, which was the location of a gun battery, built in 1870. It formed part of the defence scheme for the Severn Estuary, along with those found on the islands of Flat Holm and Steep Holm, making a line that finished at Brean Down on the Somerset coast. As you come round the point, look for the clear eddy line that runs NE and causes the water to become confused. If you move to the shore side of this you will experience a smoother ride. You can land on Penarth beach, near to the pier or use the slipway next to the lifeboat station and Penarth Yacht Club. This will have been a varied trip and you will have had an opportunity to see a full range of historical locations and events, dating from prehistoric times to the industrial revolution, as well as the second largest tide in the world.

Tide and weather

If you leave Llantwit Major soon after the SE flood stream has started you will have a free ride all the way. However any wind with an easterly component will soon cause the waves to build up. Through Sully Sound these can become quite large, especially at the eastern end, but for the competent paddler these can provide a thrilling surfing opportunity. Note that you can only pass through Sully Sound 3 hours either side of HW, so don't arrive here too soon. During the E flood stream an anticlockwise eddy builds up in Sully Bay which runs back to the Barry dock entrance.

Additional information

Another option would be to stay at Lavernock Caravan and Campsite www.lavernockpoint.com/, Tel. 029 2070 7310, where there is a swimming pool and you can launch straight from the site. This would also make an ideal stopping-off point on a longer trip or if you wanted to link this trip with a paddle out to Flat Holm and Steep Holm or over to the Somerset coast. There is also the Marconi pub here, named after the early pioneer of wireless communication. If you do not stay on the campsite there is limited car parking just past the chapel at (ST 186 681).

You could finish at the pub in Swanbridge by Sully Sound, where there is a pay and display car park, which is refunded if you buy a meal in the pub. This is a good place to watch the fast tidal flow that runs through Sully Sound.

It is also possible to start from The Knap, Barry (ST 099 663 CF62 6UD) around 3 hours before high water and complete a return trip to Penarth, using the start of the westerly ebb stream for the return.

Flat Holm viewed from Steepholm | Eurion Brown

Flat Holm and Steep Holm   50

No. 50 | **Grade C** | **19km** | **OS Sheet 182 &171** | **Tidal Port Avonmouth**

Start	△ Penarth (190713)
Finish	◯ Penarth (190713)
HW / LW	at Penarth is 15 minutes before Avonmouth
Tidal times	Between Flat Holm and Steep Holm, the SW stream starts 15 minutes after HW Avonmouth, the NE stream starts 6 hours 10 minutes before HW Avonmouth.
Tidal rates	Tidal rates will reach 4 knots between the islands and off Lavernock Point.
Coastguard	Milford Haven, Tel. 01646 690909, VHF 0150 UT repeated every 3 hours

Introduction

Steep Holm and Flat Holm are small islands in the Bristol Channel, and this is a committing trip. When looking at the islands in profile it is soon apparent where their respective names come from. The trip is full of history and provides the opportunity to experience the full force of the tidal streams in the Bristol Channel. Add to this the fact that the route crosses a major shipping channel and you are in for an exciting paddle that will give you a feeling of apprehension as you leave the Welsh coast but of great satisfaction and relief as you return. For those looking for the

Flat Holm | Eurion Brown

ultimate trip it is possible to visit the North Somerset coast as well. To achieve this in a single day would need a committed approach, however there are plenty of accommodation opportunities near Brean Down which, with good planning, makes this an attractive weekend option.

Description

You can launch from Penarth beach, near to the pier or use the slipway near the lifeboat station and Penarth Yacht Club. There is some free parking along the road just south of here, or if this fills up, use the car park at the top of the hill by the pitch and putt, where there are also some toilets. The paddle steamer Waverley departs from Penarth pier three or four times a day for cruises around the islands and would provide non-paddling companions the opportunity to follow your progress. Use the SW flowing stream as assistance to arrive at Steep Holm before local LW slack and then wait for the start of the NE flow to take you initially to Flat Holm and then back to Penarth.

As you follow the coast south from Penarth look out for the Raine buoy off Lavernock Point. The tide will flow quickly around this headland and onto Sully Island, where it can reach well over 6 knots. SE of the Raine buoy you'll see the Wolves Rocks and Flat Holm. Now is the time to break from the shore and ferry glide over to Flat Holm, using the Wolves Rock to judge your rate of progress and potential drift downstream. You will now be crossing the main channel into Cardiff, so keep a lookout for larger craft. Keep north of the Wolves to arrive by the west beach of Flat Holm. Continue around the south end of the island until you are by the lighthouse. The water can become a little rougher here. From here look for the green Holm Middle buoy. Cross the main channel at the end of the SW flow, keeping an eye open for large commercial ships heading for Avonmouth and land at the east end of Steep Holm near Tower Rock. From here there are some steps to take you up to the top of the island. It is also possible to land on a smaller stony beach on the south side of the island.

Steep Holm is a nature reserve and home to 30,000 gulls, as well as some Muntjac deer and also a former gun emplacement. It is currently owned by the Kenneth Alsop Trust and there is normally a warden on the island, so be prepared to pay a small landing fee. Its name comes from the Danish for "River Island" and was used as a base for raiding the surrounding coastline. For those looking for an easier option, it is also possible to visit the island by boat from Weston-super-Mare.

www.steepholm.online – Kenneth Allsop Memorial Trust

Leave Steep Holm, remembering to keep a lookout for larger craft, at the start of the NE flow and use this to land on the NE end of Flat Holm, where there is a stony beach and steps up to the island. It is also possible to land on the western side of the island. The tidal currents swirl around the island and seem to be particularly confusing in this area. The story behind the lighthouse here is long and at times controversial. Negotiations between local shipmasters and Trinity House started in 1733 and in 1737 a light owned by the former was built. After periods of unreliable operation the lighthouse was taken over by Trinity House in 1823, and by 1988 it was totally automated. The island was fortified during the 1860s, at the same time as Brean Down, Steep Holm and Lavernock Point, to protect the Bristol Channel ports. During refortification in WW2 the original Steep Holm guns were discarded, but can still be found nearby. Each gun was linked by a railway track and had its own underground store for munitions. There were also barracks to accommodate the gunners.

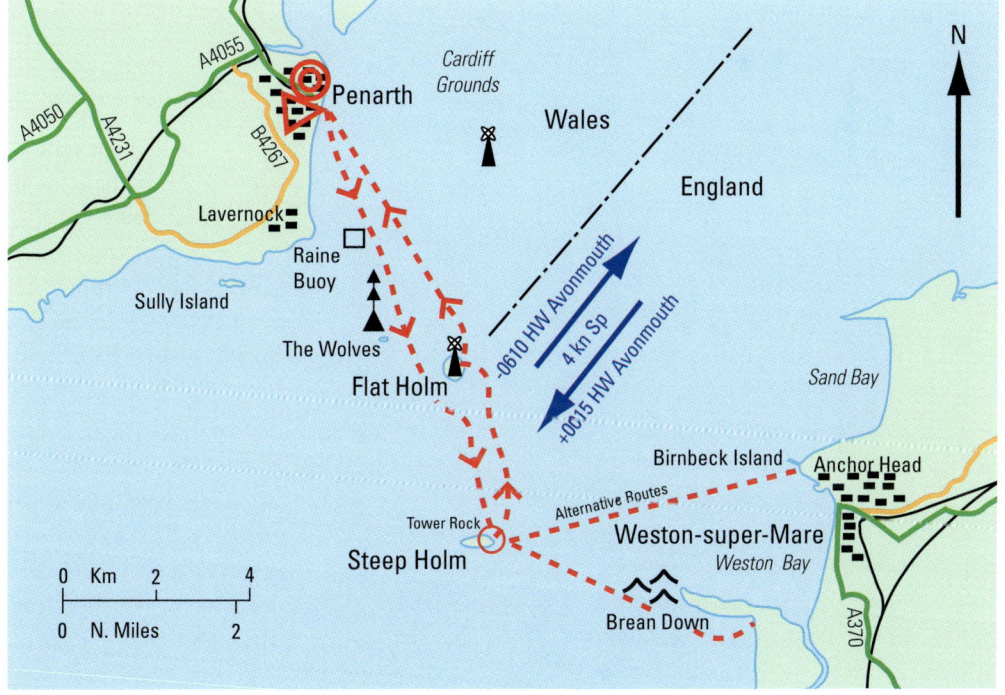

Flat Holm's farmhouse | Mark Rainsley

Flat Holm was also the location for some of Marconi's early demonstrations to show the potential of his new 'wireless' invention. In 1897 Flat Holm would play the part of a ship, as a message was transmitted from the island over the 3NM of open water to Lavernock on the Welsh coast, to prove that his invention could be used in maritime safety. In 1912 the Marconi wireless showed its worth and saved many lives after the Titanic liner sank. There is a bunkhouse on the island used by educational and natural history groups but this does need to be booked in advance. There are also some interesting displays about the island's history and you can explore many of the old gun emplacements. However, staying here overnight or not, there is a small landing fee to pay.

If you do intend to land on Flat Holm you should arrange this in advance with the Flat Holm Project, Tel. 029 2087 7912. http://www.cardiff.gov.uk/flatholm/. The project has an office at the Cardiff Harbour Authority, near the lifeboat station on Barry Island.

There is also a society that aims to promote Flat Holm and to assist the Flat Holm Project. https://flatholmisland.wordpress.com

By the time you leave Flat Holm the NE stream will be flowing at full force and, if not careful, will soon sweep you north onto the Cardiff Grounds sandbank, which should be avoided. These dry out and are well marked by various buoys. As with the outward trip judge your progress by watching the Wolves Rock and Lavernock Point. A clear eddy line develops off this headland and once inside this you should be able to relax. Reaching the relative security of the shoreline will ease the tension in your body; it will have been a wonderful day mixed with history, wildlife, tired arms but great satisfaction.

Tide and weather

You can experience rough water around both islands as well as off Lavernock Point and the Raine buoy. The tidal flow in the channel between the two islands can be strong and if you find yourself in this area even in a light wind when it is against the tide, expect a rough ride.

Alternatives

Another option would be to stay at Lavernock Caravan and Campsite, www.lavernockpoint.com/, Tel. 029 2070 7310, where there is a swimming pool and you can launch straight from the site. This would also make an ideal stopping-off point on a longer trip. There is also the Marconi pub, named after the early experiments into wireless communication.

You could launch from the pub at Swanbridge, where there is a pay and display car park, the fee being refunded if you visit the pub. Look out for the fast tidal flow that runs through Sully Sound.

It is also possible to launch from Barry and use the east-flowing flood tide to take you to Flat Holm. The easiest place to launch from is at the Knap (ST 099 663 / CF62 6UD), which is far less congested than the holiday resort of Barry Island.

From the English side

Departing from the other side of the Severn Estuary is not an easy option because of the large expanses of sand and mud that can be exposed at any time other than high water. This can turn launching or return into a long, if not impossible, carry as the surface can become soft and therefore very dangerous. There are three possible options for launching, all of which are busy tourist venues during the summer months. The local kayak shop in this area, Performance Kayaks, Tel. 01934 613612, can be found in Uphill, which is 3 miles south of Weston-super-Mare.

Burnham-on-Sea

There is a public slipway here, which strictly speaking you need a permit from the Tourist Information Office to use; this is conveniently situated next to the slipway, along with toilets and a large public car park. You could also launch 1km south of here, from the small headland at the confluence of the River Brue and River Parrett. However there is no long-term parking here.

Brean Down

There are toilets, a café and an information point here. You can also gain access to the beach by car, which will help reduce the carry. Be warned not to drive out too far, as each year a number of cars get stuck and are lost as the tide rises. A strong tide race builds up on the end of the headland as the tide flows around Howe Rock. Climb the steep steps behind the Tropical Bird Garden and you can walk out to the end of the headland, which gives you a good view of the sea state and across to both islands. There is a fort, completed in 1877 and old WW2 gun emplacements here. It is best to launch before local high water slack and ferry glide over to Steep Holm, returning as the tide turns and starts to ebb. However this is not a relaxed option, as a slow or late return will see you swept down to Berrow Flats on a falling tide.

Rudder Rock, Steep Holm | Eurion Brown

Weston-super-Mare

The best place to launch at any time other than high water is from a small slipway at Anchor Head (ST 308 621 / BS23 2ER) SE of Birnbeck Island, behind the Captain's Cabin public house on Birkett Road. There is no direct vehicle access and you will need to carry your boats down the steps to the side of the Anchor Head Hotel. There is some parking here, as well as toilets and the very pleasant Cove Café, next to the slip. Another option would be to use some steep steps, 200m north of here, that lead down to the rocks between the Royal Pier Hotel and the disused pier that goes out to Birnbeck Island. As with leaving from Brean Down, getting out to either island from here will require a committing ferry glide and misjudging this on a strong tide can have serious consequences.

Bristol Channel

No. 51 | Grade C | 50km | OS Sheet 180 & 159 | Tidal Port Avonmouth

Start	△ Mumbles Head SS 626 876 / SA3 4EN
Finish	○ Ilfracombe SS 523 477 / EX34 9
HW	at Avonmouth is 4 hours 10 minutes before Dover.
Tidal times	South of West Scar buoy, SE stream 5 hours after HW Avonmouth. NW stream 1 hour before HW Avonmouth.
Tidal rates	3 knots in the Bristol Channel and 6 knots off Foreland Point.
Coastguard	Milford Haven, Tel. 01646 690909, VHF 0150 UT repeated every 3 hours

Introduction

This is a committing trip, one of the longest open crossings in UK waters. You will be exposed to tides that can reach 6 knots and will be crossing a major shipping lane. It is a trip that is only for the experienced, who are capable of looking after themselves, performing deep-water rescues and being able to contact shore-based support services. But for those who do complete the trip they will begin to appreciate just how seaworthy a sea kayak can be when in expert hands. From here you will now have the confidence to be inspired to take on other major challenges that can be found in UK waters.

Mumbles pier

Description

It is vital to have a settled weather forecast for the trip. Some comfort is provided by the proximity of the Mumbles Head coastguard who will help keep a watchful eye over your progress. Carrying a VHF radio and flares are minimum requirements, having a GPS is also a benefit. However knowing how to use all this equipment in an emergency is essential. It is also useful to set up another method of communication, so that friends can be made aware of when you arrive or problems arise.

It is best to depart from Mumbles Head about 2 hours before HW at Avonmouth and use the last of the east-flowing flood stream to take you out towards the yellow buoy at Lat. 51.32' N, Long. 03° 56' W marked as Fl.Y2.5s on Imray chart C59, and onto the West Scar buoy. This is the point where you make a decision about carrying on or not. If one member of the group feels unsure then don't let them feel bad, turn back. The Bristol Channel will be here another day and hopefully so will you.

From here head south to cross the channel. As the west-flowing ebb stream builds, it will take you down towards Ilfracombe. It is important to stay well upstream as the fastest flow is off the north Devon coast, and around Foreland Point can reach 6 knots. It is easy to turn downstream once you are closer to the shore, turn too soon and you'll be swept past your intended destination and round Bull Point. The only option then is to try and land on Woolacombe Sands and wait for the tide to turn.

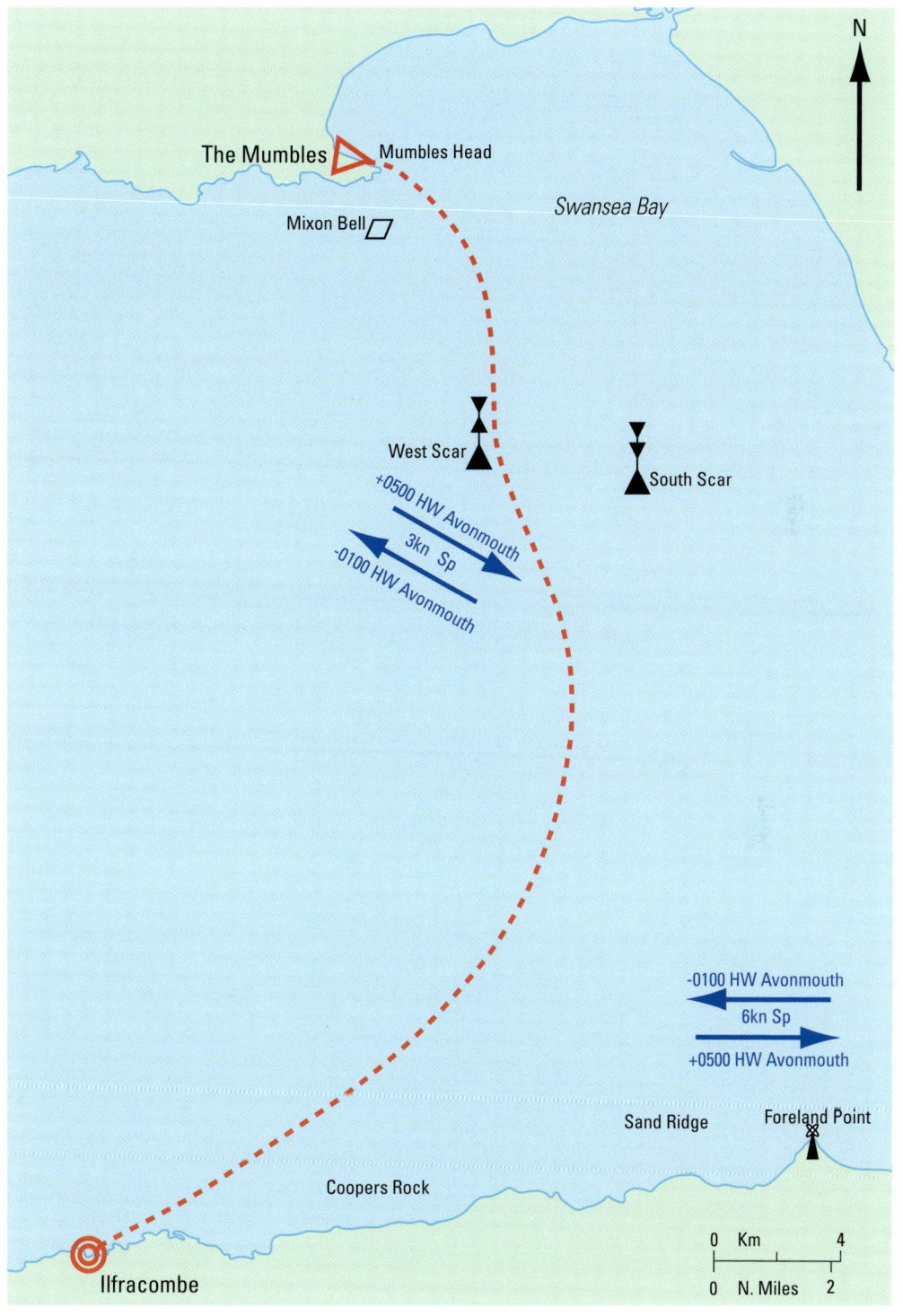

Challenging

We left Mumbles in the early morning and used the last of the flood tide to take us to the West Scar Buoy. All seemed to be going well until a SE wind picked up and it became clear that as the ebb tide built up we were being taken away from our final destination of Ilfracombe. The only solution was a concerted effort and a ferry glide of over 4 miles. When we eventually collapsed on the beach our shoulders were on fire and we couldn't move. It had been a challenging end to a great day's paddle. The B&B provided a welcome rest before the following day's return trip which passed off uneventfully as we retraced our paddle strokes.

Simon Fenton

When completing a long crossing like this it is important to take regular food and water, as well as rest. Drinking plenty is vital for a trip of this length, as dehydration can become a real problem. Keep close as a group and raft up to share refreshments. This helps keep moral high and enables each member of the group to feel valued. It is also important to check your rate of progress. This is where a GPS is useful, but it should not be your only method of navigation, batteries do fail. A carefully plotted course, allowing for drift and tidal flow, when used in conjunction with a compass will get you safely over to the other side.

Both your food and navigation equipment needs to be easily accessed from a deck bag. Don't rely on getting into your day hatch, it may become rough and removing a deck hatch is the last thing you'll want to be doing.

Once you finally fall out of your boat, your sense of satisfaction will be immense. Looking back your departure point will hardly be visible. This will be one great adventure and the holiday makers on the beach will not believe you when you explain your departure point.

Ilfracombe is a popular holiday destination, which does mean there are various accommodation options and some may opt for B&B before heading back the following day. It is a long way for a shuttle and it has been done by paddlers caught on the Somerset coast with an unsettled forecast. Other options include using the following day's west-flowing ebb stream to take you onto Lundy and then use an east-flowing ebb tide to take you back to Mumbles Head on the third day. This is a very challenging trip and you'll need a stable area of high pressure and good forecast for the whole period. The total distance for this three day trip is over 140km.

Tide and weather

The tidal flow in the Bristol Channel is at its greatest along the north Devon coast and past Ilfracombe and Foreland Point. At Lundy Island the east-flowing stream starts 1 hour 30 minutes after HW Dover and the west-flowing stream starts 4 hours 30 minutes before HW Dover. (Times are given at Dover as the best source of information offshore is the Tidal Stream Atlas).

Additional information

A trip out to Lundy Island is another serious undertaking. This solid piece of granite is popular with climbers, divers and ornithologists alike. Exposed to the full strength of the Bristol Channel

Common dolphin in the Bristol Channel off Swansea | Eurion Brown

tides, with overfalls at both north and south ends, careful planning is essential. It is best to try and arrive at slack water. Departing from Ilfracombe at local HW is a good time. There are several accommodation options including camping, all of which need to be booked in advance. If you do find yourself caught out there in bad weather, the passenger boat MS Oldenburg calls daily, weather permitting and will carry kayaks for an extra fee.

The Lundy Shore Office, The Quay, Bideford, Devon, EX39 2EY

Tel. 01237 431831 – www.landmarktrust.org.uk/lundyisland

What will tomorrow bring?

Appendix A – Coastguard & Emergency Services

In UK waters, HM Coastguard will co-ordinate rescues and emergency services. They also broadcast weather forecasts and will inform water users about potential hazards in their area. They monitor VHF CH16 and you should use this channel to make initial contact; you will then be directed to a working channel. There are four HM Coastguard stations that fall within the scope of this book, Swansea MRCC is the regional and district headquarters. Note the times here are for UT. During UK summer remember to add 1 hour.

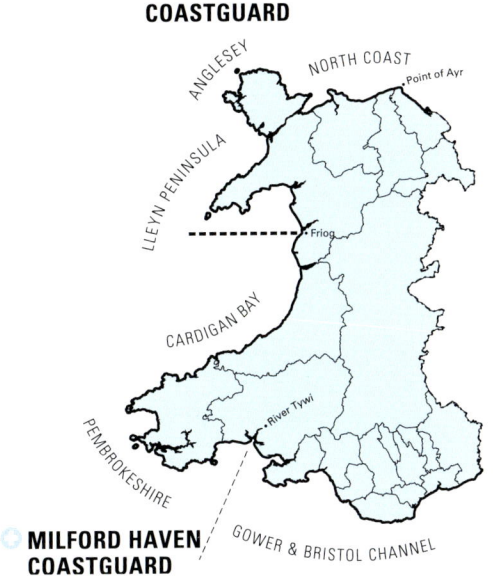

HMCG	Telephone	Weather announced on CH16 – UT
Holyhead	01407 762051	0150, 0450, 0750, 1050, 1330, 1650, 1950, 2250
Milford Haven	01646 690909	0150, 0450, 0750, 1050, 1330, 1650, 1950, 2250

Appendix B – Weather Information

The UK's weather is the most discussed topic within the communities that make up its coastline and mariners have always put their lives into the hands of those who try to predict its fickle nature. The Met. Office www.met-office.gov.uk was founded in 1854 to provide information about the weather to the marine communities. It was not until 1922 that forecasts were first broadcast by BBC radio, a tradition that is as strong now as ever. The shipping forecast and its use of areas that cross traditional national boundaries have also been used as a source for artists such as Mark Power, who visited all the areas to produce a photographic journey that explores the places and people, whose lives are dependant on its broadcast.

The Met. Office's website provides detailed predictions for the weather all over the UK. There are also a number of useful weather websites which can provide more detailed local information. These include:

www.xcweather.co.uk

www.windfinder.com

www.windguru.com

www.windy.com

If you are away from internet acccess there are a couple of other ways of obtaining a reliable weather forecast.

Radio

BBC Radio 4

0048 (92.8-96.1 & 103.5-104.9 FM & 198 LW) – Shipping and Inshore Waters Forecast
0533 (92.8-96.1 & 103.5-104.9 FM & 198 LW) – Shipping and Inshore Waters Forecast, and Weather reports from coastal stations
1200 (198 LW only) – Shipping Forecast, and Weather reports from coastal stations
1754 (92.8-96.1 & 103.5-104.9 FM & 198 LW) – Shipping Forecast (Saturday / Sunday)

Note: These times are often changed by a few minutes so please check.

VHF Radio

Owning a VHF radio and having the ability to use it is essential for anyone who wishes to venture anywhere apart from short near-shore trips. However they do not guarantee your safety, they only work in line of sight and being close under cliffs low in the water can severely reduce their effectiveness. Also be prepared to be able to recharge their batteries; even with new technology their effective working time is quite often only around 12 hours.

The coastguard will broadcast weather and navigation information every 4 hours. However remember this is only updated at 0500 and 1700 UT. An initial announcement will be made on Ch16 and then you will be told which channel the full broadcast will be made on. Before you visit an area it is worth contacting the coastguard to find out which channel they use, so you are confident about hearing the forecast.

Appendix C – Pilots

Irish Sea Pilot (2nd Edition), David Taylor, Imray, (2015) ISBN 9781846235917

Reeds PBO Small Craft Almanac, Bloomsbury (published yearly)

Cruising Anglesey and Adjoining Waters, Ralph Morris, Imray, (2021) ISBN 9781786791825

Appendix D – Mean Tidal Ranges

Tidal Port	Mean Spring Range	Mean Neap Range
Dover	6.0m	3.2m
Liverpool	8.4m	4.5m
Holyhead	4.9m	2.4m
Milford Haven	6.3m	2.7m
Avonmouth	12.2m	6.0m

Appendix E – Glossary of Welsh Language Place Names

Before the advent of maps and charts Welsh fishermen navigated the waters by local knowledge. To help them with this they used to descriptively name many of the coastal features; this way they could describe to each other where they went or how to get there. When translating the Welsh names around the coastline these days you will learn about the area from these very descriptive names. The fishermen only used to fish a relatively small area close to their villages, and therefore would just name all the features in that area. The next area's fishermen would then name the features in their area likewise. Due to this you will see lots of repetition in the Welsh names as obviously each area would have its own 'black rock' that it named. Here is a list of some of the more common Welsh names whilst kayaking the Welsh coastline. Many of the original map-makers would have been non-Welsh speaking which is why you will find variations in spelling. To make things more complicated, 'local' names, particularly for wildlife can vary from area to area!

Coastal Features

Shore/Beach	Traeth
Harbour	Porth
Island	Ynys
Current	Enlli
Estuary/River Mouth	Aber
Boat/Ship	Llong
Quay	Cai
Salt	Halen
Rock	Carreg
Stone	Maen
Salt Marsh	Morfa
Headland	Pen
Promontory	Penrhyn
Tidal Creek	Pil/Pill
Bridge	Pont/Bont
Pool	Pwll
Cave	Ogof
Causeway	Sarn

Land Features

House	Tŷ
Nose	Trwyn
Gully	Sianel
Cliff	Clogwyn
Mountain	Mynydd
Mill	Melin
Hill	Bryn
Slope	Llethr
Fort	Caer
Castle	Castell
Woods	Coed
Valley	Nant
Bog / Marsh	Gors
Cross	Croes
Church	Eglwys
Chapel	Capel
Hill Fort/City	Dinas
Well	Ffynnon
Slate / Slab	Llech
Homestead / village	Pentre(f)
Waterfall / spout	Pistyll

Common Descriptions

Red	Coch/Goch
Black	Du/Ddu
Blue	Glas/Las
White	Gwyn/Wen
Grey	Llwyd
Bishop	Esgob
Old	Hen
New	Newydd
Lower	Isaf
Upper / Higher	Uchaf
Big / Great	Mawr/Fawr

Wildlife

Seagull(s)	Gwylan(od)
Seaweed	Gwymon

Appendix F – Recommended Reading

Pembrokeshire Coast Path, Brian John, Aurum Press, 2017, ISBN 9781781315729

The Pembrokeshire Coastal Path, Dennis & Jan Kelsall, Cicerone Press, 2016, ISBN 9781852848156

Exploring the Pembrokeshire Coast, Phil Carradice, Gomer, 2002, ISBN 9781843231257

Coast - A Celebration of Britain's Coastal Heritage, Christopher Somerville, BBC Books, 2005 ISBN 978-0563522799

Wales, Walker, Dragicevich, Kaminksi & Waterson, Lonely Planet, 2021, ISBN 9781787013674

Appendix G - Trip Planning Route Card - User's Guide

The trip planning route card is designed to be used in conjunction with the information supplied in each route chapter in the book. In addition to this you will also require a set of relevant tide timetables. If the blank route card is photocopied, all the information for your route to be paddled can be worked out on it. This way it will help you plan your paddle as effectively as possible, and then allow you to have all the information you need on a handy piece of paper. This can be displayed in your map case on your kayak for easy reference. To help you use the card please refer to the following example and guidelines:

Trip Name & Number	*Bull Bay to Moelfre (No.14) & Anglesey East Coast (No. 4)*		
Page Number	*81 & 31*	VHF Weather	*0685 UT*
Date	*17 - 18 June 2006*	Weather Forecast	*Sunshine, Clear Visibility*
Coastguard Contact	*Holyhead 01407 762051*		*Force 2-3 westerly direction Sea state slight Temp 15°*

- Fill in the name, number and page of your chosen trip for easy future reference.
- When choosing the date of the trip, check in the chapter's 'Tide & Weather' section as to whether it will need specific tides that will dictate the date.
- Obtain a weather forecast using information supplied in Appendix B.
- Coastguard contacts can be found in the introductory info for each trip and in Appendix A.

Tidal Port		Mean Sp Range	8.4m	Local Port		
Liverpool		Mean Np Range	4.5m	*Moelfre*		

Tidal Port Tide Times (UT)	Height in Metres	Tidal Range in Metres	HW/LW	+1 Hr for BST?	Local Port HW/LW Time Difference	Local Port HW/LW	Sp or Np Tides
0254	8.9		Hw	0354	-0025	0329	between
0937	1.5	7.4	Lw	1037	-0025	1012	between
1527	8.4	6.9	Hw	1627	-0025	1602	between
2151	2.0	6.4	Lw	2251	-0025	2226	between

(Page 2) 18th June

Tidal Port Tide Times (UT)	Height in Metres	Tidal Range in Metres	HW/LW	+1 Hr for BST?	Local Port HW/LW Time Difference	Local Port HW/LW	Sp or Np Tides
0350	8.7		Hw	0450	-0025	0425	between
1034	1.6	7.1	Lw	1134	-0025	1109	between
1626	8.2	6.6	Hw	1726	-0025	1701	between
2252	2.2	6.0	Lw	2351	-0025	2326	between

- Identify Tidal Port from the chapter introductory information.
- Identify Mean Spring and Neap Ranges from tide timetable or see Appendix D. These will help identify Spring or Neap Tides and Estimated Maximum Speed.
- Local Port is also found in the chapter introductory information.
- Obtain the Tidal Port Times and Height in Metres from your tide timetables. Usually four times and heights, but occasionally three.
- To work out the Tidal Range in Metres subtract the LW heights from the HW heights.
- Add 1 Hr for BST? Add an hour to your Tidal Port Times if you are in British Summer Time.
- The Local Port HW/LW Time Difference can be found in the chapter introduction.
- To work out Sp or Np Tides compare your Tidal Range to the Mean Sp and Np Ranges.

Location	Direction of Tidal Stream	Tidal Stream Time Diff.	Tidal Port HW (BST?)	Tidal Stream Start Time	Tidal Rate	Est. Max Speed
	E	+0530	0354	0315	3 knots	2.25 knots
N Coast & Pt Lynas	W	-0030	1627	0928	3 knots	2.25 knots
	E	+0530	1627	1543	3 knots	2.25 knots

Location	Direction of Tidal Stream	Tidal Stream Time Diff.	Tidal Port HW (BST?)	Tidal Stream Start Time	Tidal Rate	Est. Max Speed
	SE	+0530	0354	0984	2 knots	1.5 knots
Moelfre	NW	-0030	1627	1557	2 knots	1.5 knots

Location	Direction of Tidal Stream	Tidal Stream Time Diff.	Tidal Port HW (BST?)	Tidal Stream Start Time	Tidal Rate	Est. Max Speed
	S	+0530	0450	1020	4 knots	3 knots
Puffin Sound	N	-0030	1726	1656	4 knots	3 knots

- Use the Location as indicated in the chapter introductory and tidal information.
- For the Direction of Tidal Stream there are generally four periods of tidal movement every 24 hours. Direction for the Tidal Stream Start Time soonest after 0000 hours in the first box.
- The Tidal Stream Time Difference is found in the chapter introductory and tidal information.
- Tidal Port HW can be transposed from above converting to BST if appropriate.
- The Tidal Stream Start Time is worked out by subtracting/adding the Tidal Stream Difference from/to the Tidal Port HW time.
- Tidal Rate is the average spring speed for the tidal stream, found in the chapter introduction.
- Estimate Maximum Speed based on whether it is Spring, Neap or in between tides.
- If it is Springs use the speed given in the chapter's introductory and tidal information.
- On Neap Tides halve this spring rate.
- When in between springs and neaps use the average of the spring and neap speeds.
- Note that speeds given are average spring rates. If paddling on a spring tide look to see if your Tidal Range in Metres is bigger or smaller than the Mean Sp Range. If it is bigger the speeds will be faster than average spring rates given.

ROUTE PLAN

	Location	Notes	ETA	ETD
Start	Bull Bay			1030
1st	Porth Eilian	Refreshments	1130	1230
2nd	Ynys Dulas	Seal Watching	1315	1345
3rd	Nant Bychan Farm	Camp at Nant Bychan Farm GR 516856	1620	1000
4th	Red Wharf Bay Inn	Arrive near Hw	1100	1230
5th	Trwyn Du Lighthouse		1500	1530
Finish	Trwyn y Penrhyn	Boat carry to layby	1615	

- When choosing Locations for the Route Plan use places that have tidal importance and where you may want to stop.
- When working out ETD (Estimated Time of Departure) or ETA (Estimated Time of Arrival) enter key times which need to be met for the best use of tidal stream first, as recommended in Tide & Weather. Work out other times around these.
- To work out the times an average paddling speed of 6km/h or 3 knots can be used. This can be adjusted to suit your needs, or time added for coastal exploration if desired.

Please feel free to photocopy the blank Trip Planning Route Card on the page opposite.
An A4 downloadable version is available on our website.
For this and other resources go to www.pesdapress.com, follow the links: Resources / Downloads / Printables.

www.pesdapress.com

Trip Name & Number	
Page Number	VHF Weather
Date	Weather Forecast
Coastguard Contact	

TIDAL INFORMATION

Tidal Port	Mean Sp Range	Local Port
	Mean Np Range	

Tidal Port Tide Times (UT)	Height in Metres	Tidal Range in Metres	HW/LW	+1 Hr for BST?	Local Port HW/LW Time Difference	Local Port HW/LW	Sp or Np Tides

TIDAL STREAM TIMES

Location	Direction of Tidal Stream	Tidal Stream Time Diff.	Tidal Port HW (BST?)	Tidal Stream Start Time	Tidal Rate	Est. Max Speed

Location	Direction of Tidal Stream	Tidal Stream Time Diff.	Tidal Port HW (BST?)	Tidal Stream Start Time	Tidal Rate	Est. Max Speed

Location	Direction of Tidal Stream	Tidal Stream Time Diff.	Tidal Port HW (BST?)	Tidal Stream Start Time	Tidal Rate	Est. Max Speed

ROUTE PLAN

	Location	Notes	ETA	ETD
Start				
1st				
2nd				
3rd				
4th				
5th				
Finish				

Trip Planning Route Card

Index

A

Aber Bach 167
Abercastle 165, 169, 170
Aberdaron 103, 106, 107, 108, 111, 112, 113, 115
Aberdaron Bay 103, 111, 113
Aberdaron Beach 101
Aberdovey 139, 140, 143
Aberdovey Bar 140
Aberdovey Outward Bound Centre 144
Aber Draw 170
Aberdyfi 139
Abereiddy 171
Abereiddy Bay 169, 170, 171, 173
Abereiddy Sledges 174
Aber Felin 170
Aberffraw 43
Abergwaun 161
Aber Mawr 167
Abermenai Point 41, 42, 44
Aberporth 145, 147, 151, 152
Aberporth Range Control Office 151
Abersoch 117, 118, 119, 120, 122
Aberystwyth 139, 140, 141, 142, 143
Abraham's Bosom 53, 55, 61, 65
adders 121
Adventurous Experiences (Sea Kayaking Centre) 90
Afon Dwyfor 125
Afon Gwaun 164
Afon Menai 35
Afon Nyfer 160
Afon Rheidol 143
Afon Teifi 157, 159, 160
Albion Sands 205, 210
Alfred Johnston 170
Amlwch 82, 86
Amlwch Heritage Centre 82
Amroth 227
Anchor Head 256
Angle 215, 219
Angle Bay 215
Angle Point 215
Anglesey 29, 32, 33, 34, 36, 37, 41, 42, 62, 67, 68, 71, 81, 83, 85, 86
Anglesey Sea Symposium 52
Annie's Arch' 54
Arctic terns 36, 72, 74, 76, 78
Atlantic grey seals 181
Avalon, Isle of 104
Avonmouth 253

B

Bangor Pier 37
Barafundle Bay 219
Bardsey Bird and Field Observatory 111
Bardsey Island 101, 102, 103, 104, 107, 108, 109, 110, 111
Bardsey Sound 101, 102, 103, 106, 107, 112
Barmouth 135, 136
Barmouth Bridge 135, 136, 138
Barmouth, Harbourmaster 138
barque Helvetia 236
barrel jellyfish 126, 127
Barry 248, 249, 255
Barry dock 250
Barry harbour 244
Barry Island 249, 250, 254, 255
Battle of Bosworth 211
Bay Dillyn 178, 179, 185, 186
Beacons Car Park, Conwy 25, 26
Beaumaris 35, 36, 37
Beddmanarch Bay 64
Bendrick Rocks 250
Benedictine monks 223
Benllech 32
Benllech Sand 32
Berrow Flats 255
Birnbeck Island 256
Bishops and Clerks 183, 185, 188, 189
Bitches, The 189, 197
Black Point 197
Black Rock 192
Black Rocks 244
Black Rock Sands 128, 134
Black Scar rocks 192
Black Tar Point 216
Bluebird 227
Bontddu 137, 138
Borough Head 200
Borth 140, 141, 142, 144
Borthwen 45, 46, 47, 48, 50, 61, 65, 66
Borth-y-Gest 131, 132, 133, 134
Bosherston 220
bottlenose dolphins 145, 148, 153
Bracelet Bay 241
Braich Anelog 101, 104
Braich y Pwll 101, 102, 103, 104, 110, 112
Brandy Brook 193

Breaksea Point 248
Brean Down 252, 253, 255, 256
brickworks, Porth Wen 76, 79
Bristol Channel 229, 239, 251, 253, 257, 258, 260
Britannia Bridge 37, 40
Broad Haven 197, 198, 200, 217, 219
Broad Sound 203, 205, 209
Bronze Age settlements 248
Broughton Bay 231, 233
Bruce, William 250
Brunel, Isambard Kingdom 132
Bull Bay 75, 77, 80, 81, 82, 87
Bull Hole 206
Bullock Harbour 57
Bull Point 258
burial chamber 174, 222
Burnham on Sea 255
Burry Holms 228, 231, 233
Burry Port 232

C

Cable Bay 43
Cadair Idris 136
Caer Bwdy Bay 192
Caerfai 194
Caerfai Bay 192
Caernarfon 35
Caernarfon Bay 43
café 21, 23, 28, 37, 68, 106, 117, 134, 136, 141, 142, 143, 147, 152, 160, 163, 166, 171, 174, 178, 184, 192, 196, 212, 214, 245, 248, 255, 256
Cafn Enlli 109, 110
Caldey Abbey 223
Caldey Island 221, 222, 224
Caldey Point 223
Caldey Roads 223
Caldey Sound 224
Calf of Man 87, 89
Calf Sound 87
Camarthen Bay 225, 226
campsite 152, 160, 170, 174, 194, 202, 222, 236, 240, 244
campsite, Aberafon 93, 96
campsite, Acorn Caravanning and Camping 248
campsite, Anglesey Outdoors, 56
campsite, Awelfryn Caravan Park 44
campsite, Brandy Brook 194
campsite, Cae Du 144

270

campsite, Caerfai Farm 194
campsite, Fron Caravan and Camping Site 44
campsite, Graig Wen 138
campsite, Kingsbridge Caravan and Camping Park 34, 40
campsite, Lavernock 255
campsite, Lavernock Caravan and Campsite 250
campsite, Llechrwd Riverside Camping Site 134
campsite, Morawelon 164
campsite, Mynydd Mawr 106
campsite, Nant Bychan Farm 32, 34, 86
campsite, Nant y Big 122
campsite, Outdoor Alternative 50
campsite, Parsal 96
campsite, Penrhyn Bay 66
campsite, Pen y Bont Farm 50
campsite, Porth Colmon 100
campsite, Porth Ysgaden 100
campsite, Treborth Hall Farm 40
campsite, Treheli 116
campsite, Tycanol Farm 164
campsite, Tyddyndu Farm 138
campsite, Tydu Vale 146
campsite, Ty Newydd 74
campsite, West Hook Farm 202
Cantre'r Gwaelod 142
Cardiff Grounds sandbank 254
Cardigan 157
Cardigan Bay 129, 131, 142, 144
Cardigan History Centre 158
Cardigan Island 152
Carmarthen Bar 227
Carmarthen Bay 225, 235
Carmel Head 67, 69, 70, 71, 72
Carreg Ddu 103, 104, 107
Carregedrywy 160
Carreg Fran 178, 179
Carreg-gwylan-fach 174
Carreg Gybi 168
Carreg Lydan 152
Carreg Onnen 168
Carreg Onnen Bay 167
Carreg Pen-las 163
Carreg Rhoson 185
Carreg Samspon 168
Carregwasted Point 166
Carreg yr Esgob 178
Carreg y Trai 122
Carreg y Ty 147
Castell Henllys Iron Age Fort 158
Castell Trerufydd 160
castle 123, 125, 194, 222, 227
Castle Point 164

Caswell Bay 240
cave 21, 22, 115, 233, 237, 245
Ceibwr 160
Ceibwr Bay 159
Celtic cross 202
Cemaes 80
Cemaes Bay 76, 80
Cemaes Head 157, 159
Cemlyn 72, 74, 76
Cemlyn Bay 67, 69, 71, 75
Centennial 170
Ceredigion Marine Conservation Code of Conduct 150
Ceredigion Marine Heritage Coast 145, 148, 150
Cerrig Gwylan 171
chandler 37, 48, 117, 166, 214, 216
Chapel of St Trillo 20
Chapel Point 223
Charles Holmes (wreck) 167
chough 104, 181
church 43, 77, 163, 200, 233
Church 166
Church Bay 68, 70
Church Bay Cottages Camping and Touring 70, 74
Church Bay Inn 74
Church Island 37
Cilgerran 160
Cilgerran Castle 160
Cistercian monks 223
Clarach Bay 142
Cleddau Reach 216
coastal bus service 197, 212, 219
coastguard station 241
Cobblers Hole 211
Cob, The 132
Col-huw Point 243, 244, 246, 247
Colonel Tate 166
Colwyn Bay 19, 20
common terns 76, 78
compass jellyfish 126, 127
Constitution Hill 142
Conwy 26
Conwy Ascent Race and Tour 25, 27
Conwy Castle 26
Conwy Estuary 25, 26, 28
Conwy Harbour 26, 28
Coppit Point 226
cormorant 46, 77, 82, 85
Craig Y Gwbert 153
Criccieth 123, 125, 126, 128
Criccieth Castle 125, 126, 128
Crofty 233
Culver Hole 237
curlew 46, 47, 140
Cwm Badau 170

Cwmtydu 146
Cwm-yr-Eglwys 163
Cymyran Bay 45, 47, 48, 66
Cymyran Strait 45, 46, 47, 48, 62, 66

D

Dakotian buoy 215
Dale 209, 210, 212, 213, 214, 215
Dale Fort 211
Dale Point 211, 214, 215
Dale Roads 212, 214, 216
Daugleddau Estuary 216
D-Day landings 28, 227
Dee Estuary 13, 14, 17
Deganwy 20, 26
Den's Door 197
DERA Aberporth 152
Devon 258, 260
Dinas Fach 103, 193
Dinas Fawr 103, 193
Dinas Head 159, 161, 163, 164
Dinas Mawr 167
Dolgarrog 27
Dolgarrog Bridge 25, 27
Dovey Estuary 139, 143, 144
Dovey Yacht Club 140, 144
Dream of White Horses, A 54
Druidston Haven 196
ducks 26
Dulas Bay 83, 85
Dun Laoghaire 58
Dunraven Bay 245
Dwyryd Estuary 131, 133, 134
Dyffryn 63
Dyffryn Conwy Paddlers 25, 27
Dylan Thomas 146, 242

E

East Helwick buoy 237
East Mouse 82, 85
Eel Spit 224
Elegug Stacks 217, 218
Ellin's Tower 54

F

Fairy Rock 244
Fegla Fach 136
Fegla Fawr 136
Ffestiniog Railway 132
Fishguard 161, 162, 163, 164, 165, 166
Fishguard Bay 165
Fishguard Fort 164
Fishguard Lower Town Quay 161, 164, 165, 166
Flat Holm 246, 251, 252, 254
Flat Holm Project 254

Force 4 Chandlery 229
Foreland Point 258
fort 42, 147, 160, 164, 167, 174, 211, 222, 226, 233, 250, 255
Fort Belan 42
fortification 253
forts 154, 158
Four Mile Bridge 45, 46, 48, 62, 63, 66
Fresh Water Bay 83, 85
Freshwater East 217, 219, 221, 222
Freshwater West 211, 218, 219
fulmar 93, 94, 121, 159

G

Gallows Point 37
Garland Stone 203, 205
Garn Fawr 167
Gateholm Island 203, 209, 210, 212
Gazelle Hotel 37
George III Hotel 137
Glan-y-Mor 125
Glaslyn Estuary 132
Gogarth Bay 51, 52, 54, 55, 62, 64, 65
Goodwick 166, 167
Gored Goch, Ynys 37
Gorsedd y Penrhyn 64
Goultrop Roads 199, 200
Gower 227, 229, 231, 235, 239
Gower Surfing 238
Grassholm 187, 188, 189, 190
Great Castle Head 211, 215
Great Orme 19, 21, 22, 23
Green Bridge of Wales 217, 218
Green Scar 191
Green Scar rocks 192
grey seal 72, 74, 85, 148, 149, 153, 160, 206
guillemot 21, 77, 93, 94, 218
gun battery 250
Gwahan rock 185
Gwbert 153, 157
Gwert 151
Gyrn Ddu 94
Gyrn Goch 94

H

Hafan-y-Mor 125
harbour porpoise 145, 148, 150, 178
Harry Furlough's Rocks. 72
Haven Sports 197
Haverfordwest 216
Hell's Mouth 77, 80, 113, 116, 118
Henllwyn Bay 110
Henry Tudor 211
Heritage Canoes 160
Heron 47

herring gull 85
Hilbre Island 13, 14, 15, 17
Hilbre Island Ranger 17
Hillend 236
Hobbs Point 216
Holm Middle buoy 252
Holyhead 51, 58, 64
Holyhead Bay 63, 70
Holyhead Breakwater Country Park 55
Holyhead Harbour 54, 64, 65
Holyhead Mountain 61, 62
Holyhead Port Control 61
Holy Island 61, 62, 63, 74
Hooper Sands 233
Horse Rock 179, 180, 186, 189
hotel, Ty Newydd 103, 111
Howe Rock 255
Howney Stone 200
Huntsman's Leap 218
hut circles 209

I

Ilfracombe 257, 258, 260
Inland Sea 46, 48, 62, 63, 64, 66
Inn, Duke of Edinburgh 195
Inner Haven 216
Inn, Royal Oak 166
Inn, Ship 32, 34, 147
Inn, The Mariners 196
Irish Sea 57, 58
Irish Sea Leatherback Turtle Project 126
Iron Age fort 147, 158, 160, 167, 174, 192, 197, 200, 210, 211
Iron Age forts 154
Iron Age settlements 248
Isle of Man 87, 89, 90

J

Jack Sound 203, 204, 205, 209, 210
jellyfish 126
Jemima Nicholas 166

K

Kashmir goats 21
Kenneth Alsop Trust 253
ketch, Democrat 186
King Arthur 104
King Edward I 125
Kinmel Arms 32
kittiwakes 21, 121
Knab Rock 241
Knap, The 249

L

Landshipping 216

Landsker 193, 194, 227
Langdon Ridg 74
Langland Bay 240
lapwing 181
Laugharne 194
Lavan Sands 36
Lavernock Point 250, 251, 252, 253, 254
leatherback turtles 124
Lelpie Boats 216
lesser black-backed gulls 153
liberty ship, Dan Beard 167
lifeboat 186
lifeboat station 33, 37, 178, 224, 231, 241, 244, 250, 252, 254
lifeboat station, (old) 200, 240
lighthouse 16, 22, 53, 71, 74, 83, 110, 167, 185, 208, 232, 241, 245, 253
limekiln 99, 154, 163, 170, 178, 200
Limpet Bay 248
Linney Head 217, 218
lions mane jellyfish 126
Little Eye 15
Little Haven 195, 197, 199, 200, 202
Little Hilbre 15
Little Orme 19, 20, 23
Little Quay Bay 146
Little Sound 223, 224
Live Strandings (RSPCA) 150
Llanbedrog 113, 118
Llanbedrog beach 117
Llanddwyn Island 41, 42, 43
Llandrillo yn Rhos 19, 20
Llandudno 19, 21
Llandudno Bay 19
Llandudno Beach 21
Llandudno Pier 23
Llandudno West Shore 19, 22, 23
Llanelli 232, 233
Llanfachraeth 67
Llanfairfechan 36
Llanfwrog 68
Llangennith 225, 226, 227, 235, 236, 238
Llangennith beach 228, 231, 233, 235
Llanina 146
Llanrwst 27
Llansanffraid Glan Conwy 26
Llantwit Major 243, 245, 247, 248, 250
Llareggub 146
Lleyn Peninsula 91, 96, 100
Lligwy Beach 85
Llywellyn the Great 125
Llywelyn ap Gruffydd 125
Loch Shiel (wreck) 215
Lon Bridin 93, 94, 97, 98

long-eared owls 108
Loughor Boating Club 231
Lundy Island 260
Lydstep Haven 222
Lydstep Point 222
Lynas Cove 82, 86

M

Madocks, William Alexander 132
Maen Bugail, 112
Maentwrog 132, 134
Malcolm Campbell 227
Malltraeth Bay 43
Manobier Range 224
Manorbier 222
Manx shearwater 108, 205, 206
Marconi 254
Marine Beach 125
Marloes 210
Marloes Sands 210
Martin's Haven 199, 200, 202, 204, 205, 206, 209, 210, 212
Mawddach Estuary 135, 136, 137, 138
Menai Bridge 35, 37
Menai Strait 34, 35, 36, 37, 40, 41, 44
Menai Suspension Bridge 35
Mewslade 237
Mewslade Bay 237
Middle Mouse 77
Midland Gap 178, 179, 181, 185, 186
Midland Island 203
Milford Channel Rock 211, 213
Milford Haven 210, 211, 212, 213, 214, 215, 216, 218
Milford Haven harbour 211
Mill Bay, 211
Minor Point 233
Mixon buoy 241
Mixon Shoal 241
MOD Aberporth 146, 154
Moelfre 31, 32, 34, 81, 83, 84, 85, 86
Moelfre Beach 31
Monkstone Point 226
Morawelon camping 160
Morfa Abererch 125
Morfa Nefyn 93, 94, 97, 98, 100
MS Oldenburg 260
Mumbles 239, 241
Mumbles Head 239, 241, 257, 258, 260
Mumbles lighthouse 240
Mumbles Pier 240
Mumbles Tourist Information Centre 242
Muntjac Deer 253
Museum of Speed 227

Musselwick 200
Mwnt 151, 152
Mynydd Enlli 110

N

Nab Head 200
Nant Gwrtheyrn 94, 95
Nash Point 244, 245, 246
Nash Sands 245
National Waterfront museum 242
National Welsh Language and Heritage Centre 94
National Wetlands Centre 233
Needle Rock 163, 164
Nefyn 94, 100
Nell's Point 250
Nelson, Lord Admiral 37
Newborough Forest 42, 43
Newgale 191, 193, 195, 197
Newport 157, 160, 161
Newport Boat Club 163
Newport Sands 160, 162
New Quay 145, 146, 147
New Quay Head 146
Newsurf 197
Neyland 216
Nolton Haven 195, 196
North Beach 224, 226
North Bishops 185
North Gut 189
North Haven 204, 205, 206
North Somerset 251
North Stack 51, 54, 55, 61, 62, 64, 65, 74
Nyland Bridge 216

O

Ogmore by Sea 244
Old Castle Head 222, 224
Ormes, the 19
Owain Glyndwr 125
Oxwich Bay 239
Oxwich Bay Hotel 240
Oxwich Point 239, 241
oystercatcher 36, 46, 47, 232

P

paddle steamer Waverley 252
Parliament House Cave 54
Parrog 157, 160, 161, 163, 164
Parry Thomas 227
Parys Mountain 82
Paviland Cave 237
Pembrey Sand 225
Pembroke Dock 216
Pembroke Haven Yacht Club 216
Pembrokeshire 155

Pembrokeshire Coastal bus service 163
Pembrokeshire Coastal Path 157, 227
Penally 223
Penally Range 222, 224
Pen Anglas 165, 166, 168
Penarth 247, 251, 252
Penarth beach 250, 252
Penarth pier 252
Penarth Yacht Club 250, 252
Penbennar 120
Pen Brush 168
Pen Bush 167
Penbwchdy 167, 168
Pen-clawdd 231, 232
Penclegyr 169, 171
Pen Cristin 109, 111
Pen Dal-aderyn 179
Pen Diban 109, 110
Pen Dinas Lochtyn 147
Pendine 225
Pendine Range 228
Pendine Sands 227
Penllechwen 174
Penmaenpool 135, 137, 138
Penmon 33
Penmon Priory 34, 36
Penmorfa 168
Pennard Burrows 240
Penpleidiau 192
Penrhyn Bay 20, 64, 65
Penrhyn Bodeilas 94
Penrhyn Cregyn 137, 138
Penrhyn Glas 83, 94
Penrhyn Mawr 51, 52, 53, 54, 55, 61, 64, 65, 74, 100
Penrhyn Nefyn 94
Penrhyn Twll 179
Penrhyn Ychen 164
Pen Trwyn 21
Pen-ychain 125, 126
Pen y Cil 101, 103, 104, 107, 108, 109, 111
Pen y fan 163
Pen yr Afr 159
peregrine falcons 108
Performance Kayaks 255
petrified forest 140
Pilton 237
PJ's Surfshop, 238
Plas Cymyran 63
Plas Menai 37, 40
Plas Newydd 37
Point Lynas 81, 82, 83, 84, 85
Point of Ayr 13, 14, 15, 17
ponies 233
Pont Briwet, 133

273

Poppit Sands 153, 159
Port Erin 89
Port Erin Harbour Office 90
Port Eynon 235, 236, 238, 239, 240
Port Eynon Point 237
Port Eynon YHA 238
Porthcawl 243, 244, 245, 246
Porthcawl Point 244, 246
Porth Ceiriad 117, 118, 122
Porthclais 177, 178, 179, 191, 192
Porth Colmon 99, 100
Porth Cwyfan 43
Porth Cynfor 77, 80
Porth Dafarch 45, 46, 48, 51, 52, 56, 57, 61, 62, 65, 74
Porth Diana 48
Porth Dinllaen 93, 94, 97, 98, 99, 100
Porth Dyniewaid 20
Porth Eilian 82, 83, 86
Porth Fechan 125
Porthgain 171
Porth Llanlleiana 76, 77
Porth Llechog 82
Porthmadog 132
Porthmadog Harbourmaster 131
Porthmelgan 174
Porth Meudwy 109
Porth Namarch 54, 64, 65
Porth Neigwl 113, 115, 116
Porth Oer 97, 100, 101, 102, 103, 106, 112
Porth Padrig 77
Porth Solfach 109
Porth Swtan 68
Porth Towyn 99
Porth Trecastell 43, 44
Porth Ty Mawr 100
Porth Tywyn-mawr 67, 68
Porth Wen 75, 76, 77, 79, 80
Porth Wrach 37
Porth Y Garan 48
Porthygwichiaid 83
Porth y Nant 94
Porth Ysgaden 99, 100
Porth Ysgo 114, 115, 117
Portmeirion 132, 133, 134
Port St Mary 87, 89
Port St Mary Harbour Office 90
Port St Mary Yacht Club 90
Priestholm 33
Priest's Nose 222
Prince Tudwal 121
Priory Bay 223, 224
promontory fort 158, 222

public house, Marconi 250
public house, Paddlers Return 52, 56
public house, The Sloop 171
public house, Ty Coch 93, 94
puffin 34, 152, 205, 206, 207
Puffin Island 31, 33, 34
Puffin Sound 31, 34
Pwll Deri 167
Pwlldu Head 240
Pwll Gwaelod 163
Pwllheli 123, 125, 126
Pwllheli Harbourmaster 123
Pwllheli Marina 123
Pwllygranant 159

R

Raine buoy 252, 255
Ramsey Island 174, 177, 178, 179, 180, 181, 183, 184, 185, 186, 189
Ramsey Sound 177, 178, 179, 183, 184, 187, 189, 197
range 154, 218, 220, 222, 224
Range Office 220
Rat Island 218
Ravens Point 48
razorbill 77, 93, 94
Red Lady of Paviland 237
redshank 47
Red Wharf Bay 32, 34
redwing 108
Restaurant, Mulberrys 28
Restaurant, The Old Sailor's 163
Restaurant, The Shed 171
Rest Bay 243, 244
Rev. Crwys Williams 170
Rhinogs 136
Rhoose Point 248
Rhoscolyn 45, 46, 47, 62, 65
Rhoscolyn Beacon 45, 47, 49, 50, 61
Rhoscolyn Head 45, 48, 61, 62, 65
Rhoscolyn Sound 45
Rhosneigr 43, 44
Rhosneigr Beach 41
Rhos-on-Sea 19, 20, 22
Rhos Point 20
Rhossili 232, 236
Rhossili visitor centre 238
Rhys and Meinir 95
Rickets Head 196
ringed plover 140
Ritec Fault 210
River Loughor 231, 233
River Saith 147
Roch castle 194

Roman villa 248
Ronald Lockley 208
roundhouse 174
Royal Charter (wreck) 84

S

Saint Brigid of Ireland 200
Saint Dwynwen 42
Salisbury Bank 15
sand martin 108
Sandtop Bay 223
sandwich tern 76, 78
Sandy Bay 244
Sandy Beach 67
Sandyhaven Pill 215
Sarn Cwynfelyn 142
Sarn Padrig 142
Sarn y Bwlch 142
Saudersfoot Bay 226
Saundersfoot 225
Saundersfoot harbour 226
Scotia, (wreck) 250
Scully Island 252
Sea Empress 211, 213
seals 81, 82, 86, 109, 115, 122, 160, 185, 200, 204, 206, 218, 223, 236
Seawatch Centre 81, 84, 248
Severn Bore 243, 246
Severn Estuary 243, 255
Sheep Island 218
shelduck 140
Shoe Rock 179
Silver Bay 47
Sir William Hamilton 214
Skerries, The 71, 72, 73, 74
Skokholm 203, 204, 205, 206
Skomer 203, 204, 205, 206, 207, 208
Skomer Island 199, 200, 202
Skrinkle Haven 222
Skysea Caravan and Camping 238
Sleek Stone 197
Smalls lighthouse 192
Smalls Rock 184
Smalls Rock Lighthouse 184
Smalls, The 190
smugglers 249
Snaefell 89
Snowdonia 131, 135
Soay sheep 153
Soldiers' Point 51, 52, 54, 56, 64
Solva 191, 192
South Beach 223, 226
South Bishop Lighthouse 188
South Bishops 184, 185, 186

South Caernarvonshire Yacht Club 119
South Gut 189
South Stack 51, 52, 53, 54, 55, 61, 62, 64, 65, 74
South-west Lleyn 113
SS Albion, (wreck) 210
SS Hereford (wreck) 152
SS Samtampa, (wreck) 244
Stackpole Head 219
Stackpole Quay 219
Stack Rock 214, 215
Stack Rocks 199, 200
Stacks, The 51, 52, 56, 64
Stanley Embankment 61, 62, 63, 64, 65
St Ann's Head 209, 210, 211, 212
St Ann's Head lighthouse 211
St Brides 199, 200
St Brides Bay 189, 195, 197, 199
St Brides Haven 200
St Brynach 163
St Catherine's Island 223, 226
St Cennydd 236
St Cwyfan's Church 43, 44
St David 174, 192
St David's 174
St David's Cathedral 174
St David's Cathedral 192
St David's Head 173, 174
St David's Head 174, 178, 181, 185
St Dogmaels 159
St Donat's Castle 245
St Govan's Chapel 218
St Govan's Head 217, 219
St Gybi 33
St Illtud's Church 248
St Illud 248
St Justinian 177, 186
St Justinian's 180
St Margaret's Island 223
St Margaret's Island 224
St Mary's Abbey 110
St Mary's Church 166
St Mary's Well 103
St Non's Bay 192
St Patrick 77
St Samson 168, 223
St Seiriol 33
St Trillo 20
St Tudwal's Island East 121, 122
St Tudwal's Islands 117, 119, 120
St Tudwal's Island West 120
St Tudwal's Sound 113, 117, 122
steam railway 249

Steep Holm 251, 252, 253, 255
Stephenson, Robert 37
Stranded Marine Animals 150
Strumble Head 165, 166, 168
Strumble Head lighthouse 167
Stuart, The (wreck) 100
Sully Bay 250
Sully Island 247
Sully Sound 250, 255
Summerhouse Point 248
surf beach 116, 122, 195, 217, 222, 228, 233, 237, 239, 240, 248
Swanlake Bay 222
Swansea 242
Swansea Bay 239, 241
Swansea Tourist Information Centre 242
Swellies Rock 37
Swellies, The 35, 36, 37, 40

T

Talacre Marsh 17
Tal y Cafn 26
Tal y Cafn rapids 26
Tanskey Rocks 14, 15
Tanskey's (café) 18
Teifi Marshes Nature Reserve 160
Telford, Thomas 35, 37
Tenby 221, 223, 225, 226
Tenby South Beach 221, 225
Tenby Tourist Office 224
terns 46, 67, 78
The Bitches 177, 178, 179, 180, 181, 186
The Burrows 223
The Knap 250, 255
The Lucy, (wreck) 204
The Neck 204
The Wick 206
Thomas Knight 249
Thorn Island 214, 215
Three Cliffs Bay 240
Titanic 254
toilets 21, 32, 37, 82, 85, 90, 102, 126, 134, 136, 141, 142, 147, 160, 163, 166, 170, 171, 174, 178, 184, 192, 194, 196, 197, 202, 204, 216, 218, 219, 222, 240, 244, 245, 248, 252, 255, 256
Tower Point 200
Tower Rock 253
Traeth Bach 160
Traeth Bychan 32
Traeth Dulas 85
Traeth Lligwy 85, 86
Traeth Mawr 132

Traeth Penbryn 147, 150
Traeth yr Ora 85
Trearddur 48
Trearddur Bay 46, 48, 49, 52, 63
Trecco 244
Trefin 170
Trefor 93, 94, 96
Trefriw 27
Treheli 117
Tremadog 131
Tresaith 147
Trewent Point 219
Tripods 103
Trwyncastell 171
Trwyn Cemlyn 72
Trwyn Cilan 113, 116, 117, 122
Trwyn Dinmor 33
Trwyn Du 33
Trwyn Du Lighthouse 33
Trwyn Dwlban 32
Trwyn Eilian 83
Trwyn Llanbedrog 117
Trwyn Maen Melyn 103
Trwyn Penmon 34
Trwyn Porth Dinllaen 96, 98, 99, 100
Trwyn-Sion-Owen 177
Trwyn Talfarach 115
Trwyn y Gorlech 94, 109
Trwyn y Penrhyn 31, 34, 35, 36
Tudweiliog 99
turnstone 36
Tusker Rock 205, 243, 244
Ty'n y Groes 26

U

Up & Under 229

V

Valley 46, 63
Valsesia, (wreck) 249
Victoria Bank 72

W

waders (birds) 17, 26
Wallog 142
Waverley steamer 250
Welsh National Watersports Centre 40
Welsh Strandings Network 150
Welsh Surfing Federation School 238
West Angle Bay 217, 218
West Beacon Point 223
West Coast Surf' shop 116
Westdale Bay 210
West Kirby 13, 14, 15, 16, 17

West Kirby Sailing Club 13, 14
West Mouse 72, 74
Weston-super-Mare 256
West Scar buoy 258
West Wales Wind Surf and Sailing 212, 214
whalers 214
wheatear 108
Whistling Sands 97, 101, 103, 112
Whiteford 232
Whiteford Burrows 231, 232
Whiteford lighthouse 231, 232, 233
Whiteford Point 232, 233
Whiteford Sands 232
White Ladies, The 67, 72
Whitesands 181, 183, 184, 185, 186
Whitesands Bay 173, 174, 183, 187, 188
Whitmore Bay 249
wildfowl 17
Wildgoose tide race 203
Wildlife Trust 206
Williams-Ellis, Clough 133
Wirral 15
Wiseman's Bridge 227
Witches Cauldron 157, 160
Wolves Rock 254
Wolves Rocks 252
Woolacombe Sands 258
woollen mill 192
Worms Head 225, 228, 235, 238
Wylfa Head 76

Y

Y Felinheli 37
Ynys Amlwch 82
Ynys Arw 73
Ynys Badrig 77
Ynys Benlas 37
Ynys Bery 181
Ynys Byr 223
Ynys Deullyn 170, 171
Ynys Dewi 181
Ynys Dulas 83, 86
Ynys Eilun, 179
Ynys Enlli 101, 108
Ynys Gifftan 133
Ynys Gwales 187
Ynys Gwylan Fach 115
Ynys Gwylan Fawr 115
Ynys Gybi 62
Ynyslas 140
Ynys Lawd 53
Ynys-Lochtyn 145, 147, 148
Ynys Meicel 167, 168
Ynys Moelfre 85
Ynys Môn 29
Ynysoedd Gwylanod 47
Ynysoedd y Moelrhoniaid 71, 72
Ynys Seiriol 31, 33
Ynys Wellt 54
Ynys y Brawd, 138
Ynys y Fydlyn 68, 70
youth hostel 28, 143, 170, 197, 210, 240
Yr Eifl 93, 94
Y Swnt 85

MORE SEA KAYAK TITLES

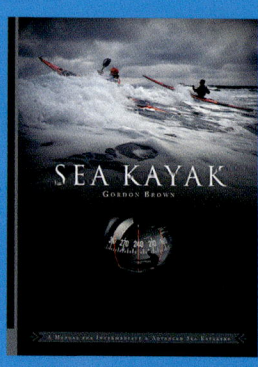
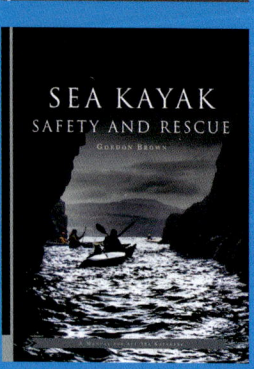

www.pesdapress.com

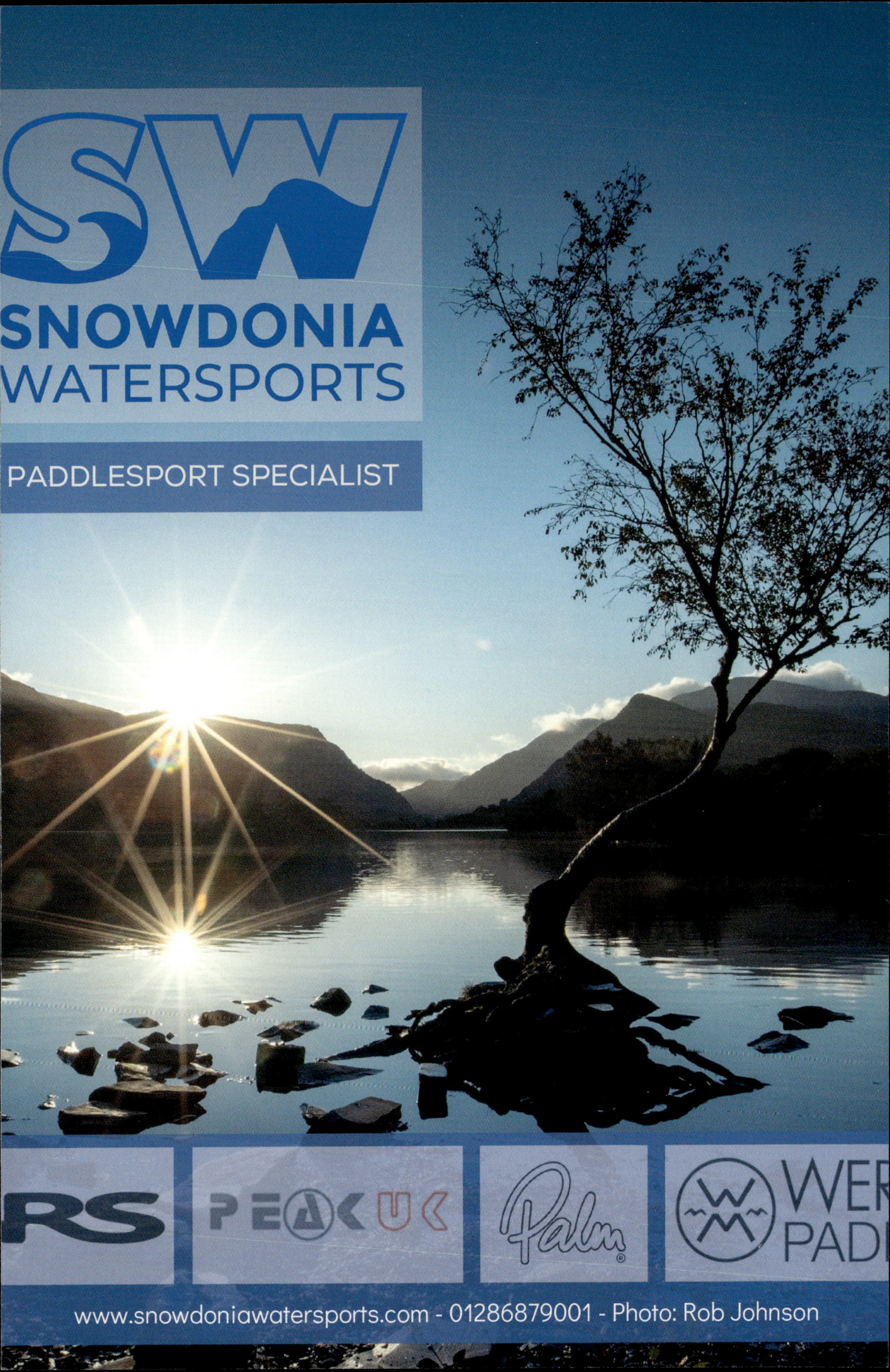
SW
SNOWDONIA WATERSPORTS
PADDLESPORT SPECIALIST
PEAK UK
Palm
www.snowdoniawatersports.com - 01286879001 - Photo: Rob Johnson

The Specialists in British Sea Kayak Design

Founded in 1968, P&H quickly established a range of successful canoes and kayaks spanning various disciplines, with standout models such as the Phazer slalom kayak, and the MKII Surfer still being fondly remembered today.

Producing the Orinoco under licence from Pyranha in 1975 was the beginning of an enduring relationship between the companies, and several more of Pyranha's models were produced under licence by P&H in the following years.

It was in 1979 that P&H produced its first sea kayaks (the same year that current Production Manager, Perran Shreeve joined the company), namely the 'Umnak' and 'Icefloe' designed by Derek C. Hutchinson.

In the mid-90s the Capella set the benchmark for polyethylene sea kayaks, followed by the composite Capella in 1997; a few years later in 2003 Dave Patrick retired, selling the company to Pyranha who continue P&H's heritage to this day through world-renowned models such as the Cetus and Aries.

Here's to another 50 years of P&H!
#ExploreTheSea

www.phseakayaks.com   *Designed and built in Britain, paddled Worldwide*

More Sustainable

- Recycled fabric & zips
- CFC Free, water repellent DWR finish
- Bioprene outer seals
- Zero packaging

t: +44 1629 732611 | e: info@peakuk.com

 peakuk  peakukkayaking  peakuktv